India's Culture

The State, the Arts and Beyond

India's Culture

The State, the Arts and Beyond

B.P. SINGH

DELHI
OXFORD UNIVERSITY PRESS
CALCUTTA CHENNAI MUMBAI

Oxford University Press, Great Clarendon Street, Oxford OX2 6DP

Oxford New York
Athens Auckland Bangkok Calcutta
Cape Town Chennai Dar es Salaam Delhi
Florence Hong Kong Istanbul Karachi
Kuala Lumpur Madrid Melbourne Mexico City
Mumbai Nairobi Paris Singapore
Taipei Tokyo Toronto
and associates in
Berlin Ibadan

ISBN 0 19 564147 7

Typeset by S.J.I. Sevices, New Delhi 110024
Printed in India at Pauls Press, New Delhi 110020
and published by Manzar Khan, Oxford University Press
YMCA Library Building, Jai Singh Road, New Delhi 110001

Dedicated to
Karunaji
and
our granddaughter Gauri Singh

THE DALAI LAMA

Foreword

by His Holiness The Dalai Lama

The relationship between the artist and his or her patron is complicated and delicate. Analysing it presents a challenge to any critic and art historian. This is the very area in relation to Independent India that Mr B.P. Singh has chosen to survey in the present book. He documents and analyses the state's policy and achievements in connection with the protection, preservation and support for the Indian artistic and architectural heritage from the earliest times to the present day. Independent India's approach has been to create specific institutions to address this need: the National Museum, state museums and academies for the major arts and crafts.

In India, as elsewhere, royalty and the nobility have historically been the traditional patrons of learning and the creative arts and crafts. The hereditary right to land, wealth and power brought with it a responsibility to the people under their care. As well as defending them from attack and offering help in times of disaster, this included protecting and supporting local culture. Needless to say, not all those who inherited such responsibilities fulfilled them, but invariably those who did retained popular respect and affection. The arts have long played a major role in Indian culture in the ways people understand and express themselves and the physical and spiritual aspects of their existence. Similarly, it is through the universal language of art that different peoples and cultures can come to know each other at a deeper, more intimate level.

As the author observes, the nature of the patron–artist relationship changes when society is governed by a democratically elected government and traditional royal patrons no longer have the resources to support the arts and education as they once did. Here he examines the crucial problem of state patronage and promotion of art and culture. Where some people have declared that the State and culture are antagonists, Mr Singh claims that contemporary Indian experience is just the opposite. In his book he casts light on the ideals and intentions behind the formation of the Central Department of Culture and its workings, and the ways in which those ideals have been fulfilled. This will be of great interest and value to readers concerned about the state of Indian culture today.

Early in his book Mr Singh celebrates the rich qualities of India's ancient and pluralistic culture. He then examines the impact that independence and economic liberalization have had on that heritage, citing the Nehru–Azad dialogue as an example. When he turns to the prospective development of Indian culture in the twenty-first century, he asks whether this is likely to lead to greater harmony or conflict. I share his optimism and belief that human nature is predominantly gentle and creative, and that our own need for love and friendship goes hand in hand with our instincts to be compassionate towards others. However, I have also observed that when we place too great an emphasis on external development and physical comfort, there is a corresponding decline in our sense of basic human values. Therefore, I believe, it is very important that technological and economic development is accompanied by a corresponding inner development.

In his prescription for the future role of Indian culture, the author has drawn inspiration from Buddhist scriptures and the writings of Mahatma Gandhi. He writes: 'In the long history of ageless Indian culture, two personalities stand out as world figures: Gautama Buddha and Mahatma Gandhi. If their messages are properly harmonized with the social and economic realities of our life and times, they seem to have the potential to avert any future clash among civilizations and also to strengthen the forces of democracy, ecology and culture.

India has indeed a long and rich ethical tradition exemplified by self-sacrifice and non-violence. These remain among the most potent forces for good in the world today. But it is not enough to talk admiringly about these qualities, we must incorporate them into our daily lives. We must apply them to our relations within our own families and communities. Indeed, the application of non-violence is not restricted merely to other human beings. It also has to do with ecology, the environment and our relations with all the other living beings with whom we share the planet. Non-violence can be employed whatever our position or vocation. It is even relevant to medical procedures, education systems, legal affairs and so forth. If we look forward to greater peace, justice and honesty in society, we must start by applying these values ourselves.

24 June 1997

Preface

For the past 18 months, I have been thinking, speaking and writing about one or the other facet of India's culture. The exclusiveness of such a concern is unprecedented in my life, including my long years of service and years spent in academic pursuits, except perhaps in my childhood days in the company of my parents and particularly of my grandfather. This book is not only a reflection of my recent mental journey but also relates to my whole being.

The book, however, has prosaic and unromantic origins. I had reluctantly accepted the invitation of the Federation of Indian Chambers of Commerce and Industry (FICCI) to inaugurate a two-day seminar at New Delhi on 11 April 1996 entitled 'Art, Culture and Business in a Liberalized Economy: Towards Synergy'. I had then articulated two interrelated ideas: one, that India is one of the unique nations in the world in that it possesses a developed culture and a developing economy; and second, that in the last decade of the twentieth century one could clearly see that culture is emerging as a third factor in determining the status of a nation in the world after market and military strength, the market having replaced military strength from its position of supremacy in the post-Cold War world. These ideas have led to the writing of this book.

Every student of India's culture has found India both fascinating and baffling, with its the multiplicity of languages and dialects, gods and goddesses, values and beliefs, customs and practices, sensuality and asceticism. One is enchanted with high levels of thinking among Indian *rishis* and *arhats*, the imagination as well as earthiness of painters and poets, the achievements of sculptors and architects, musicians and dancers, weavers and artisans. The Ajanta and Ellora

caves and several Buddhist stupas are physical manifestations of the
Hindu concept of the Absolute. This becomes evident when one
looks at the way in which these sites were built with a grand design
to sculpt mountains, to construct edifices of reason as well as prayer
in conformity with Hindu thought, its architecture and sculpture.
Octavio Paz catches this ethos beautifully when he writes:

> The Indian genius is a love for abstraction and, at the same time, a passion
> for the concrete image. At times it is rich, at others, prolix. It fascinates
> us and tires us. It has created the most lucid and the most instinctive art.
> It is abstract and realistic, sexual and intellectual, pedantic and sublime.
> It lives between extremes, it embraces the extremes, rooted in the earth
> and drawn to an invisible beyond. On the one hand, a repetition of
> forms, a superimposition of concepts, a syncretism. On the other, the
> desire for totality and unity. And in its highest moments; the incarnation
> of a totality that is plenitude and emptiness, the transfiguration of the
> body into form that, without abandoning sensation and the flesh, is
> spiritual.[1]

In the interpretation of history and culture, a particular aspect
about the past can be described in a certain way depending on the
nature of the questions that engage and motivate that enquiry. In
writing the first chapter I have been guided solely by a desire to
provide factual information about the attainments of Indians prior to
the beginning of the Christian era and how these have influenced the
succeeding generations of Indians. These attainments have imparted
a distinctive personality to Indians and to people of Indian origin.
The fact that through all these years the original character of Indian
culture has been retained and continuously renewed, is of considerable significance.

During the freedom struggle special emphasis was laid on the
unitary features of India's culture and superiority ascribed to the
Indian mind; the observations of foreigners in this regard were
liberally quoted. This was necessary as the colonial rulers continuously highlighted the disparate elements of India's culture and
justified their presence as a civilizing mission and for the preservation
of Indian unity. We are not under any such obligation today. Yet

at the same time, the need to describe certain achievements of the past is important in order to understand the issues facing the Indian nation today. The concept of a nation state is of recent origin; and if one compares the Indian culture of the times of Chandragupta Maurya with that of the ancient Athenians, or Romans, or Germans, one would understand very clearly that, despite the diversity of languages and religions, the multiplicity of caste and ethnic ties, and the wide economic differences, there is an over-arching unity of Indian culture. Amartya Sen has rightly observed:

> The interpretation of India's past cannot but be sensitive to the concerns of today. Our identities cannot be defined independently of our traditions and past, but this does not indicate a linear sequence whereby we interpret our past first, and then arrive at our identity, equipped to face contemporary issues. On the contrary, our reading of the past and understanding of the present are interdependent, and the selectional criteria that are central to interpreting the past have to take note of the relevance of the different concerns in the contemporary world. While we cannot live without our past, we need not live within it either.[2]

India's role in the world of the future lies in the hands not only of politicians, bureaucrats and military men, but rests very significantly with creative persons in the realm of art and culture, philosophy and science, media and education.

Both the market and the state have played pioneering roles in the promotion of art and culture in India's ageless history. During the last fifty years the policies pursued by the Government of India have facilitated cultural progress under the guiding philosophy that it is not for the state to guide culture but only to provide an environment which would facilitate dialogue among creative persons and encourage freedom of their expression. We in India are fortunate to have had leaders and creative persons like Mahatma Gandhi, Rabindranath Tagore, Jawaharlal Nehru, Sri Aurobindo, Satyajit Ray, Ravi Shankar, Maulana Azad, Rukmini Devi Arundale, Kamaladevi Chattopadhyaya, Amrita Sher Gil, Lata Mangeshkar, Bismillah Khan and many others to illuminate our political and cultural world.

The leaders of the early Republic were not only freedom fighters and persons of vision but also individuals of distinction in the realm of culture.

The second chapter of this book is mainly concerned with the situation obtaining after 1947. This chapter provides an account of institution building efforts by Jawaharlal Nehru and Maulana Abul Kalam Azad, and the care with which they handled matters of art and culture to the minutest detail. The result is for all to see. Many Indians occupy pre-eminent positions in the world in the respective fields of their creative activity. The role of the market is gradually unfolding itself and economic liberalization in India has created new opportunities for the market in the realm of art and culture. Some concerns about the role of the market and the growing influence of westernization on India's culture as also the interventionist role of the Indian state are discussed as well.

Stalwarts like Jawaharlal Nehru, Maulana Azad, Rajendra Prasad and Sarevapalli Radhakrishnan often chose to pen their inner thoughts on official files. These remarks have helped officials and creative persons to jointly establish and shape national akademies and organize cultural pageantry on national days. Chapter 3 of the book is a faithful portrayal of dialogues between officials and leaders about art purchase policies and cultural aspects of the Republic Day parade, and is, a kind of replay of history. The aim is to provide an insight into the cultural climate of the early years of the Indian Republic. At a time of deepening rivalries between individual wielders of power and the reckless use of authority for personal gain, the ideas and conduct of leaders and officials in the early days of the Republic have both relevance and value. The need to strengthen the forces of integrity and public service in the polity, and even to influence the conduct of the market is imperative. We have to activate national forums to allow artists and writers representing the vast diversity and plurality of the nation to meet and reflect upon the nation's problems, and to guide the instruments of national unity and cohesion.

Decolonization and the fall of communism are two great events of the twentieth century. India played a major role in bringing to a close the colonial system which in turn meant the end of Europe's domination over large parts of the globe. The post-Second World War scene was marked by two superpower blocks, and the countries of Eastern Europe were subjected to Soviet hegemony which was only another variant of the colonial order. The fall of communist control over the East European countries in a way completed the task of decolonization. It can be said today with some certainty that a genuinely new era of history has begun in the last decade of the twentieth century. One sees the emergence of three powerful lights, of democracy, ecology and culture.

The post-colonial and post-industrial society demands a new kind of understanding. Information technology, markets, banking systems and even international organizations can only facilitate but cannot provide a spiritual ethos among individuals and the community. The spiritual ethos alone can guarantee respect for individual opinions, ethnic identities, recognition of various art forms and other creative manifestations. Every religion and culture visualizes in one form or another the submission of an individual before the creator, whether one is a believer or a rationalist or both. Our consciousness relates to the fact that we are citizens of a world abounding with nature's beauty and human works of heritage. The respect for this creation is a basic prerequisite for human survival as well as for meaningful change. It is, therefore, necessary to create conditions which will allow mutual respect for and tolerance of different cultures. In this task science and technology could be effective instruments provided culture is accorded a primacy of place. The respect for genuine cultural pluralism would strengthen the forces of peace and harmony in the world.

Chapter 4 of the book also discusses the value system in the third millennium in a global perspective, and whether Indians would continue to retain their distinctive character in an age in which modern methods of communication and media would knit the world even closer. Would the Indian cultural values make a meaning-ful impact in the world of tomorrow, or would they themselves be transformed so as to lose the Indian identity hitherto preserved? The answer is in favour of India retaining her 'Indianness' and also making a contribution to world civilization in terms of her genius. This belief is based not only upon the lives and deeds of persons like Buddha, Gandhi, *rishis* and *arhats* but also on the values practised by the people of India. The people are the custodians of India's spirit of beauty, poetry, sculpture, dance, music and crafts. It is the fragrance of this India, particularly of its women, which will be the source of strength in the third millennium of history.

In 1977 when the dark clouds of the Emergency gave place to the bright sunshine of freedom, democracy was a 'taste of honey'. Appendix A, 'Culture and Administration: A Study of Interaction as a Means of Social Change in India' was written in those days of euphoria. That paper recognizes the role that the administration plays in a developing economy situated as it is at the centre of social and economic activities. As an instrument of the state, its organiza-tional sensitivities towards culture would provide a certain direction to change which would facilitate an individual to attain his full potential in terms of his capabilities and inheritance. Culture as a paradigm of development is a prerequisite that field administrators have to take note of, and such an approach in turn shall enrich the consciousness of individual civil servants as well.

Appendix B, 'The Monumental Challenge: The Role of the Archaeological Survey of India', is the result of the first major three-day Conference of Superintending Archaeologists held on 27–29 May 1996. This conference gave me an insight into the magnitude of the task and the various challenges that the Archaeological Survey of India is facing. The conference focused on specific problems relating to (i) management of monuments and sites; (ii) conservation of monuments and sites including conservation policy; (iii) manage-ment of museums including their security and documentation; (iv) antiquarian laws and problems of illicit traffic in antiquities; and (v) excavation and exploration with special reference to policies and priorities in excavation of sites, problem-oriented surveys and village to village survey for antiquarian remains.

Gauri, my granddaughter, was born on 22 December 1993. During 1996 there has been a phenomenal growth in her consciousness. She would invariably be the first person to receive me on my return from office. And whenever I come home·with new books and magazines in my hand Gauri would insist that I write Gauri Singh on the cover of the book and hand the book over to her. Karunaji—her grandmother—would lend support to Gauri's entreaties and I usually gave in . This book has grown in these environs and is aimed at capturing some of our cultural sensibilities. The book is accordingly dedicated to Karunaji and our granddaughter Gauri Singh.

This book makes no attempt to relate the history of contemporary Indian art and culture, or to resolve historical puzzles which characterize different disciplines. It is aimed at providing a glimpse of some aspects of India's culture and highlighting the relevance of culture in the social and political life of the nation. The manifestations of culture are not mere pursuits of individual artists or scholars, they constitute a social concern and provide a base for meaningful dialogue. The belated recognition of culture as an important factor in development, and also as a major ingredient of the national personality, will certainly alter the national scene in significant ways in the coming decades. Artists and creative writers will play a more direct role in the nation's affairs and their works will not only be prize collections of universities, museums, and libraries but of individual homes and of society itself. India has a large number of gifted individuals in the realm of art and culture. This will serve to strengthen her stability and faith in her future.

In realizing the immense beauty of the subject and my own shortcomings in dealing with it, I am reminded of Sant Tulsidas, the great Hindi poet, and the verse from his epic work *Ramacharitamanas*:

कीरति भनिति भूति भलि सोई। सुरसरि सम सब कहँ हित होई।।
राम सुकीरति भनिति भदेसा। असमंजस अस मोहि अँदेशा।।

कीर्ति, कविता और सम्पत्ति वही उत्तम है, जो गंगाजी की तरह सबका हित करनेवाली हो। श्रीरामचन्द्रजी की कीर्ति तो बड़ी सुन्दर (सबका अनन्त कल्याण करनेवाली ही) है, परंतु मेरी कविता भद्दी है। यह असामंजस्य है (अर्थात् इन दोनों का मेल नहीं मिलता), इसकी मुझे चिन्ता है ।।५।।

'Fame, or Poetry, or Power, is of any value only if it, like the Ganga, brings benefit to all. Fair is Rama's glory, but my verses are clumsy; such disparity fills me with anxious doubt.'[3]

Notes

1. Octavio Paz, *In Light of India*, Harcourt Brace and Company, New York, 1997, p.185.
2. Amartya Sen, *On Interpreting India's Past*, The Asiatic Society, Calcutta, 1996, p.38.
3. Tulsidas, *Ramacharitamanas*, Gita Press, Gorakhpur, Varanasi, 1996, p.21.

Acknowledgements

In writing this book I have received kind and generous support from a large number of friends and colleagues.

My colleagues in the Department of Culture—Shri Ashok Vajpeyi, Shri Rajeev Yadav, Shri Vijay Kumar, and Smt Kalpana Das Gupta—were extremely helpful. Shri B.M. Pande, former Director (Publication), Archaeological Survey of India; Dr S. Sarkar, DG, National Archives of India; Dr G.N. Pant, Director, National Museum Institute of History, Art, Conservation and Museology, New Delhi; and Dr (Smt) Saryu Doshi, Honorary Director, National Gallery of Modern Art, Mumbai, assisted me in numerous ways.

I delivered a series of lectures covering the themes enunciated in this book at the Nehru Centre, London, on 10 February 1997, at the Asia Society, New York, on 14 February 1997, and at the A.N. Sinha Institute, Patna, on 9 March 1997. The directors of these centres as well as the participants at these events greatly helped me in acquiring new insights and in clearing several of my doubts. Professor Ralph Buultjens, a perceptive thinker and long-time friend, was very keen that the conclusions indicated by me needed to be developed in the form of a book. Professor Ravinder Kumar, a noted historian, and Dr H.K. Kaul, an eminent librarian, warmly supported this idea.

Special thanks are also due to my colleagues Shri Vijay Kumar Tulreja and Shri Sanjeev Batra who worked hard in typing and giving shape to the manuscript. My son, Rajeev Prasad Singh, a member of the Indian Revenue Service, went through the manuscript and prepared the index.

Contents

The photograph depicts Brahma (Prajapati) with Bhudevi (in the form of a cow). The work was done by an unknown artist from Mewar (Rajasthan) sometime during **AD** 1725–35.

(Courtesy National Museum, **New** Delhi)

1

India's Culture: Some Facts, Some Perspectives

I

Introduction: The Enduring Imprints on Consciousness

What is India's culture?[1] This is a question that cannot be easily answered. And yet India's culture which blossomed more than 3000 years ago, has given successive generations of Indians a mind-set, a value system, and a way of life, which has been retained with remakable continuity, like enduring imprints on Indian consciouness, despite the passage of time, repeated foreign invasions, and the enormous growth in population. It gives to Indians as well as to people of Indian origin a unique personality today, as it has done in the past.

By the year AD 1, India was a highly developed culture. The achievements in the realm of literature, art, dance and drama, poetry, economy, astronomy, and religion before the beginning of the Christian era have continued to influence its people during the last 2000 years. The national pencil or the pencil of Indian culture has been extensively used during the last 2000 years with sensitivity and care, and its manifestations are examples of continuity and renewal, and yet no major innovation seems to be a departure from the past.

India, Egypt, Iraq, Greece, and China have been recognized as the five cradles of human civilization. The ancient civilization of

India, however, differs from the others in that its traditions have remained intact to the present day. In this respect it is like China. In fact, both India and China can claim to have the oldest continuous cultural traditions in the world.

As a student, I found India's cultural history quite bewildering. This was chiefly because cultural attainments were required to be viewed, and were generally associated with kings and rulers, and occasionally one missed names or wrongly related a poet or a philosopher to a particular king who had reigned a century or two later or earlier. Even the essays in our textbooks which dealt largely with cultural ideas and less with historical figures, projected measures that were invariably abstract. Notwithstanding these, one fact stood out clearly—that well before the beginning of the first millennium of the Christian era, India had scaled great heights in her cultural attainments, of which succeeding generations of Indians had every reason to feel proud.

As a post-graduate student and subsequently as a lecturer in Patna University, four eminent personalities and their work on Indian culture exercised a profound influence on my thinking. They were: Professor A.L. Basham and his book, *The Wonder that was India* (1953); Jawaharlal Nehru and *The Discovery of India* (1946); Rabindranath Tagore and his numerous poems, essays and lectures; and, above all, Ramdhari Singh 'Dinkar' and his monumental work: *Sanskriti ke Char Adhyaye* (1955). In listing these influences I have relied upon certain impressions that have remained fresh in my mind all through these years, particularly, Basham's emphasis on looking at culture in the perspective of ecology and his assessment of India's contribution to world civilization; Nehru's view of India's culture in the context of the people of the villages; Tagore's description of the eternal values of India's culture; and Dinkar's belief that India's culture has a message for the world because that is India's destiny.

I had the privilege of interacting at a personal level with Professor Basham and Ramdhari Singh 'Dinkar'. In fact, my meetings with Professor Basham during his visit to the Patna University, and with

'Dinkar' when he visited our home in Bihat village, Bihar, and conversations with him in Patna, enlarged as well as deepened my comprehension of the Indian thought processes. I found both Basham and 'Dinkar' more intelligible in their conversation than their books; 'Dinkar', of course, proved more appealing as his approach was emotional and left a lasting imprint on my mind. I attended several meetings addressed by Jawaharlal Nehru, but unfortunately I never had the opportunity to discuss any matter with him. And I was not destined to have an encounter with Gurudev Rabindranath Tagore, for he had died some months before I was born.

Prof. Basham's view of India's culture was holistic and his approach with its emphasis on environment was unusual for its time. He examined India's culture within the framework of its geographical situations, eco-systems, bio-diversity, climate, soil, and sunshine and assessed their influence on the people, their lifestyle, their philosophy, and above all, their ideas and art. This provided a new vision to students of Indian history and culture of our time. To quote the following opening sentences from Prof. Basham's classical work:

> The ancient civilization of India grew up in a sharply demarcated sub-continent bounded on the north by the world's largest mountain range—the chain of the Himalayas, which, with its extensions to east and west, divides India from the rest of Asia and the world. The barrier, however, was at no time an insuperable one, and at all periods both settlers and traders have found their way over the high and desolate passes into India, while Indians have carried their commerce and culture beyond her frontiers by the same route. India's isolation has never been complete, and the effect of the mountain wall in developing her unique civilization has often been over-rated.
>
> The importance of the mountains to India is not so much in the isolation which they give her, as in the fact that they are the source of her two great rivers. The clouds drifting northwards and westwards in the rainy season discharge the last of their moisture on the high peaks, whence, fed by ever-melting snow, innumerable streams flow southward, to meet in the great river systems of the Indus and the Ganges. On their way they pass through small and fertile plateaux, such as the valleys of Kashmir and Nepal, to debouch on the great plain.[2]

Prof. Basham, an admirer of India's civilizational attainments, has repeatedly asserted that India's cultural life goes back far beyond that of the west. In his introduction to *A Cultural History of India,* he said,

> No land on earth has such a long cultural continuity as India, though there were more ancient civilizations, notably in Egypt and Iraq, these were virtually forgotten by the inhabitants of those lands, and were overlaid by new intrusive cultures... On the other hand, in India the brahman still repeats in his daily worship Vedic hymns composed over 3,000 years ago, and tradition recalls heroic chieftains and the great battles fought by them at about the same time. In respect of the length of continuous tradition China comes second to India and Greece makes a poor third.[3]

Jawaharlal Nehru's *Discovery of India* is essentially a mental journey as the notes and references do not provide the sources of his information but, instead, supplement his thought processes and insights. Nehru, in particular, related India's cultural attainments to the hardships encountered by the rural population with whom he, as a freedom fighter, came face to face in numerous Indian villages. Among Nehru's several pragmatic observations was his statement that we in India have both progressive and regressive features, and these have flourished side by side. The need to rid Indian thinking of obscurantist ideas and irrational beliefs was a challenge that appealed to him the most, and in that sense he became an important link in the movement started by Raja Rammohan Roy in the eighteenth century. While Nehru could clearly see the spirit of resignation and acceptance of things as 'predetermined' by fate, he understood and was moved by the mellowness and gentleness which flowed from a cultural heritage of thousands of years, which no amount of misfortune had been able to 'rub off'. Reflecting upon the manner in which a common Indian carries his culture as an integral part of his world-view, Nehru wrote:

> Thus I saw the moving drama of the Indian people in the present, and could often trace the threads which bound their lives to the past, even while their eyes were turned towards the future. Everywhere I found a cultural background which had exerted a powerful influence on their

lives. This background was a mixture of popular philosophy, tradition, history, myth, and legend, and it was not possible to draw a line between any of these. Even the entirely uneducated and illiterate shared this background. The old epics of India, the Ramayana and the Mahabharata and other books, in popular translations and paraphrases, were widely known among the masses, and every incident and story and moral in them was engraved on the popular mind and gave a richness and content to it. Illiterate villagers would know hundreds of verses by heart and their conversation would be full of references to them or to some story with a moral, enshrined in some old classic. Often I was surprised by some such literary turn given by a group of villagers to a simple talk about present-day affairs. If my mind was full of pictures from recorded history and more-or-less ascertained fact, I realised that even the illiterate peasant had a picture gallery in his mind, though this was largely drawn from myth and tradition and epic heroes and heroines, and only very little from history. Nevertheless, it was vivid enough.

I looked at their faces and their figures and watched their movements. There was many a sensitive face and many a sturdy body, straight and clean-limbed; and among the women there was grace and suppleness and dignity and poise and, very often, a look that was full of melancholy. Usually the finer physical types were among the upper castes, who were just a little better off in the economic sense. Sometimes, as I was passing along a country road, or through a village, I would start with surprise on seeing a fine type of man, or a beautiful woman, who reminded me of some fresco of ancient times. And I wondered how the type endured and continued through ages, in spite of all the horror and misery that India had gone through. What could we not do with these people under better conditions and with greater opportunities opening out to them.[4]

Rabindranath Tagore is rightly perceived as one of the tallest literary figures after Kalidas in the cultural pantheon of India. He influenced various forms of cultural expression and continues to do so even today. He believed passionately that India's culture owes its continuity to the support that it has always received from the masses and also because there is something eternal in this land. Mahatma Gandhi, after reading a poem of Tagore which is reproduced below, remarked that Tagore would have become immortal even if he had written nothing else:

Where the mind is without fear and
the head is held high;
Where knowledge is free;
Where the world has not been broken
up into fragments by narrow domestic
walls;
Where words come out from the
depth of truth;
Where tireless striving stretches its
arms towards perfection;
Where the clear stream of reason has
not lost its way into the dreary desert
sand of dead habit;
Where the mind is led forward by
thee into ever-widening thought and
action —
Into that heaven of freedom, my
Father, let my country awake.[5]

'Dinkar' made the understanding of historical perspectives much more direct by looking at the history of India's culture in terms of four major encounters: between the autochthons and the Aryans; between Vedic beliefs and the philosophy propounded by the Buddha, as well as by Mahavira; between Hinduism and Islam; and finally between the European civilization and the Indian way of life and learning. These encounters at different periods of history have imparted strength to India's culture. The most striking feature of India's civilizational history has been its marked tolerance and human approach with its potential to impart a message to the world. 'Dinkar' wrote:

Examples of inter-mixture and cultural harmony among peoples belonging to different races, languages, and faiths are available in some other countries too (such as Mexico and ancient Greece), but not to the same extent as in India. In the world there are but four colours of people—white, wheatish, black and yellow—and all four are profusely inter-mixed in the Indian populace. Even linguistically, the offspring of all the major language families live together in this country. And as for religion, India as a whole has always been, from the beginning, a land common to all the major religions of the world. The Indians of Tiruvankur had become Christian long before the people of England, and Islam had perhaps already arrived among the Moplas while Prophet Mohammed was still alive. Similarly, the followers of Zoroaster have been inhabiting India since the tenth century. When the Arab Muslims occupied Iran and began to propagate their own religion there, the Parsis fled Iran and came to settle in India. When the Jewish temples began to crumble under the Roman tyranny, a number of Jews fled to India in order to save their faith, and ever since they have been living happily in South India. Therefore, Christianity, Islam, Judaism and Parsi religions have as much a claim over India as Hinduism or Buddhism has.

It would seem as though nature has made an experiment in unity in this land of India, so that unity of the world becomes possible. If the composite culture of India is true, then some day the idea of world-culture and world-humanity must also come to be true. India has shown the way. And the way is that of truth and non-violence.[6]

It is not very clear when the Indian mind started delving into fine arts, poetry and philosophy. The myths and legends, cults and rituals, as well as agricultural practices and handicrafts indicate that civilizational attainments in India commenced earlier than 5000 years ago. The divine narratives were pieced together out of unconscious allegory, poetic symbolism, personification of Nature, or disguise of language. But in all these, the human mind played as important a role as inanimate Nature. It is this feature of the Indian mind which is responsible for the rapid growth of Indian philosophical pursuits and the development of the Hindu way of life. Indian history begins with evidence from the Indus civilization which **flourished during 3000–1500** BC. The archaeological excavations at various sites connected with that civilization, such as at Mohenjodaro, Harappa and Dholavira, have amply proved that there existed a well-developed city life, irrigation system, and agricultural operations in India during this period.[7] Much later, the notes recorded by the Greek ambassador, Megasthenes (3rd century BC), and the Chinese pilgrim, Fa-hsien (5th century AD) as well as the rock edicts of Ashoka (3rd century BC) indicate the richness of India's culture in ancient days.

By the year AD1, India's pre-eminent position in the world was established by her cultural attainments in the spheres of language, religion and spirituality, literature, philosophy, music, dance, drama, sculpture, and the sciences including astronomy. It is another matter that at that time, due to undeveloped communications, the world was not well-knit and easily accessible physically. This, however, did not prevent Indian sages and saints from viewing the world as a family when they proclaimed वसुधैव कुटुम्बकम्.[8] According to them, environment and peace were global in character and that vision revealed itself in the song which reads: 'the earth is my mother and I am a son of the world' (माता भूमि: पुत्रों अहं पृथ्वीयाः).[9]

The cultural attainments of the people of India can be viewed in the context of language and literature; religion and spirituality; visual arts; performing arts; and philosophy, science, and economics.

II
Language and Literature

The beginnings of Indian literature are found in the *Vedic* hymns composed around 1500 BC. Early literary forms include Tamil verses from the south, Prakrit and Pali tales from the mainland of India and tribal lore from the hills and uplands.

Sanskrit, Greek and Latin are ancient languages, Sanskrit being the oldest. Literature in early days was primarily religious.[10] The Hindus recognized two kinds of authoritative religious literature: *shruti* (hearing) which is eternal and self-existent and divinely revealed; and *smriti* (recollection) which is a product of human authorship and thus at a lower level than *shruti*. The entire Vedic literature is *shruti*. The *Ramayana*,[11] the *Mahabharata*[12] including the *Bhagavad Gita*,[13] and the *Upanishads Dharmashastra*[14] represent the finest examples of *smriti* tradition.

Sanskrit literature conforms to the rules of grammar particularly to the work authored by Panini[15] around 500 BC which, even now, is regarded as highly authoritative. Sanskrit literature is flexible, polished, expressive, and direct.

Sanskrit became the medium of expression of poets, authors, storytellers, as well as of valuable treatises on philosophy, astronomy, science, town-planning, architecture, music, drama and dance. It dominated India's literary traditions in the ancient period. Classical Sanskrit was the language spoken by a cultured minority. Classical poetry catered to the interests of this small group and was characterized by intellectual speculation and a play on the senses. Alongside, folk literature flourished in popular dialects and in languages like Pali and Prakrit. However, Sanskrit, Pali, and Prakrit grew and developed at the same time. Pali became the sacred language of Buddhism and Prakrit, of Jainism. Sanskrit, Pali, and Prakrit, contributed to the growth of modern Indian languages like Hindi, Marathi, Bengali, and Assamese, and have influenced their script, grammar and literature.

Pali is no longer a medium of conversation, but is still used in the Buddhist scriptures of Sri Lanka, Myanmar and Thailand. It is widely believed that Pali was the mother-tongue of, and was used by, the Buddha. The *Rupasiddhi* is the oldest text on Pali grammar and its author Buddhapriya compiled it from the ancient work of Kachhyayana, a contemporary of Lord Buddha. The *Tripitaka* in Pali consists of three *pitakas* (baskets), and is the most authentic document on Buddhism. The basic teachings of Buddhism are incorporated in the *Dhammapda* which is a part of the second *pitaka*. There are several poetical works in Pali dealing with the life and teachings of Lord Buddha. It may be mentioned that several Buddhist scriptures, in addition to Pali, employ Prakrit and Sanskrit.

Prakrit was initially a form of speech which was commonly used by the masses in various parts of India. Prakrit works are divided into two broad classes: canonical and non-canonical. The canonical literature comprises the religious works of the two sects of Jainism: Shvetambara and Digambara. The most famous work of the Shvetambara sect is known as *Siddhanta* which deals with the main tenets of Jain philosophy and its way of life. This was followed by various commentaries on these texts. Two notable authors who wrote commentaries were Bhadrabahu (300 BC) and Jinabhadra Kshamashramana (AD 609). The religious literature of the Digambara sect consists of *Prathamanuyoga* (containing *Puranic* stories), *Karananuyoga* (dealing with cosmogony and cosmology), *Dravyanuyoga* (philosophical works, including those of Kundakunda) and *Charananuyoga* (on religious rites), and together they are known as the four *Vedas* of Jainism. The literary works in Prakrit cover poetry, anthropology, drama and short stories.

Both Pali and Prakrit were the languages of the masses. However, Prakrit became the language of administration in Ashoka's time. This continued for some centuries till it was replaced by Sanskrit again.

Vedic literature, both prose and poetry, was composed exclusively in Sanskrit and handed down orally. If today, one reflects upon the capacity of the people who transmitted the vast corpus of Vedic literature from one generation to the next, one is not only filled with admiration, but is also awe-struck by the enormity of the task.

While Pali, Prakrit and Sanskrit are known as Aryan languages, the earliest Dravidian language was Tamil. It grew rapidly and evolved in three stages—old, middle and modern. The old Tamil is largely in the form of unitary poems and stems from folk-songs and stories. The old Tamil was not at all influenced by Sanskrit. In fact, Sanskrit influence is evident more in Kannada, Malayalam and Telugu than in Tamil. However, while Tamil became a well-developed language before the Christian era, the other languages, namely Telugu, Kannada and Malayalam, came later. The ancient Tamil literature comprising several classics is known as *Sangam* literature. According to historians, it was composed some time between 500 BC and 200 AD and its rhythmic structure has cast its influence on subsequent literary activity in Tamil as well as in Malayalam, Telugu and Kannada. Tolkappiyar, a renowned scholar, wrote the famous grammatical work entitled *Tolkappiyam* for the Tamil language.

Tribal habitats are scattered over the entire length and breadth of India. There is no single tribal language, but each tribe developed its own linguistic code. The process of change in tribal dialects and languages became discernible when social intercourse between tribals and non-tribals occurred. For example, in north-east India, most of the Tibeto-Burman languages came under the influence of Sanskrit and its two major offshoots, Assamese and Bengali. Similarly, Tamil influenced the tribal dialects and languages in Tamil Nadu, Kerala, Karnataka, Pondicherry, and the island group of Sri Lanka, Maldives and Lakshadweep. In the Nilgiri hills of South India, a large number of tribal languages are spoken, but for inter-tribal communication, the non-tribal language of the area—Tamil, Kannada, or Malayalam—is employed. In states like Bihar, Madhya Pradesh and Orissa the fusion between tribal languages and Sanskrit is evident. The linguistic changes in tribal languages not only signify an evolving form and content, but also a major social change.

The migratory tribals or gypsies found all over India, are of different kinds. Although each gypsy group has its own dialect which serves as the mode of communication within the group, they possess the gift of quickly coming to terms with the language of the area in which they operate.

Before the Christian era, Sanskrit acquired pan-Indian fame and importance, with Tamil holding sway in areas below the Vindhyas. The indigenous oral folk traditions found expression in the languages of the masses such as Pali, Prakrit and tribal dialects. Through dialogue with the common people in their language or *bhasa*, Sanskrit and Brahmin scholars were able to impart the fragrance of folk-tales and traditions to their work. At the same time, the linguistic expressions of the common people benefited by their interactions with savants. It was always a two-way process.

The linguistic attainments of the people of India can be surmised from the fact that more than 2500 years ago the scholars of Bihar, particularly in Pataliputra and Mithila, composed the finest religious scriptures and philosophical treatises in Sanskrit, Pali and Prakrit. This not only reveals the religious pluralism of that period in India, but also the presence of linguistic diversity even within that small geographical unit. There is enough evidence to indicate that during this period India had developed a system of conferences and free discussions to which specialists came from all over the country. The summaries of those conferences were known as *samhitas*, the compilers being editors, not authors.

III
Religion and Spirituality

In the realm of religion and spirituality, the Hindu view of life, and the two other religions—Jainism and Buddhism—dominated Indian thought processes and human activities.

In ancient India, the theme governing Hindu activity and world view centred around four concepts: (1) *dharma* (righteousness); (ii) *artha* (economic and political goals); (iii) *Kama* (pleasure); and (iv) *moksha* (freedom from the cycle of life, death and re-birth). *Dharma*, inclusive of *artha* and *kama* is the grand design of life and *moksha* is its culmination. In many ways *dharma* is the basis of the universe, for it refers to the rules of social intercourse laid down for every person in terms of his/her *varna*[16] (social status), *ashrama*[17] (the stage of life), and *guna*[18] (the qualities of inborn nature).

It may be pointed out that all the four goals pertain to legitimate human activities but, on the scale of values *moksha* takes precedence over the rest. In the attainment of freedom from the cycle of life, the body is not an obstacle but an instrument. *Moksha* can be attained both through *gyan* (knowledge) or through *bhakti* (devotion). *Moksha* is a state of knowledge or more correctly a sense of realizing the truth. *Moksha* is essentially self-knowledge. Liberated persons

perform their duties in a state of tranquillity and detachment and trans-
mit light to all those who come in contact with them.

The notion of *karma* (deed) is integral to the Hindu view of life.
Dharma and *karma* are inseparable as they together determine the
domain of human life. All Indian religious traditions believe that
human actions have consequences that are inescapable—good acts
lead to joy and evil acts to sorrow. Whatever cannot be enjoyed or
suffered in this life flows on to the next birth which may not
necessarily be in a human form.

The Hindu religious philosophy is expounded in a large number
of texts and legends among which the Vedas, the *Upanishads*, the
Ramayana, and the *Mahabharata* with its *Bhagavad Gita,* are the most
significant.

The Vedas

The Vedas—the root *vid* of Sanskrit means 'to know'—are the most
sacred scriptures of the Hindus in all matters pertaining to religion,
philosophy, forms of worship, and way of life. The Vedas are a
product of the great Indian cultural tradition of *shruti* (hearing),
which is eternal and divinely ordained, and *smriti* (recollection)
which is handed down from generation to generation. The Vedas,
along with the *Upanishads,* form the basis of *Vedanta*[19] philosophy
whose main thesis is that God (*Brahm*) alone exists, that the human
soul (*atman*) is a spark of *Brahm* and that all the physical world is a
mere illusion (*maya*). According to *Vedanta,* liberation (*moksha*) consists of freedom from the illusion of the physical world and the
merging of the soul with the godhead.

The oldest and the most important of the four Vedas is the
Rigveda—the Veda of hymns, the final version of which was made
around 1000 BC. The subject matter of the *Rigvedic* hymns—1017 in
number—consists of panegyrics and prayers addressed to the natural phe-
nomena such as the sun, the water of the seas, the winds, the fire, and
the earth. Today, their relevance is realized by movements which

protest against the degradation of the environment and advocate its conservation as well as world peace.

The *Samaveda*—the Veda of chants or songs, contains 9425 verses. They indicate the manner in which these stanzas are to be chanted and recited, and have helped in the growth of music in all its forms not only in India but also in several other countries of Asia.

The *Yajurveda*—the Veda of prose formulae, is a text book for priests who performed the rituals of sacrifice. The *Yajurveda*, and texts formulated on its ideals, have provided continued employment to a class of Brahmins over all these centuries. At the same time, the rituals of sacrifice and other meaningless rites have been the root cause of blind faith, giving rise to obscurantist modes of thinking in the country. The power of Vedic sacrifice was such that it became the fundamental law, not only of individual destiny, but of the universal order. For this reason, the Brahmins or priests, the 'invokers' of the gods, enjoyed particular prestige which established their absolute superiority over other caste groups.

The *Atharvaveda*—the Veda of rituals, which contains 730 hymns (approximately 6000 stanzas) both in poetry and prose, deals with religion on a personal and private level rather than in the domain of the State and the public. These hymns are used against enemies, demons, and diseases or for success in love, procreation, and material prosperity. This has also, unwittingly, contributed to irrationality in thinking.

The *varna* hierarchy is well-defined in a hymn in the *Rigveda*, where it demarcates society into four sections; priests (Brahmin), rulers and warriors (Kshatriya), merchants or craftsmen (Vaishya), cultivators or servants (Shudra). The *Jatis* (castes) owe their origins to the *varna* classification and are important features of Indian social, economic and political life.

The Brahmanas and the Upanishads

The *Brahmanas* are commentaries on Vedic rituals composed between the 8th and 6th centuries BC. They deal with the use of Vedic hymns, the sequence of rituals, and the philosophy therein. They employ the device of story telling for interpreting the significance of sacrifice. They contain regulations for Vedic ritual, along with myths and other traditional matter, and they also reveal the meaning of *mantras*.

The *Upanishads*, composed in 800 BC, are the most classic texts and form the inner core of Brahmanism. There are a large number of *Upanishads*, of these 108 are in print. Ten of these *Upanishads* (*Ishavasya, Kena, Katha, Prasna, Munda, Mandukya, Taittiriya, Aitareya, Chhandogya*, and *Brihadaranyaka*) have particularly influenced the development of Indian philosophy. The *Upanishads* point out that the *Brahman* and the *atman* are the same: The Supreme manifests Himself in every soul, and the student of religion is dramatically told 'Thou art That' (*Tat twam asi*). The *Bhagavad Gita*, composed a few centuries after the *Upanishads*, discusses not the unreality of the world, but man's duties in the world. The indestructibility of the soul is stressed, selfless work is enjoined as an ideal, and the duties of every human being are emphasized.

Adi Sankaracharya, born in AD 788, was the foremost exponent of the *Vedanta* philosophy and developed the doctrine of *advaita*[20] (non-duality) which denies the existence of the world as separate from god. He helped unite the length and breadth of India by setting up different monastic orders in far-flung areas of the country. He also popularized philosophical dialogues and discourses with scholars and thus enriched the Indian mind. Some form of this tradition continues to this day in the order set up by Adi Shankaracharya, which addresses modern issues in the light of the *Vedanta* philosophy.

One of the tenets of Vedic philosophy has been that every person takes birth with three *rinas* (debts), and that it is his/her sacred duty to redeem these debts. These debts are to the (i) *devas* (celestials); (ii) *pitra* (parents); and (iii) *samaj* (society). The debt to celestials is repaid by performance of *yajnas* (fire sacrifices) which includes conservation of nature and peaceful conduct towards other living creatures. The debt to parents is redeemed by becoming a good student and raising a family. The debt to society is discharged by helping the poor, and by providing money to the needy in society. It would, therefore, appear that Vedic literature deems family, society and ecology as integral to human conduct.

The Ramayana, the Mahabharata and the Bhagavad Gita

It is widely believed that the *Ramayana* and the *Mahabharata* were already a part of the collective Indian consciousness prior to the 8th century BC. However, their actual composition took place subsequently, some time between the 3rd century BC and the 3rd century AD.

The *Ramayana* was first composed in Sanskrit by Valmiki some time during the second millennium BC. It consists of 24,000 couplets and is divided into seven *kandas* or books. The *Ramayana* is called *Adi Kavya* (the first epic) and Valmiki *Adi Kavi* (the first poet). It contains ethical and philosophical conclusions epitomized in the life and deeds of Lord Rama and his wife Sita. The *Ramayana* has been translated into various languages, and the *Ramcharitamanas* of Tulsidas in Hindi and the *Ramayana* of Kamba in Tamil in particular have guided generations of Indians in differentiating right from wrong, moulding the attitude of children towards their parents and siblings, defining the duties of kings, and explaining the role of religion in this life and thereafter. The *Ramayana* spread beyond the confines of South Asia, and is a living part of the human consciousness in southeast Asian countries, Africa and Europe.

The *Mahabharata* consists of over a lakh of verses and is divided into 18 *parvas* (books). It is widely believed that it was composed by Vyasa. Historians are of the view that the composition of the *Mahabharata* in poetic verse was spread over a period of 800 years, from 1000 BC to 200 BC.

The story of the *Mahabharata* centres around a heroic battle between two Bharata families, the Kauravas and the Pandavas, with the hero-god Krishna, King Dhritarashtra, and the two insuperable archers—Karna and Arjuna, playing leading roles. The *Mahabharata* contains the teachings and beliefs of various tribes and societies of that era and is a rare work of history and mythology, politics and law, as well as philosophy and theology. Many great works of enduring value in poetry, painting, sculpture, music, drama, history, philosophy, cinema and jurisprudence have been inspired by it and are cast in its image.

A portion of the *Mahabharata*—the *Bhagavad Gita* (the Lord's holy song), comprising 18 chapters, elucidates the spiritual law of action beyond the rigid confines of a single religion. It was revealed by Krishna to Arjuna on the battlefield of Kurukshetra (in Haryana). The philosophical significance of this great epic poem is central to the Indian psyche. As Vamadeo Shastri has observed, the *Bhagavad Gita* is

> a poem that is still universally read, praised, and quoted in educated Hindu society, in the form of truisms. And I ask, where else in poetry, or in religious legend, will you find a divinity, on the eve of a desperate battle, persuading the hero that it is his duty to fight, not for the promise of victory or the justness of his cause, but by demonstrating that life and death, the slayer and the slain, are philosophically indistinguishable. That the incongruity of such a discourse, at a time when the two warring sides were poised for imminent collision, has not affected the great power of the poem shows, I would like to point out, what solace the Hindu mind has drawn, at all times and in all places, from the story.[21]

The recent television shows serializing the *Ramayana* and the *Mahabharata* proved so popular that at the time of their telecast traffic in towns used to come to a standstill! In rural areas, working people and children invariably sat spellbound in front of a television set at a community centre or in a home. They wept and laughed as the situation demanded and even the electricity supply, which is irregular at the best of times in the rural areas, would function normally during the telecast. Perhaps the employees of the Electricity Board did not wish to incur the wrath of the public and of the gods by their failure to ensure the viewing of the epic tale.

Besides the four Vedas, we also have works on the sciences of music, archery, and *Ayurveda* (medicine). Mathematics and astronomy were in a highly developed stage and the value of *shunya* or zero was a fundamental contribution made by India even before Aryabhata (AD 499). In addition to the *Ramayana* and the *Mahabharata*, the *Puranas*[22] constituted an important branch of classical literature, and these are eighteen in number. Ashvaghosha's *Buddhacharita* and *Saundarananda* are two *kavyas* composed in the Ist century AD. The most celebrated *kavyas* are *Raghuvamsha* and *Kumarasambhava*, both composed in the 5th century AD. Kalidasa's *Meghadoota* is a classic of lyrical beauty. Similarly Kalidasa's *Abhijnanashakuntalam* is the greatest work of drama not only of ancient times but of subsequent times as well. The *Panchatantra* of Vishnusharma and the *Hitopadesha* are fables of eternal value.

Jain literature in Sanskrit is comparatively very little. Hem Chandra's book *Parishista Paravana*, Hari Bhatt's *Hari Bhattiya* and Sidh Sen's *Nyayavatara* are some important Jain works. Another reputed Jain author is Pujya Pad.

The earliest work in Tamil which we hear of is *Kural*, an ethical classic. It consists of 33 chapters which deal with politics and economics. It was written by Tiru-Valluar in the second century BC. The third century BC witnessed the flourishing of the famous grammarian Tolkappriyar, whose book *Tolkappiyam* is a reference work on Tamil grammar even today. The richest and the best epics in Tamil are *Silappadhikarama* and *Manimekhala*.

Buddhism, Jainism and Non-Vedic Philosophy

Buddhism: Gautama Buddha (566–486 BC) was born in Kapilavastu in north-eastern India at the foot of the Himalayas and attained enlightenment while deep in meditation under a *peepal* tree in the year 531 BC at Bodh Gaya in Bihar. Thereafter, for 45 years until he attained *Mahaparinirvana* he taught the world the way to obtain release from suffering. Logic and rationality formed the kernel of the Buddha's teaching.

The *Dharmachakra-pravartana-Sutra*, and the Buddha's repeated instructions to his followers to pursue practical methods in order to arrive at the truth, provide the exposition of the Eight-fold Path (*Arya ashtangika marga*), and the Middle Path (*madhyama pratipada*), both of which keep clear of the two extreme ways of life—one being that of luxury and the other of rigorous asceticism.

Before explaining the Eight-fold path, the Buddha expounded the four noble truths (*chaturaya satya*): (1) misery (*dukha*), (2) cause of misery (*dukha-samudaya*), (3) negation of misery (*duhkha-nirodha*) and (4) the path which leads towards negation of misery (*duhkha-nirodha-gamini-pratipada*). The last one is itself the Eight-fold Path consisting of right speech, right action, right means of livelihood, right exertion, right mindedness, right meditation, right resolution, and right point of view. The first three paths lead to *shila* (physical control), the second three to *samadhi* or *chitta* (mental control), and the last two to *prajna* (intellectual development).

The most famous of all Buddhist scriptures is the *Dhammapada* (way of duty), a Theravad Buddhist scripture. Even in his last statement, the Buddha wanted a person to strive earnestly towards his goal. The *Dhammapada* thus prescribes:

> Earnestness is the path of immortality, thoughtlessness the path of death. Those who are earnest do not die, those who are thoughtless are as if dead already.
>
> If a man is earnest and exerts himself, if he is ever-mindful, his deeds are pure, if he acts with consideration and restraint and lives according to the Law, then his glory will increase.[23]

Jainism: The world 'Jain' comes from the root word 'ji' (to conquer), and Jainism literally means a philosophy to conquer desire. Its exponent Mahavira at birth was named Vardhamana (599—527 BC). He was an older contemporary of the Buddha, and propounded his religious philosophy in Bihar at the same time as the Buddha. Jainism has two sects, the Shvetambaras (whose monks are white-clad) and the Digambaras (whose monks are sky-clad or naked). The Digambaras deny that women can reach liberation from the cycle of life.

The philosophy of Jainism can be technically called *Syadavada* (the theory of 'maybe') in which no definite or absolute statement can be made about any question. Jain logic was a subtle and disguised protest against the dogmatism of Vedic principles. The world, according to Jainism, consists of co-existing but independent categories of the *jiva* (conscious) and the *ajiva* (unconscious). There is no god or creator, and man is the maker of his own destiny. The best life is the life of renunciation. *Ahimsa* or non-injury is the greatest virtue. For obtaining freedom from the cycle of birth and death, three principles should be followed, namely right knowledge, right belief, and right action. These three principles are described as the three jewels of Jainism. The *jiva* (soul) inhabits the body, be it human, animal, or plant, and is subject to the law of *karma* and rebirth. It suffers by its contact with matter and is born again and again to suffer. Its highest endeavour is to free itself from this bondage and obtain salvation which can be attained by higher knowledge and meditation.

The path to happiness does not lie in acquiring wealth, but in controlling desire. For example, one of Jainism's dictums states:

> Happiness dependent upon others leads to pain. Only independent happiness is commendable. Else how could the ascetics be called happy?[24]

Non-Vedic philosophy: Along with Vedic culture, the agnostic (*nastika*) creeds and opinions also developed around 800 BC, both independently and also as a reaction to the Brahminical order.

These philosophical thoughts are associated with *Charavaka*[25] or *lokayata*. *Charavaka* comes from the world *charv* (to eat) and reflects the hedonistic philosophy of 'eat, drink, and be merry'. The term *lokayata* is derived from the root word *loka* (world) and reflects the belief that only this world exists. There is hardly any formal literature on Indian hedonistic philosophy, but its essence is encapsulated in a few popular sentences, as for instance

> As long as life remains let a man live happily; let him feed on ghee even though he runs into debt; when once the body is reduced to ashes, how can it ever return again?[26]

These ideas are still familiar to people all over the country and are being carried forward through an oral tradition.

There are three main schools of thought of this philosophy: epistemology, ethics, and metaphysics. The first school (*pratyakshavada*) maintains that perception is the only source of valid knowledge, the second (*sukhavada*) recommends the pleasures of the senses to be the ultimate aim of life; and the third (*jadavada*) points out that the world is only material in nature. This philosophy which has existed since pre-Buddhist times is mentioned in different contexts in Sanskrit literature, but it has no authentic or comprehensive text of its own.

IV
Visual Arts

Early Indian architecture can be seen in the remains of the cities of the Indus Valley civilization. The streets ran in straight lines and crossed one another at right angles. Major towns were built entirely of bricks, a larger number of which were properly fired. The drainage system, as demonstrated at Mohenjodaro and Chanhudaro, was sophisticated in its design. Every street had a brick-lined drainage channel to which were connected the smaller tributary drains from the houses on either side. Larger brick culverts (5'long, 2'wide) with corbelled roofs were constructed on the outskirts of the city to carry away storm water. The great bath (40 × 23 feet), a palatial building (220 × 115 feet)—all at Mohenjodaro and a store house (168 × 134 feet) at Harappa reveal the architectural skill of the Indus people.

Obscurity shrouds the period between the decline of the Harappan culture around 1500 BC and the emergence of the Mauryas in the 3rd century BC. The excavations at Patna and Kumrahar nearby have revealed that in the 3rd century BC, the Mauryas had built a fine capital. The discovery of huge wooden palisades and a large pillared hall built on a wooden substratum prove that wood was extensively used in buildings.

A new form of architecture that developed at this time was rock-cut sanctums excavated from the hard rock of hills. Ashoka and his grandson Dashrath commissioned for Ajivika monks a group of seven caves in Gaya in Bihar, four of which are at Barabar and three at Nagarjuna. The entrance to the most famous cave at Barabar, called the Lomas Rishi, is beautifully carved in low relief. It emulates the wooden doorway of a simple hut. From these early beginnings developed a tradition of rock-cut architecture which spread all over India and constitutes one of the greatest movements in Indian architecture. Though examples have been discovered in Orissa, Andhra Pradesh and Gujarat, this architectural movement was most prolific in the Western Ghats at Ellora and Ajanta. These Buddhist complexes comprise *viharas* (residential caves) and *chaityas* (cave temples).

Stupas were raised to enshrine the body relics of Buddha or of Buddhist teachers. Ashoka is said to have built 84,000 *stupas* in the country, but only a few have survived. The finest *stupa* is at Sanchi. It consists of an *anda* (solid hemisphere) and stands on a *medhi* (circular base). On its flattened top rests a *harmika* (kiosk) and a *chhatravali* (stone umbrella). The stupa itself is plain and devoid of any ornamentation but the *vekika* (railing) that surrounds it is richly decorated with sculptured figures and lotus patterns.

Ashoka erected about forty stone pillars at different places in India including Sarnath, Sanchi, Vaishali, Rampurva, and Amaravati. These pillars are about 40 to 50 feet tall, broad at the base, and tapering at the top. The shaft is plain and monolithic (i.e., made of one single stone), and is surmounted by a capital shaped like an inverted lotus. The shaft is joined to the capital by a thick and strong pin-type copper dowel. Upon the capital is placed the figure of an animal.

In caves and rock shelters at Mirzapur (Uttar Pradesh), Bhimbetka (Madhya Pradesh) and Kupgallu (District Bellary in Karnataka) some remarkable cave paintings of prehistoric times have been found. A thousand such painted caves have now been reported. These simple yet forceful drawings of palaeolithic men inaugurate the panorama of Indian cave paintings. They were the forerunners of Ajanta and Ellora.

Indian literature is replete with reference to the existence of wall paintings in royal palaces, houses of noblemen and places of worship. Of all the ancient monuments of India the thirty rock-cut caves at Ajanta have earned a unique place by virtue of their having the earliest historical and the most perfect specimens of Indian cave painting. Ever since the fortuitous discovery by the officers of the Madras army in 1819, the name of Ajanta, attesting the acme of artistic excellence attained by the ancient painter's brush, has cast a spell on the Indian mind.

The excavation of caves in rock was itself a laborious and time-consuming process; then the walls and ceilings were plastered and the bare walls were converted into an eloquent canvas. The narrative scenes were drawn from the Buddha's present and previous lives. The earliest painting (caves 9 and 10) are attributed to the 2nd century BC (Satavahana period), belonging to the Hinayana phase of Buddhism wherein Gautam Buddha is not represented in human form. The Mahayana phase, which started in the 4th century AD, synchronizes with the rule of the Vakatakas (caves 1,2,16 and 17). These caves were neither painted at one time nor by one person; nevertheless, they maintain a unity of vision and have stood the test of the highest art standards. Among the many masterpieces are 'Bodhisattva Padmapani' (cave 1), 'Consort of Bodhisattva' (cave 1), 'Black Princess' (cave 17), 'Palace Scene' (cave 17), and 'Toilet Scene' (cave 17). The paintings on the ceiling of the ante-chamber (cave 21) and on the verandah (cave 17) are also notable.

The paintings at Ajanta mirror contemporary life as it was lived in the palaces, towns, villages, and hermitages. They serve as an illuminative documentary on the divinities of the Buddhist panthe-on featuring Bodhisattvas, gods, and *yakshas*[27] (semi-gods), *kinnaras*,[28] *gandharvas*[29] and *apsaras*[30] (heavenly dancers). The paintings present a living record of the temples, forts, huts, *stupas*, and houses as they existed at that time. They record the dress and ornaments, arms and armour, utensils, and musical instruments of that period.

Ajanta's legacy is visible in the murals at Bagh, Ellora, Badami, Leepakshi, and Alchi in India. Beyond India, art centres such as the Dun Huang caves in China, Bamiyan in Afghanistan, Tsparang in Tibet, and Sigriya in Sri Lanka bear witness to Ajanta's influence. Mural painting continued through the centuries and is practised even today, but the Ajanta murals have hardly any peer in the realm of world art, if one were to consider their artistic quality and antiquity.

The sculptural art of India occupies a prominent place in the history of world art. The earliest sculptures come from the Indus Valley culture (3000–1500 BC). The human and animal figures in bronze, stone, and terracotta unearthed from that region reveal a high degree of finish and excellence. They exhibit the ability of the sculptor in the rendering of anatomical details, as also the depiction of expression and movement with vigour and effect. A mutilated male torso in red sandstone from Harappa and another torso in greyish limestone—the first dancer in art form—are truly marvels of human industry at that early age. The bust of a priest in stone from Mohenjodaro is an impressive figure, stylistic and formal. There are innumerable terracotta figures of animals such as the bull, buffalo, monkey, dog, and rhinoceros as well as birds and reptiles. They reveal the sculptor's consummate ability to represent them with realistic effect. The figures of animals carved on the steatite seals convey the technical skill of the artisans. A bronze buffalo with its ponderous body is a remarkable specimen of fine modelling. The 'Dancing Girl' in bronze from Mohenjodaro is a work of surpassing beauty.

No specimen of art has so far been traced in the intervening period between the Indus Valley culture and the Mauryan age, when, in the 3rd century BC, a sudden efflorescence of art occurred under the patronage of the Mauryan ruler Ashoka. This period constitutes a notable epoch in the sculptural art of India. Ashoka commissioned the erection of monolithic pillars at various places, and inscribed his edicts upon them. Thirty of these pillars are still intact. The art of polishing hard stone was carried to great perfection imparting to it a mirror finish. The ruins of the many-storeyed buildings of Nalanda University—the world's finest university until the twelfth century AD—and its official seal indicate that it was an architectural wonder.

A remarkable achievement of Mauryan court art is the Lion Capital, now displayed at the Sarnath Museum. It is the emblem of the Republic of India. Besides court art, there existed a popular form of art, specimens of which are encountered in the *yaksha* and *yakshi* figures such as Besanager Yakshi (Indian Museum, Calcutta), Parkham Yaksha (Mathura Museum), Didarganj Yakshi (Patna Museum), the Jain Tirthankara from Lohanipur, as also portrait heads. All of these have the distinctive Mauryan polish. The Didarganj Yakshi is, artistically, the best of these figures.

The Mauryans were succeeded by the Shunga rulers (1st–2nd centuries BC) in the north. The gateways and railings of the Buddhist *stupas* at Sanchi and Bharhut constructed during this period present a vast panorama of life. In the Deccan, the rock-cut sanctuaries of the Buddhists, Jains, and Hindus are notable for their sculptures. The sandstone hills known as Khandagiri and Udaigiri in Orissa are full of Jain caves containing beautiful figures. In Andhra Pradesh the Buddhist *stupas* at Amaravati and Nagarjunakonda erected by the Satavahana and Ikshavaku rulers respectively are masterpieces.

The beginning of the Christian era witnessed the emergence of two schools of sculpture—one at Mathura and the other at Gandhara. The Gandhara school bears a distinct stamp of Greek influence. The rulers of the Gupta, Gurjara-Pratihara, Chandella, and Eastern Ganga dynasties have left a legacy of superb temples at places such as at Bhitargaon, Khajuraho, and Konarak. Each of these temples is embellished with sculptures of the finest quality.

V

Performing Arts

Music

The technical word for music throughout India is *sangita*, which originally included dance as well as vocal and instrumental music. Siva is the creator of this threefold art and his mystic dance symbolizes the rhythmic motion of the universe.

Earlier, it was believed that Egyptians were the first to give music to the world in the second millennium BC. The Dravidian people of the Indus Valley culture had evolved a music and dance system in the third millennium BC. The bronze figure of the Dancing Girl, the Dancing Male Torso in stone and a number of motifs on the seals resembling musical instruments prove beyond doubt India's claim of being the land where music originated.

Vedic literature furnishes a wide range of musical instruments. These have been classified into percussion instruments such as the *dundubhi* (drum) and *aghati* (cymbals), stringed instruments such as the *vina* (lute), and wind instruments such as the *nadi* (flute).

The hymns of the *Rigveda* and the *Samaveda* are the earliest examples of words set to music. The *Ramayana* refers to the sublime chanting of the Vedic hymns. The *Mahabharata* (*c.* 1000 BC) speaks of the seven *svaras*. The theory of consonance is also alluded to. The first reference to musical theory is in the *Rikpratishakhya* (*c.* 400 BC) which mentions three voice registers and the seven notes of the gamut. It was approximately at the same time that Pythagoras in Greece (510 BC) worked out the Greek musical system. The *Pali Pitaka* (*c.* 300 BC) refers to two disciples of the Buddha attending a musical performance. The *Mahajanaka Jataka* (*c.* 200 BC) mentions the four great sounds (*param maha shabda*) of the drum, horn, gong, and cymbals.

In the Tamil books *Purananuru* and *Pattupattu* (*c.* AD 100) three kinds of drums are recorded—the battle drum, judgement drum, and the sacrificial drum. The Tamil work *Paripadal* (*c.* AD 150) gives the names of seven *Palai* (ancient Dravidian modes) and a peculiar instrument, the yazh, like the *vina* but now obsolete. The *Shilpadikarama (c.* AD 300), a Buddhist drama, mentions the drum, flute, *vina*, and yazh, and also notes specimens of early Tamil songs. This book records some of the earliest expositions of the Indian musical scale, giving the seven notes of the gamut and also a number of the modes and *ragas* in use at that time. *Tivakaram*, a Jain lexicon of the same period, provides detailed information about early Dravidian music. It also gives the Tamil names of the seven *svaras* with the equivalent Sanskrit sol-fa initials (*Sa, Ri, Ga*, etc). This evidence, taken together with the frequent references to the science of music and to musical performances, both vocal and instrumental, clearly indicates that before the Christian era musical culture had reached a high level among the Aryans in the North and the Dravidians in the South.

The oldest detailed exposition of Indian musical theory is found in *Natyashastra*[31] (Science of Drama) attributed to the sage Bharata who lived at the beginning of the Christian era. Seven chapters of the *Natyashastra* (Chapter 28–34) are devoted to music. These contain an in-depth exposition of *svaras, shrutis, gramas, murchhanas* and *jatis.*

Classical music in India has maintained its distinct identity and is continuously reaching greater heights. Observers have described Indian classical music as the oldest of the old and the newest of the new.

Theatre

In its origins, Indian theatre was the theatre of the Indian people. According to a legend quoted at the very beginning of the text of the *Natyashastra*, all the gods went to Brahma, the creator, complaining that the 'People all over the world have taken to vulgar ways; they have grown greedy, avaricious, jealous and quarrelsome; they do not know whether they are happy or miserable. Please let us have some diversion which could be both heard and seen.'[32] So Brahma created drama.

In my childhood in Bihat village, in Bihar, I was exposed to two forms of theatre. The first of these was the *Ramlila* which was based on the *Ramcharitamanas* by Sant Tulsidas. The *Ramlila* performances extended for nearly a month and we used to witness it every evening. The second was *natak*, staged by enterprising and educated boys of the village; the girls never participated in it. It was much later, when I was posted in Assam, that I had the pleasure of witnessing the *Raasleela* based on the loves of Krishna. The finest and the most impressive rendering of the *Raasleela* that I have attended was in 1966. This was organized by Dakhinpata Satra at Majuli, believed to be the biggest river island of the world, where unlike in my village boys played the male roles, and girls played the female roles.

The famous *Pururavas and Urvashi* hymn (*Rigveda*, X.95) embodies one of the most romantic love stories which provides excellent material for dramatization. In the Vedic period, Indians developed the form of dialogue-drama. The art of puppet plays was also developed a couple of centuries before Christ and the dialogues which were intoned by the *sutradhara* (performers), manipulating the strings tied to the puppets, gave a decided impetus to the emergence of drama in ancient India. The Indonesian genius has developed puppetry in a meaningful manner based on this tradition.

In the Jogimara and Sitabenga caves in Bihar (3rd century BC) there are inscriptions containing love songs which are highly suggestive of the existence of a developed dramatic form. The earliest specimens of drama are found in the fragments of the Buddhist play entitled *Sariputra-Parakrama* attributed to Ashvaghosa, the court poet of Kanishka (Ist century AD). The earliest available complete dramatic works are the thirteen plays ascribed to Bhasha (*c.* AD 100). These plays reveal a dual character—epic and artistic. Most of the plays are drawn from the *Ramayana*, *Mahabharata*, and *Harivamsha*. Next in chronology comes Shudraka (*c.* AD 150) whose

Mrichchhakatikam (Little Clay Cart), a comedy, depicts Indian society of the 2nd century AD.

It was during the Ist century AD that Bharata composed his *Natyashastra* with thirty-seven chapters comprising 5569 verses in short metre called *shlokas*. In addition, there are prose passages which read like explanatory notes. It is the first audio-visual script. It is *lok vritta, anukarna* (the imitation of men and their doings). All the media of expression—speech, gestures, movements and intonations—must be used. Bharata's genius does not leave out any aspect concerned with drama. He recommends three kinds of theatre houses: *vikrishta* (large), *tryasra* (small) and *chatarasva* (medium-sized). He also instructs the audience as to how a play must be seen and enjoyed. There can be little doubt that the performing arts in India have been primarily guided by the *Natyashastra*. This classical treatise is relevant for all times and one can get its flavour in the following goal which it prescribes for drama:

> occasionally piety, occasionally sport, occasionally wealth, occasionally peace of mind, occasionally laughter, occasionally fighting, occasionally sexual passion, occasionally slaughter.... [Theatre] will produce wholesome instruction, create courage, pastime [entertainment] and pleasure.[33]

With Kalidasa (4th century AD) drama reached the pinnacle of artistic creation. His three plays—*Malavikagnimitram, Vikramovarshiyam* and *Abijyanshakuntalam* are famous in world literature. He was followed by Bhavabhuti, Vishakhadatta, Harsha, and many more.

The *Natyashastra* of Bharata plays the same role in the realm of the performing arts as the Vedas in religious philosophy. However, the fact that the tribals and other ethnic communities have developed their own theatre, dance and music needs to be kept in view. Some of these are still a part of a living culture in India's north-east and in parts of Bihar, Madhya Pradesh, Orissa, Andhra Pradesh, Kerala and Karnataka. It may be recalled that ethnic and tribal drama flourished side by side with Sanskrit drama from 200 BC–AD700.

Dance

Classical Indian dance is the most beautiful and significant symbol of the spiritual and artistic approach of the Hindu mind. Shiva, the eternal *nataraja*, personifies cosmic rhythm in its endless movement of involution, evolution and devolution.

Both the *Aitareya* and *Kausitki* of the *Rigveda* contain references to dancing. The *Shatapatha Brahmana* has the legend of Urvashi dancing for Pururava. The *Upanishads* refer to the *nritta* (music) and *nata* (drama). In the *Grihya Sutras* the art of music and dancing are diligently cultivated and are present at every stage of domestic life. No ceremony, no ritual, no festivity is complete without music and dance.

The *apsaras*, *nata*, *nartaka*, *ganika* and *gayika*—all dancers and singers—adorn the *Ramayana*. Indra sends Rambha to entice Vishvamitra with her dance. The elaborate feast of dance and music with which Rishi Bharadvaja entertains Bharata is incomparable to any festivity of the same grandeur in literature. There are innumerable allusions to and descriptions of dancing in the *Mahabharata*. Menaka, Urvashi and Rambha—the celestial dancing *apsaras*, the *gandharvas* headed by Tumburu, and the *kinnaras*, (singers by birth) were all skilled in music, dancing and chanting. Arjuna as Brihannala (impotent) proved an expert teacher in song (*gita*), instrumental music (*vadya*) and dance (*nritya*). Krishna is the supreme dancer in the *Puranas*.

The *Ashtadhyayi* provides a wealth of information on the music and dance known to Panini. Kautilya advises the State to maintain *nartana* (dancing girls) and use them even for diplomacy.

Courtesans such as Amrapali and Salavati feature in Buddhist legends. Their fee for dancing was high but the classical tradition of dancing and music was preserved by them. The *Rayapaseniya*, a Jain canonical work, records thirty-two types of dances.

Indian sculpture derived its inspiration from dance and vice versa. In fact the theory of Indian dancing cannot be understood in isolation; it has always to be comprehended as a complex synthesis of the arts of literature, sculpture and music. The writer of the *Natyashastra* is fully conscious of the all-embracing quality of this art when he says at the very beginning of his treatise that this art of dance and drama will be enriched by the teaching of all scriptures (*shastra*) and will give a review of all arts and crafts.[34] The bronze Dancing Girl and the stone Male Dancer from the Indus Valley culture ascribable to the 3rd millennium BC, are the first representations of Indian dancers in art form. The *shalabhanjikas, apsaras, devis* as well as gods such as Shiva, Ganesha and Krishna have been portayed as dancers in ancient Indian sculpture.

According to the *Abhinaya Darpana* (and also the *Sangitaratnakar* of later date) Indian dancing is divided into three distinct categories: *natya, nritya* and *nritta. Natya* corresponds to drama, and *nritya* is interpretative dance performed to the words sung in a musical melody. *Nritta* on the other hand signifies pure dance, where the body movements do not express any mood (*bhava*) nor convey any meaning. All these aspects use movements of the limbs and poses of the human body as their medium.

Another classification in dance is *tandava lasya. Tandava* the vigorous dancing of Shiva signifies the masculine aspect while, the gentle, delicate dancing of Parvati is recognized as the *lasya* or feminine aspect of dance.

VI
Philosophy, Science and Economics

Philosophy

In ancient times, Indian religious thought, metaphysics and philosophy had a symbiotic relationship with one another. Before the beginning of the Christian era, the learned Brahmins of India, drawing upon their *shruti* and *smriti* traditions, as well as Buddhist and Jain philosophies, developed six systems of philosophy dealing with the nature of the world, logical methods of analysis, and knowledge.

These six systems of philosophy are (1) *Nyaya*, (2) *Vaiseshika*, (3) *Samkhya*, (4) *Yoga*, (5) *Purva-Mimamsa*, and (6) *Vedanta*.

Nyaya means logic. According to the *Nyaya* school of philosophy, the four sources of knowledge are: perception (*pratyaksha*), inference (*anumana*), analogy (*upamana*) and credible testimony (*shabda*). The process of reasoning and the analysis of the process itself are the basic tenets of *Nyaya*. The first and the most authoritative exponent of *Nyaya* was Gautama (different from Gautama, the Buddha), who composed the *Nyayasutra* in the third century BC. Much later, in the twelfth–thirteenth century AD, Pandit Gangesh of Mithila provided a cogent analysis. It was a great pleasure in my childhood to talk to Sanskrit scholars, particularly the *Nyayacharyas* in my village.

The *Vaiseshika* deals with the nature of the cosmos. According to this philosophy, four kinds of atoms determine the value of all material objects; these are earth, water, fire, and air. But there are substances in the world which are not material, such as space, time, ether, mind, and soul. The most outstanding exponent of the *Vaiseshika* school of philosophy was Kanada. His monumental work, the *Vaiseshikasutra,* has served as the basic document of this philosophy ever since its composition in the 3rd century BC. The founders of *Nyaya* and *Vaiseshika* have shown great heights of analytical ability with respect to physical and metaphysical issues and these, in turn, have helped the development of the faculty of analysis as well as contemplation among succeeding generations of students of these disciplines.

The *Samkhya* philosophy recognizes two categories in the universe: human beings (*purusha*) and nature (*prakriti*). Prakriti represents a fundamental substance, and under the influence of *purusha* it keeps evolving. The *Samkhya* philosophy also highlights three qualities, namely purity (*sattva*), energy or passion (*rajas*), and anger or darkness (*tamas*). Each of these three conflicting aspects of *purusha* play different roles in evolution. The *Samkhya* school was founded by Kapila in the seventh century BC and deals with the interaction between humans and nature. Several of its ideas are of great relevance in the conservation of ecology and in restraining certain traits of human behaviour through education and moral conduct.

The philosophy of *Yoga* believes in evolution, and that God is the creator. The *Yoga* system of discipline consists of exercises of the mind and the body, through which it believes freedom is achieved. *Yoga* prescribes various methods of concentration, and its exercises have world-wide appeal. Outside India it is widely accepted by students, executives, and scholars.

The *Purva-Mimamsa* deals with the interpretation of the Vedas and more particularly, the nature and manifestation of *dharma* (right action). The *Aerwa-Mimasa-sutra* of Jaimini composed in the 4th century BC provides the basic text of this philosophy.

The *Vedanta* philosophical system springs from the *Upanishads* and its central thesis is the *Upanishadic* doctrine of the *Brahman*. This is the most important philosophical system and is widely prevalent in India and abroad.

Indian philosophy has, over the years, produced some of the finest minds. These six schools of thought have sharpened the Indian intellect and made it capable of analysing new ideas of different cultures. The Indian mind has expressed itself from time to time, drawing from Greek, Roman, Confucian, Islamic, Christian, and other philosophies; the basis being the sound intellectual and analytical methods provided by these six philosophical systems.

Science

The Indus Valley civilization offers clear testimony to the fact that the principles of standardization, including weights and measures, were prevalent, otherwise, it would not have been possible to build cities in conformity with a universal plan resembling the layout of a chess-board, and using well-fired bricks of uniform size and specification in construction. Pottery used in the homes of that time goes further to support this point of view.

In the Hindu philosophy of cosmology, Mount Meru occupies a central place. This was further developed by the Jains and the Buddhists. As H.J.J. Winter has observed, the atomic theory developed by the Indians during this time had met with a divergence of views. He writes:

> atoms could be grouped together to form molecules, and whilst the atoms envisaged by the Jains and *Vaiseshikas* were eternal, those of the Buddhists, being included in a phenomenalist view of nature, appear and disappear by cycles.[35]

Astronomy

India made significant contributions in the realm of astronomy as well. The earliest source dealing exclusively with astronomy is *Jyotisha Vedanga* which might have been composed in the 5th century BC. This book deals with the rules for calculating the position of the new and full moon amongst the 27 *nakshatras*. The *Surya-siddhanta* is reckoned as one of the most ancient astronomical treatises. Parasara, the author of the *Parasaratantra*, lived earlier than the 2nd century BC. His name is linked with the Vedic calendar. After Parasara came Garga, the author of *Garga-Samhita*, in the first century BC.

Among the Jain texts, it is unanimously believed that works like *Surya-Prajnapti, Chandra-Prajnapati, Jambudvipa-Prajnapti, Sthananga, Uttaradhyayana, Bhagavati, Anuyogadvara* and *Sama-Vayanga* contain astronomical texts and were composed between the sixth and second centuries BC.

Medicine

The *Atharva Veda* talks about medicine. Dhanvantari is regarded as the custodian deity of the elixir of immortality. We also have records to establish that by first century AD, surgical equipment including 20 different types of knives and needles and 26 articles of dressing were in use. It was, however, due to the genius Charaka, a court physician to King Kanishka (Ist century AD) that Ayurveda became a well-codified system of medicine and continues to be so.

Economics

Kautilya's *Artha-shastra* and Aristotle's *Politics* could well be the two most outstanding works on science, economics, statecraft, and the art of administration prior to the Christian era. Kautilya was the Prime Minister of the Mauryan emperor Chandragupta, who ruled from *c.* 321 to 300 BC. The *Artha-shastra* contains in detail, the duties of a king and the methods available at his command for practising statecraft, as well as for ensuring the welfare of the people. Kautilya also went on to prescribe both righteous and not so righteous methods that could be employed by the king for the governance of the country as well as for the maintenance of its sovereignty. Interestingly, the book also mentions the need for a bureaucracy to uphold *dharma*. The book is a storehouse of information about communication by land and sea, agriculture and irrigation, ores and mining, plants and medicines, mechanical contrivances to be used for war, as well as implements for use in agriculture, architecture, and mining.

VII
India in Asia

It was quite natural for a civilization of this magnitude and depth to extend its influence beyond its territories. By the beginning of the Christian era, the civilization of India had begun to spread across the Bay of Bengal into both the mainland and the islands of South East Asia. Both Hindu and Buddhist religious philosophies dominated the consciousness of the people of Thailand, Indonesia, Burma, Malaysia, Cambodia and Vietnam. Even the system of governance that developed in these countries was based on Indian polity. Many commentators have described the eastward spread of the Indian civilization as a series of waves and the countries mentioned above as a part of 'greater India' in cultural terms. One of the latest publications sponsored by the Government of Indonesia acknowledges this in the following passage:

The great store of Indian religion and literature provided the subject-matter for classical Indonesian architecture, art and dance, and the artistic techniques applied were likewise developed from Indian foundations, but it is clear that these traditions and techniques quickly received a special interpretation on Indonesian soil, in conformity with locally perceived needs and values... On the Indian subcontinent the same process was occurring. The great traditions of Hinduism and Buddhism, emerging from their centers of origin in more or less pristine form, would be altered to suit local belief and tradition by the cultures that adopted them. Translation from Sanskrit or Pali (the 'official' languages of Hinduism and Buddhism respectively) into a local tongue was itself a symptom of this process. Since the first Indian textual sources referred to in Indonesia were those originating from the centers of high Indian culture, the cultural remove was similar to that between an outlying Indian culture and the source in Indonesia, acculturation proceeded from these sources along uniquely Indonesian lines, even as cultural interchange with all parts of the subcontinent followed in its course.[36]

The monarchy in Thailand, like the monarchy in Nepal, has Indian origins. The Ramayana formed the basis of Thai monarchy and continues to do so despite Buddhism having become the religion of Thailand. Satya Vrat Shastri in the Preface to his monumental work in Sanskrit, *Sriramakirtimahakavyam*, observes as follows:

> It is said, and correctly so, that if there is any truly Asian epic, it is the Ramayana. It is all too familiar to the peoples of the region who have added to it much of their own, a proof, if ever the same were needed, of their having completely owned it.

He goes on to add,

> it is not just an accident that I have chosen to compose a Mahakavya on the Thai Ramayana, the Ramakien or the Ramakirti. What I have done in the present case is that I have chosen to concentrate on as many of the episodes of the Ramakien as are not to be met with in the Valmiki Ramayana or other Indian Ramayanas, highlighting thereby the contribution of the Thais to the development of the Rama story.[37]

The interaction between the Indian brahmins and pandits, monks and scholars, and the indigenous population of these countries led to a process of Indianization in these areas. Several scholars have documented the mechanics of cultural fusion between India and South East Asian countries in the domain of art and architecture, religious beliefs and forms of worship, linguistics and literature, methods of crop cultivation and land administration, and polity management. Even the conversion to Islam of several of the island areas in South East Asia in a subsequent period has the impact of Indian influence. The role played by traders in the dissemination of Indian culture was of great value.

Similarly, Indian cultural influence extended to Central Asia. As early as in the third century BC a number of Indians had settled in some parts of Central Asia. The travelogue of Fa-hsien reveals that by the 5th century AD practically the whole of Central Asia had come under the influence of Indian religion and culture. Indian settlements were evident in Yarkand, Kashgar, Khotan, Kuchor, Karashar, and Turfan. Sanskrit and Prakrit, along with local dialects flourished in Central Asian countries well before the Christian era. Indian culture made a deep impact on Afghanistan, Iran, Greece, Turkey, and several other countries.

The Chinese civilization, which is as old as that of India, also drew its main substance from India as indicated by J. LeRoy Davidson:

> Buddhism was India's contribution to China. Moreover, it was a contribution that had such shocking and seminal effects on the religion, philosophy, and arts of the adoptive country that it penetrated the entire fabric of Chinese culture.[38]

The two Indian Buddhist monks, Matarya and Kashyaka, made an immense contribution towards the introduction of Buddhism in China in the first century AD. Their efforts also paved the way for a large number of Buddhist monks from India to visit China in subsequent years. At the same time, the quest for drawing further knowledge from India was a dominant concern among Chinese scholars and mendicants. The visits of Fa hsien and Huien Tsang to India are most outstanding in this regard as both of them undertook this difficult journey at the risk of their lives, with the sole objective of acquiring knowledge from India which would give substance to China's civilization—a task in which their success is indeed of historic dimensions.

Recognizing India's contribution to the world civilization, Will Durant puts it very well when he says,

> India was the motherland of our race, and Sanskrit the mother of Europe's languages; she was the mother of our philosophy, mother through the Arabs, of our mathematics; mother, through the Buddha, of the ideals embodied in Christianity, mother, through the village community of self-government and democracy. Mother India is in many ways the mother of us all.[38]

VIII
Authority and Respect

I am fascinated by two aspects of the Indian way of life which are integral to India's culture, namely authority and respect; and *sruti* and *smriti*.

There has always been a line of demarcation between authority and respect, and this division has acted as an integral part of Indian mythology. The kings depended upon sages and mendicants for guidance and treated them with considerable reverence. The position of a sage, therefore, was higher in public consciousness than that of the king. The king and his consort rose at the sight of a sage and went to his hermitage whenever they needed guidance. The sage, in turn, taught the scriptures to the royal children and imparted to them training in statecraft as well as in the use of armaments. Whenever a sage felt that something needed to be conveyed to the king, he undertook a journey to the palace and was invariably treated with great deference by the king and his ministers. The names of Vashistha, Vishvamitra, Agastya, Sandipani, Dronacharya, Krishna, Buddha, Shankaracharya, and Ramanuja naturally come to one's mind. This tradition received institutional expression during the reign of Chandragupta

Maurya. The relationship between Chandragupta Maurya and his guru, Chanakya, was a rare combination of authority being invested in the king, and respect being shown to the teacher. This tradition was a hallmark of life in the villages where power rested with the village chief but the most respected person was always the learned brahmin of the village.

In a pre-democratic society, people were driven to take up political offices by their longing for a comfortable life and desire to enjoy the respect that such an office bestowed upon the one who held it. The proximity to the king or the queen had its own glamour. During the freedom struggle, the Indian people were attracted to politics by their resolve to pursue the national goal of independence from colonial rule, and by an irresistible desire to fight for the same regardless of its consequences. Mahatma Gandhi not only made truth and non-violence instruments of action in his valiant fight against colonial rule but also exhorted persons in public life to work for the spread of education, better sanitation and the use of *swadeshi* (indigenous) products. During the last five decades of the working of the Indian democracy, one has clearly witnessed that people long for political power largely for three reasons: to pursue certain values or ideals in which they believe, to satisfy the longing that every human being has for self-affirmation, and finally, to acquire the power and numerous perquisites that accompany political positions, even in a democratic order. The easy movement of politicians from one party to another, and the bizarre fight for retention of perquisites at public cost, have gone to establish that people belonging to the first category are becoming rare in Indian public life.

The fact that Mahatma Gandhi commanded more respect and authority than a Governor General or a Prime Minister is widely believed to be in consonance with India's rich cultural tradition of making a distinction between authority and respect. This cultural tradition, perhaps, seems to have ended at the national level with the demise of Vinoba Bhave and Jaya Prakash Narayan. There is considerable doubt about its re-emergence, even though it continues to be observed in several Indian villages.

The Indian scriptures and subsequent knowledge related thereto have their origin in *sruti* and *smriti* traditions. The Vedas are believed to be divine revelations (*sruti*). The term *smriti* signifies an oral tradition wherein the teachers passed to their students the texts which they themselves had received from their masters. The *guru-shishya parampara* (teacher-student tradition) was a significant institution that emerged out of the *sruti* and *smriti* traditions. Teaching was then perceived to be a religious duty placed upon the brahmins and the students were sent to live with a *guru* and learn not only the scriptures but also statecraft, music, warfare, science, and agriculture. In time a student would attain the status of a *guru*, and carry on the tradition of transmitting his knowledge to his disciples. The institution of *guru-shishya parampara* covered the entire gamut of creative activity, namely religious discourse, history, dance, drama, poetry, painting, and sculpture. In this process, the learned mind renewed the sacred texts in the light of new social, religious, and economic realities as the *guru* was required to interpret the scriptures to find answers to emerging problems.

The institution of the *guru-shishya parampara* declined over the years and it is now seen mainly in the realm of music and dance. New schools and institutions, seminar and discussion forums, have however emerged replacing, in a way, the traditional modes of learning. The development of writing manuscripts, followed by the technology of printing books and journals, and today the storage of classics in computer software have ensured that we do not lose anything of the past as human memory cannot always be relied upon to carry forward all of what it has received. However, the present system has its own inadequacy in storing information, as the renewal that occurred through dialogue in the old tradition is not a part of computer software.

There is no denying that archives, libraries and computer technology play an important part in the conservation and interpretation of the past. But their role has been more in the realm of maintenance of texts rather than in its renewal. For renewal comes by using, by doing, and by making the past an effective memory and an effective force in the present.

It is true that maintenance and renewal are inter-related. But renewal is not revival. What is necessary is to free a thought from specificity of its context and to help what is immanent in that thought to emerge in the new context in order that it meets the social and intellectual requirements of the present. Such developments in new directions have infinite possibilities in India. Renewal also presupposes the capability of a civilization to reject an ideal. It should also be our endeavour to learn from other civilizations—the Chinese, the Islamic, the Latin American—by studying their experience and thereby enriching our own.

In a wider sense, history encompasses the development of human consciousness, a handing over or easy passage of ideas and beliefs from one generation to the other. As a remarkable feat of conservation of memory, the Hindus, through the tradition of *Smriti* and *Sruti*, have passed on the *Ramayana*, the *Mahabharata*, the *Bhagavad Gita* and other sacred texts to the present day. This aspect of historical consciousness of Indians was highlighted by Rabindranath Tagore in his paper, 'A Vision of Indian History', where he writes:

> I love India, not because I cultivate the idolatry of geography, not because I have had the chance to be born in her soil, but because she has saved through tumultuous ages the living words that have issued from the illuminated consciousness of her great sons.[39]

Notes and References

1. There is no single comprehensive definition of culture. The author has relied upon the following four descriptions:

   (i) Edward B. Taylor, *Primitive Culture: Researches into the Development of Mythology, Philosophy, Religion, Language, Art and Custom*, Murray, London, 3rd ed, vols. 2, 1871, p.1.

   According to Taylor, culture 'is that complex whole' which includes 'knowledge, belief, art, morals, laws, customs, and any other capabilities and habits acquired by man as a member of society'.

(ii) A.L. Kroeber, *Anthropology: Race, Language, Culture, Psychology, Prehistory*, Oxford & IBH Publishing Co, Calcutta, by arrangement with Harcourt, Brace & World, Inc, New York, 1948, p.253.

Kroeber holds that one can roughly 'approximate what culture is by saying that it is that which the human species has and other social species lack. This would include speech, knowledge, beliefs, customs, arts and technologies.'

(iii) Nirmal Kumar Bose, *Culture and Society in India*, Asia Publishing House, Bombay, reprint, 1977, p.15.

Bose views 'Culture' as a 'term in anthropology which covers everything from the traditional manner in which people produce, cook or eat their food; the way in which they plan their houses, and arrange them on the surface of their land; the manner in which men are organized into communities, to the moral or religious values which are found acceptable, or the habitual methods by which satisfaction is gained in respect of the higher qualities of the mind.'

(iv) D.D. Kosambi, *The Culture and Civilization of Ancient India in Historical Outline*, Vikas, New Delhi, reprint, 1990, p.11.

Kosambi asserts that 'the basis of any formal culture must lie in the availability of food supply beyond that needed to support the actual food producer. To build the imposing *ziourrat* temples of Mesopotamia, the Great Wall of China, the pyramids of Egypt or modern skyscrapers, there must have been a correspondingly imposing supply of food at that time. Surplus production depends on the technique and implements used—the means of production, to adopt a convenient though badly abused term. The method by which surplus—not only surplus food but all other produce—passes into the hands of the ultimate users is determined by—and in turn determines—the form of society.' 'Ideation is a physiological process resulting from the awareness of environment. But once they are formed, ideas exist by themselves, governed by their own laws. The dynamics of ideas run parallel to the process of social evolution, the two influencing each other mutually. But in no particular point of the process of the integral human evolution, can a direct causal relation be established between historical events and the movement of ideas. (idea is here used in the common philosophical sense of ideology or system of ideas.) Patterns of culture and ethical values are not mere ideological super-structures of established economic relations. They are also historically determined—by the logic of the history of ideas.'

2. A.L. Basham, *The Wonder that was India*, Sidgwick and Jackson, London, 1954, p.1.
3. A.L. Basham (ed), *A Cultural History of India*, Clarendon Press, Oxford, 1975, p.2.
4. Jawaharlal Nehru, *The Discovery of India*, OUP, Delhi, 1981, pp.67–8.
5. Rabindranath Tagore, *Gitanjali*, Macmillan and Co., London, 1953, p.xx.
6. Ramdhari Singh 'Dinkar', *Sanskriti ke char adhyayay*, Rajpal & Sons, Delhi, 1956, pp.12–13.
7. Unlike the urban centres of Egypt and Mesopotamia, Mohenjodaro was a planned city. The city had bazaars as well as artists' quarters where bead-makers, cotton weavers, coppersmiths and other artisans peddled their wares. The archaeological evidence indicating the large granary goes to establish that there was a powerful government which was able to demand agricultural surplus from farmers for use in urban centres. It is also well-established that Indian goods used to go from the port of Lothal to Mesopotamia and other places. Indian archaeologists have discovered similar settlements at Dholavira in district Kutch, Gujarat. It appears that the settlement of Dholavira started in the first quarter of the third millennium BC and came to an end around 1500 BC. The full-fledged city of Dholavira is unique in being a proportionately resolved multidimensional settlement with a citadel, a stadium, a middle town and a lower town. These are all surrounded by water reservoirs within a massive fortification and it is considered to be one of the five largest cities of the Harappans. Some of the objects discovered in excavation like mirrors and cosmetics, and other decorative motifs conform to the Harappan standards of craftsmanship and art work. The Archaeological Survey of India is working on this site and its report is expected shortly.
8. B.P. Singh, *Role of History in Understanding of Society*, Professor K.K. Dutta Memorial Lecture, K.P. Jayaswal Research Institute, Patna, 8 March 1997. The relevant portion reads as follows:

   Trackless centuries ago, Indian philosophers had declared, in words the meaning of which is as modern as the day after tomorrow, and that declaration freely rendered from Sanskrit verse would be as follows:

   It is the small-minded who trivialize this world by their preoccupation with many kinds of divisions and demarcations which separate the peoples of the world. Those who are generous of spirit and have a larger vision regard the whole world as one family.

9. The famous astronomer Carl Sagan in his television series entitled 'Cosmos' gave prominence to Hindu cosmology. In a recently published dialogue Carl Sagan acknowledged that Hindu cosmology gives a time-scale for the earth and the universe which is consonant with that of modern scientific cosmology. Talking about 'Nataraja' which he adopted for the Cosmos television series, Carl Sagan observed:

   The traditional explanation of the Nataraja is that it symbolises the creation of the universe on one hand and the death of the universe on the other—the drum and the flame—and after all, that is what cosmology is all about.

   'Indian Cosmology', *New India Digest*, Pune, India, No. 57, March–April 1997.

10. *Vedic literature*: Vedas are four in number: *Rigveda, Samaveda, Yajurveda* and *Atharvaveda*. Each of these vedas has branches called *Samhitas* (collections) and *Brahmanas* (treatises relating to prayer and sacrificial ceremony). *Aranyakas* are appendices to the *Brahmanas, Upanishads* are books on philosophy. Thus each of the vedas has *Samhitas, Brahmanas, Aranyakas* and *Upanishads*. All these are, in a way, expositions of the Vedas and hence are termed Vedic literature. The *Rigveda* was orally composed in the 2nd millennium BC.

11. *Ramayana*: First poetic composition (*Adi Kavya*) in India, the *Ramayana* was authored by Valmiki in Sanskrit around 1500 BC. Written in 24,000 verses, the epic is divided into seven *kandas* (sections) of five hundred chapters.

12. *Mahabharata:* This epic was composed by Krishna Dvaipayana Vyas in around 1000 BC. It contains over one lakh verses. In size the *Mahabharata* is double that of Homer's *Iliad* and *Odyssey* put together. It comprises eighteen *parvas* (books) and 2109 chapters. It was written in around 300 BC.

13. *Bhagavad Gita:* This is a poem consisting of 650 verses divided into eighteen chapters. The *Gita* covers chapters 25–45 in the *Bhishma Parva* of the *Mahabharata* and is in the form of a discussion between Arjuna and Lord *Krishna*.

14. *Upanishads:* There are many *upanishads* of which only 108 are in print. Of these the most important are: (i) *Ishavasya*, (ii) *Kena*, (iii) *Katha*, (iv) **Prasna**, (v) **Munda**, (vi) *Mandukya*, (vii) *Chhandogya*, (viii) *Taittiriya* (ix) *Aitareya*, and (x) *Brihadaranyaka*.

15. *Panini:* Born in Salature (now in Pakistan) in about 500 BC, Panini was a great grammarian. His work *Ashtadhyayi*, a reference book on grammar, has 4000 *sutras* (formulae) divided into eight chapters.

16. *Varna:* Initially the society was divided into four *varnas* (classes), called *chaturvarnya; brahmana, kshatriya, vaishya, shudra,* each on the basis of duties assigned to them. There was no restriction on food, dress and marriage, one could conveniently change one's *varna.* Later *varna* was replaced by *jati* (caste), where the *jati* of a person was determined by birth. Once born a *brahmana,* he/she remains a *brahmana* all through life.

17. *Ashrama:* The four stages of life were called the four *ashramas: brahmacharya* (student life), *grahastya* (married and family life), *vanaprastha* (detachment from worldly pleasures), *sanyasa* (renouncing the family and leading the life of an ascetic).

18. *Guna:* The good qualities (gunas) are ten in number: *satya* (truth), *vinaya* (modesty), *devataradhana* (worship of god), *adhyayana* (study), *kulashuddhi* (purity of family), *sushila* (good conduct), *shakti* (strength), *dhana* (wealth), *shruava* (valour) and *yuktiyukta sambhandha* (intelligent and rational talk).

19. *Vedanta:* This means the end and completion of the Vedas. The *Upanishads* are called *Vedanta* because they are the end of the Vedas; they contain philosophical speculation about the conception of God, soul, life and death. *Vedanga:* The word Veda includes the *Vedanga* (ancilliary of the vedas); these are *shiksha* (phonetics), *kalpa* (ritual), *vyakarna* (grammar), *nirukta* (etymology), *chhanda* (metrics), and *jyotisha* (astronomy).

20. *Advaita:* This is the most influential of the schools of *Vedanta.* Its main text is that non-duality or monoism is the final reality. This is expressed in the *Upanishads* mainly *Mandukya.* Adi Sankaracharya is the greatest exponent of this school.

21. Vamadeo Shastri, *Asiatic Studies* (2 volumes). First published in 1882 and reprinted in 1976 by Cosmo Publications, New Delhi, pp.21–2. Vamadeo Shastri is the assumed name of Alfred C. Lyall.

22. The word purana in Sanskrit means 'ancient'; and the title *Purana* signifies 'ancient lore', indicating that these books contain ancient lore as handed down to us in the highest tradition of *Sruti.* There are eighteen Puranas, i.e. the Brahma, Padma, Visnu, Siva, Bhagavata, Naradiya, Markandeya, Agni, Bhavisya, Brahmavaivarta, Linga, Varaha, Skanda, Vamana, Kurma, Matsya, Garuda, and Brahmanda (Vayu). Western thinkers have often compared these to Aesop's Fables as the *Puranas* give popular versons of tales, legends, anecdotes and fables of Indian mythology and thought processes.

23. William Gerber (ed.), *The Mind of India,* Southern Illinois University Press (first printed in 1908) reprinted in 1977, Basic Texts, p. 49.

24. Ibid., p.86.

25. *Charavaka:* He was a philosopher in ancient India, an atheist. He controverted in a powerful manner the belief in the existence of heaven and hell after death.

26. *The Mind of India,* p.100 Gerber, William (ed.), Southern Illinois University Press, London, 1908.

27. *Yaksha:* A class of demi-gods. The feminine counterpart is a *yakshi.*

28. *Kinnaras:* Musicians by birth. They always carry a *vina* (lute) or some other musical instrument. Their female counterpart *kinnari* is half bird and half woman and is extremely beautiful.

29. *Gandharvas:* Semi-gods adept in music and dance. Their head is *Tumburu.* They are half human, half animal; their female counterparts are *gandharvis.*

30. *Apsara:* A nymph (*devastri*). These were born at the time of the churning of the ocean of milk.

31. *Natyashastra:* Written by Bharata in the first century AD, it contains 37 chapters and deals with dance, music and drama.

32. Girish Karnad, 'Theatre in India' in *Daedalus, Mother India, Journal of the American Academy of Arts and Sciences,* Fall, 1989, pp.331–52.

33. Ibid., pp.331–52.

34. A.K. Warder, 'Classical Literature', in A.L. Basham (ed.), *A Cultural History of India,* Clarendon Press, Oxford 1975, pp.170–96.

35. HJJ Winter, 'Science', in A.L. Basham (ed.), *A Cultural History of India,* pp.141–61.

36. V.I. Vernadsky, *Pusaka Art of Indonesia,* Haryati Soebadio (ed.), English translation published in Singapore, 1992, p.22.

37. Satya Vrat Shastri, *Sriramakirtimahakavyam,* Moolamall Sachdev Foundation and Amarnath Sachdeva Foundation, Bangkok, 1990, p.xv–xvi.

38. J. LeRoy Davidson, 'Indian Influences on China', in A.L. Basham (ed.) *A Cultural History of India,* p.455.

39. Quoted in A.L. Basham (ed.) *A Cultural History of India,* Chapter I.

40. Rabindranath Tagore, 'A Vision of India's History', in Sisirkumar Ghosh (ed.) *Tagore for You,* Visva-Bharati, Calcuta, 1966, p.37.

A mural on the wall of the monastery at Tabo in the remote mountains of Spiti in Himachal Pradesh. This monastery celebrated 1000 years of its existence in 1996.

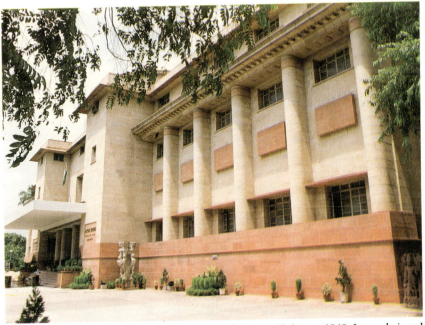

The National Museum of India, which came into being on 15 August 1949. It was designed by the architect Shri Deolalikar and the foundation was laid by Jawaharlal Nehru.

(Courtesy National Museum, New Delhi)

2
State and Market in India's Culture

I
Culture and Power

One of the unique things about India is that it possesses a developed culture but not yet a developed economy. This cultural status is of special relevance today within a world that has changed substantially after the end of the cold war, and radically since 1991. It is now widely assumed that the status of a country will be determined not by its military arsenal but by the power of its economy, which in turn has come to mean that countries with sophisticated technology and the largest share of world trade will be the most powerful and important. While I am not one of those who overlook the importance of market forces or world trade, or who ignore military arsenals as factors in international politics, I do believe that culture is going to be an important variable, along with market and trade, in determining the position of a country within the comity of nations. This aspect needs to be kept in view not only by our leaders in the arenas of culture and trade, but also by our politicians, planners, civil servants, the media, and the academic world. It is in this context that India has to consciously adopt a policy of placing culture at the centre of things not only for enlarged economic growth but also to create an environment that encourages self-expression by individuals and communities. Pride in India's culture is a concomitant of this, but we must realize that we cannot be treated deferentially by others simply because of the fact that our ancestors were great people.

In one of my papers, I argued that culture is power.[1] A number of scholars and civil servants told me that I had misused the word 'culture'. I still hold to my opinion because for me the term culture, in its most comprehensive sense, refers to the diverse creative activities of a people—to literature; to the visual and performing arts; and to various forms of artistic self-expression by the individual (specialist or lay) or by communities. These activities give a sense of purpose to human existence and, at the same time, provide the reflective poise and spiritual energy so essential to the maturing of a 'good society'. I also hold the view that when an artist is involved in reflective activities, even in the solitude of his home or in the workplace, he is not alone. His mind is activated by what happens around him and his creativity has an element of that. When his work is shared with society, it influences events in the wider community outside his home or workplace.

Culture is a dynamic variable, enormously potent and influential. When it is articulated in a manner aimed at achieving an objective, it releases the dormant energies of a community. It is thus comparable to energy and power, and has a similar place *vis-à-vis* development programmes. India's culture is deeply rooted in an age-old pluralistic ethos, providing creative expression, value-sustenance and belief patterns to the thousands of communities which constitute contemporary Indian society.

Looking at Indian culture, we may take two opposite views. One is the segmented view of culture in terms of religion, i.e. a Hindu view of culture, a Muslim view of culture, a Christian view of culture, etc.; or in terms of region, i.e. an Assamese or Bengali or Tamil culture, and so on. The second view is that Indian culture is composite. Cultural activities can be compared to two kinds of activities which I call 'ant activity' and 'bee activity'. Ants collect food particles from different places and deposit them in one place, but even within a heap of sugar so deposited by ants, one can distinguish each particle and separate it from the others in the heap. The bee collects nectar from one flower after another, assimilates it, and thus honey is made. Within the honey you cannot separate the specific contribution of each flower or plant, unless you apply genetic engineering processes. Indian culture in my perception is the accomplishment of 'bee activity' rather than 'ant activity'. The taste of honey varies with the time of year, the place, and the flowers visited by the bees, so that honey from Srinagar will taste different to that from Shillong or Mahabaleshwar. In the same way the taste of the honey of Indian culture on the banks of the Brahmaputra in Assam, or at Lok Tak in Manipur or the Ganga at Allahabad, or the Cauvery at Thanjavur is different because of the country's pluralistic culture. They are all varieties of Indian cultural honey but each tastes different because of local variations, climatic influences, linguistic expressions, and bio-diversity factors. This is what makes Indian culture so fascinating. I can do no better than quote Tagore, who beautifully highlighted the living organism of Indian culture when he wrote :

> The Aryan, the non-Aryan, the Dravidian,
> The Huns, the Pathans and the Moguls—
> They all have merged here into one body.[2]

Some of us are in the habit of asserting that we have a superior culture because our forefathers were very cultured people, and that in the fabric of Indian culture we have combined all their values, skills and ideas. This is a debatable matter as in relation to our personal behaviour and conduct, or in relation to developmental programmes or paradigms of development, we find that there is a great deal of difference between what our forefathers said, wrote, and did on the one hand, and what we say, write, and do today. There is, in fact, much divergence between the values of our ancestors and the practice of these values amongst us.[3] If we look at our development profile over the last 50 years, we find for instance that despite the so-called, 'sacredness' of our rivers, most of our ferrous and non-ferrous industries, as well as our oil refineries, have been located in areas which had the necessary raw materials, yet in relation to which care was not taken to set up effluent treatment plants. Effluents from these industries have therefore been freely discharged into those very 'sacred' rivers. The result has been that river waters on which large rural populations depend are no longer safe. Our age-old tradition of respecting the wetlands and treating some of these rivers as our 'mothers' has not prevented us from polluting them, while bestowing the title 'temples of modern India' on these polluting industrial complexes!

When we examine this state of affairs somewhat more deeply, two things are found contributing to the acceleration of this dichotomy between our conduct and our belief-system within our long history. One is that we repeatedly stress a distinction between culture and civilization. We argue that culture is a thought process, while civilization is conduct. And we have thought that our culture can remain pure even if our conduct suffers degradation. As the Indian mind proverbially functions at different levels, it is possible to rationalize this paradox between belief and conduct, between *kathni* and *karni* (speech and action). Although the conceptual distinction between culture and civilization is valid, their interdependence is not adequately emphasized. The need to establish the interrelationship between culture and civilization is imperative to bridge the gap between what we say and what we do. It is heartening that this interrelationship is now being increasingly appreciated.

The other aspect is that, for a very long period, science was not viewed as a part of culture, even though science and technology are expressions of a country's cultural personality. For long, in our perspective, science and technology stood apart from culture, and in a culture-dominated society the fallout of this was inevitable. We lagged behind other countries in our achievements within these fields. Science and culture are not two separate and distinct expressions of human consciousness and human endeavour: both are products of the creative expression of human minds which remain constantly open to the truth. It was not fully appreciated that science, which made such a profound impact on humankind and on the utilization of natural resources, should not be viewed outside the ambit of culture, since culture concerns the entire gamut of human activity and achievement.

Such distinctions between science and culture did not exist either in our mythology, or in the times of Chanakya or Ashoka. One is conscious of the fact that our decline in science and technology cannot be explained solely in terms of divorcing science from culture, but viewing the two together, particularly in our context, was bound to have encouraged scientific temper and progresss in the fields of science and culture within a longer time-frame. This aspect of the 'togetherness' of science and culture was explicitly stated in the Scientific Policy Resolution adopted by Parliament on 4 March 1958, which stated: 'It is an inherent obligation of a great country like India with its traditions of scholarship and original thinking and its great cultural heritage, to participate fully in the march of science...'.[4] One is happy to observe on the national scene, that groups of gifted individuals are concerned both with human values and with pursuing scientific knowledge. The work of art and literature in their hands is bound to bridge this gap between science and culture. The spiritual sensibilities of our well-known scientists is a guarantee that they will not drive their scientific techniques blindly or ruthlessly, without goal or purpose.

India has forged the necessary premises to enter into a new stage of development—that of pushing ahead with industrialization and modernization. The shift to a market economy, on the one hand, encourages dynamic and efficient production and business; on the other, it causes social and cultural problems.

Shifting to a market economy in which science, technology and information are decisive factors for development, we should reso-lutely affirm the need for cultural preservation and development with a full understanding that the economy and culture are closely linked with each other; the economy cannot grow by itself without a cultural foundation, and cultural development is not a by-product of economic growth. If the ultimate goal of development and economic growth is the well-being and happiness of every member of society, change cannot be imposed from outside or from above; and the rate of change must accommodate the human capacities of a particular society.

Culture has to play a spiritually balancing role to actively minimize the negative elements of commodity-money relations in society. Culture also contributes to shaping a path of national development in line with the national characteristics, and with world development trends. As such, culture constitutes both a balancing and a driving force of development, and an objective of development itself. Above all else, for the health of culture and the quality of the natural environment, all our people must retain their sense of dignity, and their sense of self-confidence. They must feel that they have some control over their lives, and over their environment. There will be neither sustainable economic growth, nor social progress and durable peace, if we do not maintain growth in tune with our heritage.

II
Culture and the State

In India's long and uninterrupted cultural history, religion, trade and the State have played a major role in the promotion of culture and the arts. The temples, monasteries and churches were not only centres for worship but also for cultural activities of the region. Similarly, the maharajas and badshahs, the colonial rulers and the zamindars, were often patrons of the arts and literature; some even indulged in poetry and music, dance and drama. The task of protecting India's heritage when India became a Republic fell upon the State, as both the religious institutions and princely orders were not seen as capable of continuing with their traditional role. The princely states were merged and their titles, honours and purses gradually faded into history. The State became a secular institution and religious organizations were left to fend for themselves to propagate their beliefs.

Our national leaders were aware of the fact that stimulus and support was needed to be given to artistic creativity. Jawaharlal Nehru, Maulana Abul Kalam Azad, Rajendra Prasad and Sarvepalli Radha-krishan[5] were deeply conscious of the fact that the old institutional forums of cultural creativity, such as princely courts, temples, churches and monasteries, would not be in a position in these changed economic and political circumstances to bestow the patron-age which they once had extended to poets, painters, dancers, musicians, scholars and other creative individuals. They were also aware that the market in India was undeveloped, and that there were dangers in leaving matters concerning cultural creativity to market forces. A major intervention by the State was therefore both necessary and desirable. Autonomous institutions like the Sangeet Natak Akademi (1953), the Lalit Kala Akademi (1954), the Sahitya Akademi (1954), the National School of Drama (1959) and the National Museum (1954) were set up to provide forums in order to facilitate a dialogue among persons engaged in creative activity, and for the publication and display of their work. These institutions were formed in the belief that the result of cultural endeavours would shape for the community a sensibility which would renew India's heritage. Our leaders deliberately provided a working arrangement in which Government control over these institutions would be minimal. As a result, although these institutions were fully funded by the Government of India, they have functioned almost on the pattern of non-government organizations.

The role of society was not ignored either. Maulana Abul Kalam Azad put it succinctly when he said: 'in a democratic regime, the arts can derive their sustenance only from the people, and the State—as the organized manifestation of the people's will—must, therefore, undertake its maintenance and development as one of its first responsibilities'.[6] In fact the role played by Maulana Azad in the field of literature and the arts, and by Kamaladevi Chattopadhyaya[7] in the restoration of crafts, are significant achievements of the 1950s and these, in turn, helped create and sustain an environment for creativity. The fact that India today is one of the few countries in the world which can claim it has more than a hundred creative persons who are the world's best in their respective fields is a tribute to the vision that our leaders had cherished in the 1950s.

The Constitution of India, though belatedly, incorporated a few significant cultural provisions in the Constitution (Forty-second Amendment) Act, 1976. These were: (i) to value and preserve the rich heritage of our composite culture; (ii) to protect and improve the natural environment including forests, lakes, rivers and wildlife, and to have compassion for living creatures; and (iii) to strive towards excellence in all spheres of individual and collective activity so that the nation constantly rises to higher levels of endeavour and achievement.

The Haksar Committee reviewed the working of the Akademies, namely the Lalit Kala Akademi, the Sangeet Natak Akademi and Sahitya Akademi, and of the National School of Drama. In its report submitted in July 1990, this Committee observed that, in their perception, although all these Akademies had done some good work, their impact on Indian culture had not been widely felt. It also observed that the interaction of the Akademies with sister institutions in the States and Union Territories was far from adequate, not only because of their own fault, but because of the poor state of many of these institutions. The National School of Drama too, it was felt, should enlarge its vision and widen its horizons.[8] These observations are valid even today.

The 1980s witnessed three significant government initiatives in the realm of culture. First, a major move was made in 1985 by creating a separate Department of Culture in the Ministry of Human Resource Development in the Government of India;[9] hitherto the cultural affairs had constituted a wing of the Department of Education. This was a welcome development as the Department of Culture, besides having eight government organizations under its control, is accountable for the working of 39 other cultural organizations spread across the country. The creation of a separate Department of Culture was widely appreciated, both within India and abroad, and many viewed it as a landmark development towards the establishment of an independent Ministry of Culture in India.

Under the new administrative arrangement, major organizations of the Department of Culture made significant strides. In the task of conservation, preservation and maintenance of nearly 5000 monuments in the country, including sixteen World Heritage Sites, the Archaeological Survey of India showed both its professional ability and capacity to operate efficiently at minimal cost. Several voluntary organizations got support from the Department of Culture, including INTACH (Indian National Trust for Art and Cultural Heritage). The 43-volume *People of India* series of the Anthropological Survey of India[10] has already made its mark among students and scholars as well as media persons in India and abroad. The Nehru Memorial Museum and Library, New Delhi, has emerged as the finest library of Contemporary Indian History in the World. In fact, the Department of Culture, through its network of institutions and schemes, has made a meaningful attempt to build linkages between the past and the present in terms of their bearing on future development.

Second, the concept of the Festival of India was introduced to remove a public perception, particularly among foreigners, which generally depicted a stereotype of India as 'a fossilized monolith', a romantic and exotic land of maharajas, tigers, snake-charmers, the Taj Mahal and, of course, grinding poverty. Festivals of India[11] were held in the UK, the USA, France, Japan, Sweden, Germany, China, and the former Soviet Union, under the framework of Cultural Agreements/Cultural Exchange Programmes. These Festivals tried to depict, through exhibitions and performances, the theme of continuity and change in the culture of India as a living continuum of creativity over the past 5000 years. Such artistic and cultural manifestations of India's people, which have been part of their lifestyle, drew enthusiastic crowds. The Festivals have contributed to the popularity of our folk traditions and arts abroad. Another important gain was a certain boost to the tourist traffic into India. The Festivals, in a way, made both traditional and modern India more intelligible and approachable. The festival model developed by India has become a valid concept in international cultural exchanges, with many countries organizing such festivals. However, as Pupul Jayakar puts it, we must remember that :

> To organise a festival is to float oil lamps in tiny boats on a river; for an instant to illumine the ripples on the water and the rapt faces of those that participate in the launching; to set before the mirror of attention, times past and times present; and when the festival ends, to disappear, like the boats, into the night.[12]

In 1985 it was also decided to establish seven Zonal Cultural Centres (ZCCs) to cover each State and Union Territory. These Zonal Centres were meant to provide facilities for the creative development of the performing arts, graphic arts, and other literary works, and to deal with the entire spectrum of creativity from ancient times to the present, particularly with reference to the traditions of folk and tribal art. These Centres were to lay special emphasis on people's participation and on the revival of vanishing arts. They were an outreach, rather than strong physical campuses, of India's culture. In fact, these Centres were seen as focal points for the participation of common people from all regions of India, the purpose being to celebrate the pluralities of cultural forms and expressions within the whole country. A meaningful togetherness among artists and craftsmen has been facilitated by these Centres, particularly by organizing melas and holding festivals. Hitherto, people who were specialists in local culture, or in folklore and folk studies, tended to be very narrowly limited to the ethnolinguistic group of their own region, and never had a chance to be exposed to anthropological perspectives and methodologies in the research and documentation activities prevalent elsewhere. The Zonal Centres have stimulated new kinds of dialogue across regional and ethnolinguistic boundaries. However, as the Ananthamurthy Committee has observed,[13] these Centres should have evolved, in the span of a decade, a composite audience with a sensibility to the folk as well as classical forms of art, and at the same time to contemporary expressions in literature, theatre and painting. It should have taken certain pan-Indian inter-zonal mega narratives like the *Mahabharata*, the *Ramayana* and the *Bhagavatha*, and traced their existence, interconnectedness and mutations in various forms of cultural expression. The Centres should also have functioned in closer collaboration with the national academies than has actually happened.

The government's role in setting up and maintaining public libraries, archives and museums, in organizing archaeological and anthropological surveys, and in creating and supporting prestigious academic institutions, has also been applauded. The Haksar Committee hoped that more public funds would be invested in creating and maintaining a useful infrastructure for cultural activities, and assisting voluntary institutions and individuals, rather than in organizing cultural events.[14] This is, in fact, the Government's policy on culture, and this policy continues.

There is a growing acceptance of the role of the State in the domain of culture by the community of artists in India. The State must fulfil the function of patronizing the arts, and one of the methods suggested is the purchase of artefacts by State-funded organizations such as the National Museum, National Gallery of Modern Art, Lalit Kala Akademi. At present, every organization has an Art Purchase Committee consisting of eminent artists, which decides on the purchases of works of art at yearly intervals. While supporting this policy, the well-known scholar Krishna Chaitanya raised an important question, namely that there should be a clear policy about the price of art objects, for the money of honest tax payers is involved. He also very rightly observed the relationship between art and poverty:

To return to the issue of state patronage, a close encounter will show that the problem can be agonising. Poverty has been there since the beginning of history. Should art and creativity be totally suspended till a better social order is created? If we decide it that way, life will be infinitely impoverished. Somehow we have to manage to spare some of our energy for art even while we are struggling for bread. But there is great need for a balance, a sense of proportion, here. I wish the artist well and hope that he will be able to sell his work.[15]

III
Culture and Trade

Culture and trade have an old and enduring relationship: the one literally facilitates the other, even in areas as remote as the Himalayas. For example, we celebrated, in the year 1996, the thousandth anniversary of the establishment of the Tabo Monastery in the western Himalayas of the Lahul-Spiti region in Himachal Pradesh. Tabo is the oldest continuously functioning Buddhist monument in India and the Himalayas, with its original decorations and iconography intact, including its paintings, sculptures, inscriptions and extensive wall texts. A thousand years ago Tabo became a meeting place of migrants and Tibetan inhabitants.[16] Indian pandits came to Tabo to learn Tibetan. The laborious process of translation was always conducted by a team of Indian and Tibetan scholars, along with religious studies. As a result, the art which was created at Tabo used Indian forms in conjunction with Tibetan wall texts. The style and iconography of the paintings and sculptures brilliantly indicates this cultural synthesis.

Evidence from several sources has revealed that trade facilitated the movement of persons and helped create a market at Tabo. It needs to be mentioned that the Buddhist ecclesiastical elite of India had attained a high level of intellectual sophistication and had the wisdom to see merit in Tibetan lamas. This led to the presence of unique and gifted personalities at different periods of time at Tabo.

Not only was there the will to create a symbolically coherent ritual space, but also the means to gather artists and materials of the highest quality. Tabo Monastery also clearly establishes the belief of the Buddhist teachers and patrons in the artistic means to disseminate Buddhism. The artists who worked at Tabo Monastery devoted both their talent and labour unconditionally to serving their beliefs. All these led to the expansion of the provincial boundaries of this West Tibetan dynasty into the cosmopolitan world of Indian monastic Buddhism. This tradition has continued in the modern period as well. The improved standard of living in the valley—the result of many Government initiatives—and the educational and spiritual activities which commenced due to the activism of a variety of people intermixing (on account of market and trade) have facilitated a renewal of creativity in this region.

Similarly, in the southern parts of India, close interaction between market, state formation and religion was an important factor in cultural attainments from early times. For example, Kanchipuram or Kanchi sustains an unbroken continuity as a seat of learning and as one of the sacred cities of India. The archaeological excavations have revealed that as early as in the 4th century BC trade in iron flourished at Kanchipuram and thereabouts, although it was predominantly an agricultural society. The neighbouring port at Mahabalipuram was used extensively for trade with the Romans, and goods meant for export through Mahabalipuram used to pass through Kanchipuram, a central place located in between the port and the southern portion of what is now Andhra Pradesh.

The Pallavas made Kanchipuram the seat of their political power in the 6th century and it continued as such until the end of the dynasty five hundred years later. The court of the Pallavas was adorned by many poets like Dandin, and some of the rulers (like Mahendravarman) were themselves poets. The court of the Pallavas was famous throughout India for its patronage of Sanskrit literature and of Buddhist, Jaina, Vaishnava and Shaiva scholarship, rituals, and temples. Kanchi became an active centre for Sanskritic religious learning with the establishment of a *pitha* by Adi Sankara. In fact, Ramanuja lived here for a long time and attracted scholars from all over India to Kanchi. Well-positioned at the crossroads of land and sea trade, Kanchipuram over the years became a religious and cultural centre of significance both for north and south India. Kanchi played a major role in the transmission of Indian culture into Thailand, Cambodia, Java, and Vietnam.

The commercial activities related to trade and the patronage of the rulers greatly influenced literary and cultural activities. The influence of religion was central as it provided inspiration in the realm of creativity and found magnificent expression in temple architecture, poetry, drama, and paintings. Many towns and cities in the South came into existence as complements to the construction of temples at well-established holy spots. George Michell has rightly observed:

> The most important temple towns in Tamil Nadu have always had a commercial identity; religious centres were, and still are, market towns with festivals coinciding with great fairs. The simultaneous growth of pilgrimage and trade is an outstanding feature of urban life in the region. Kanchipuram provides an excellent example of a significant religious-commercial centre dealing in locally woven textiles and other goods. Festivals in temple towns are generally sensational events that also benefit business. Processions take place in the streets, in full view of crowds of visitors who pay homage to gods and goddesses before proceeding to the business of buying and selling. Structures located on axis with temple gateways are often reserved for commercial activities.[17]

Kanchipuram continues to be an important place for Hindus as a sacred seat of the goddess Kamakshi, and as an important centre of learning where one of India's Sankaracharyas lives and preaches. It is also well known for the manufacture of and trade in its world-famous silk saris.

In the long history of India, one sees that trade and travel routes have carried not only philosophical thought and religious beliefs out of the country but they have also been transmitters of many of our traditional handicrafts (such as the famous textile designs) as well as styles in architecture and sculpture.

About 5000 years ago during the Harappan days, Indian goods and merchants used to go from the port of Lothal to Mesopotamia and other places. Since the Indus script is yet to be deciphered, it has not been possible to know all that occurred during that period regarding the role of market and trade in the promotion of ideas and crafts.

The export of Indian ideas a few centuries after the Buddha's *Parinirvana* is extensively covered by literature. During this period, well before the Christian era, traders and monks carried Buddhist philosophy along the silk routes to the far east. Somewhat later, Ashoka despatched emissaries to Lanka and made a concerted effort to disseminate the philosophy of Buddhism outside India. Indian traders and goods reached as far west as Rome. The exchange of ideas and goods between India and Greece is well known. Foreign emissaries and scholars from Europe came to the Indian coast and carried goods as well as Indian ideas in philosophy and astronomy back with them.

The second half of the 20th century has witnessed widespread dissemination of Indian mystical ideas throughout the world, and rapid westernization in India itself. Words like 'yoga', 'vegetarianism', 'transcendental meditation', as well as Indian music and dance forms have become familiar in western countries.

The liberalized economy has brought in its wake a consumer awareness hitherto unknown. These consumer industries—regional, national and multinational—are trying to attract clients and gain their loyalty. Sponsorship of the arts has become an important medium of communication. Such sponsorship is being increasingly determined by the demand–supply relationship. As one sensitive artist has put it:

> Arts sponsorship is the payment of money by a business to an arts organization for the purpose of promoting the business name, its products or services. It can also be a means of fulfilling a business's sense of corporate social responsibility. Sponsorship is therefore part of a

marketing strategy, and generally a part of a business's general promotional expenditure.[18]

A recent three-year survey conducted in Britain by ABSA
(Association for Business Sponsorship of the Arts) had revealed that,
all things being equal, 60 per cent of consumers are more likely to
choose the product of a corporation involved in promoting the
arts.[19]

Until recently what got sponsored in India was mostly classical
dance and music in the form of two- or three-day festivals every year.
Today the scope is much wider and sponsorships could include
literature, theatre, film festivals, crafts, the plastic arts, monuments,
books, street festivals, art competitions, museums, and theatre spaces
and their combinations. Arts sponsorship by corporate houses to
advertise products could go a long way in removing the element of
vulgarity from advertisements, besides helping artists and art organizations.

There are, however, certain genuine fears in allowing creators of
art objects to be increasingly controlled by the market, or to place
them at the mercy of the market. There are disturbing features
already evident in the West. Even in the United States, where
corporate underwriting has produced some magnificent results for
American libraries, museums, ballets, theatres, and orchestras, sensitive Americans are now critical of the corporate sector's too fervid
obsession with popular, prestigious events, for their goal is almost
only to make money. As a result of such market considerations, we
have in India recently noticed artistic mass production, whether it
be painting, or sculpture, or song, or books. This impairs the quality
of what is produced, supposedly within the aesthetic domain. The
autonomy of practitioners of classical dance forms or folk art forms,
too, is being whittled down, and their conformity to market
requirements is on the rise.

Even selective patronage, especially in a set-up where the
dispensers of economic benefits may sometimes be uninitiated, can
be harmful for the propagation and perpetuation of culture. In fact,

our history is also witness to the fact that the patronage of unenlightened rajas and maharajas converted art objects into decorations for their mansions and material for their sessions of romantic poetry, music, dance, and love-making. Poets and historians eulogized the virtues of their masters both within poetry and works of history, perhaps regardless of the realities. There were, however, some courageous and rare exceptions, such as Bana's *Harsha Charita*, in which sufferings imposed on the people by the mobilization and movement of a large army, and resentment felt by peasants and farmers, were also expressed.[20] Today, business houses are seen as potential patrons of art and culture. Patrons are expected to be connoisseurs of art, and it is, to my mind, necessary that decision-makers in the corporate world are made aware of their role in assisting the promotion of creativity and aesthetic values, as also the pitfalls inherent in such a role.

Artistic patronage has always inspired honour and respect. To provide support to an aspiring or established artist is sufficient to bring merit to the benefactor in every civilized society. No study of cultural performances in India today can ignore the importance of financial support rendered by individuals, societies, industries, and the public, as audiences, critics, benefactors, and financial underwriters. There are numerous ways of encouraging patronage. In India and elsewhere, concert and theatre programmes list categories of supporters, benefactors, and patrons, and thank them for their support. While ticketed programmes are still regarded as less prestigious then invitational programmes, the number of ticketed programmes are on the increase, particularly in Bombay.

Since art management as a profession is not yet recognized in India, individual arrangements for production, programmes and publicity are the order of the day. Some public organizations like the Indian Council for Cultural Relations, the Sangeet Natak Akademi and the National School of Drama, provide some of the services of management in organizing performances sponsored by the government.

The houses of Birla, Tata, Godrej, Bharat Ram and Charat Ram, and more recently, the Indian Tobacco Company and Vazir Sultan Tobacco Company, have emerged as major patrons of the arts with varying interests and goals.

The market, as a primary influence upon artistic and cultural activity, has its limitations. In the generation of cultural values—more so than in the generation of material values—the market needs to be tamed and harnessed to serve the interests of creativity. I say this because of my deep conviction that cultural and artistic creativity, as a self-reflexive activity, is an important constituent of the influences which shape the 'good society' in harmony with nature. It is my belief that, in cultural production, there must be free scope for bold innovation and daring experimentation by artists who bring to bear upon their work novel and lofty ideas and social concerns.

Business houses of multinational corporations that promote the use of modern science and technology for industrial growth at the global, national, regional and local levels need to be sensitive to the cultural ethos of the region. Sometimes, industrial development takes away the local regional flavour by merging it with the larger perspective of economic growth. For example, what happens when a multinational corporation comes into a remote area of, say, Madhya Pradesh or Orissa to set up a big textile or synthetic-fibre industry, where a small tribal community living in the interior weaves little-known designs and motifs on handlooms? Apart from the onslaught on tribal aesthetics, the whole religio–cultural environment may well change along with the economic impact of industrialization; the rituals, myths and performance of individuals or of small communities are often thus annihilated. The pluralistic nature of culture has to be reiterated and honoured in such circumstances. If we really want people to think globally, we have to give them the confidence that they will not be swamped by the wider world.

The utilization of resources available with government, society, and the market would require a participatory system for the promotion of art and culture. The National Culture Fund and similar organizational efforts may well provide that institutional framework to convert new challenges and situations emerging within a liberalized economy, and thus serve the cause of India's culture.

It also needs to be emphasized that business houses in India are looked upon as rational organizations and, as such, are expected in their functioning to take into account the traditions of the local people, and not merely become imitations of western businesses. The sensitivity of these business houses to local practices and skills would go a long way not only in preserving long-established cultural mores of people, but also towards meeting the needs of their own business. The harmonious relationship between corporate managers, artists, and craftsmen would ensure higher levels of productivity while promoting creativity through traditional talents.

IV
Plurality and Culture

Among the factors which have contributed to the continuity and richness of our culture, the most important one is our plural character—ideas, languages, forms of worship, architecture, agricultural practices, dress, handicrafts, medicine, industry, science, and instruments of production and consumption. It used to be strongly believed that every ethnic group was entitled to express itself in its own manner, according to its own genius. Now, relations between different ethnic groups in a shrinking world have become much more problematic. As economic growth accelerates and people migrate across cultural boundaries, there is a natural tendency to turn towards a group's own cultural identity and to resist what is perceived by culturally embattled ethnic groups as a threat to their integrity, to the continuity of their cultures and heritage. Recent decades have seen dramatic changes in demographic ratios, and in the social and cultural mix of people in several regions. This has caused local populations to feel endangered and beleagured. What has happened in the recent past in the North-East,[21] or in the Kashmir valley, or in Punjab, are expressions of this phenomenon.

The democratization of polity has sharpened the consciousness of each ethnic group within India's multi-ethnic state to gain control of state power as a means of securing for itself a larger share of income and wealth. In this scenario, the need for harmony and peace among ethnic groups has become crucial. The answer lies in secular and fair policies in respect of rights over land, employment, economic benefits, education, use of language, political representation, and freedom of religion. The most durable way is for the state to continue the policy pursued during the freedom struggle, which was to create a sense of the nation as a civic community based upon some shared cultural consciousness. Such a sense of community is best achieved if the concept of nation is freed from connotations of ethnic and religious exclusivity. One of the virtues of a plural culture is that it encourages us to understand and value our own family traditions, our own ethnic and cultural practices, yet also to stand outside these and be able and willing to judge them. The prospect of a blanket westernization of India via television, and fears of regional groups such as those among the people in the South about Hindi-ization from the North, or among the tribals of Assam about Assamization—such fears continue to haunt sections of our people and will continue until the perceived threat to our plural culture is removed. Such fears have their repercussions beyond India's boundaries, and it would not be unnatural to expect debates on Indianization in Pakistan, Nepal, Bangladesh and Sri Lanka due to other ethnic, religious and political considerations.

Writing in 1921, Mahatma Gandhi virtually laid down India's cultural policy:

> I want the cultures of all lands to be blown about my house as freely as possible. But I refuse to be blown off my feet by any. I refuse to live in other people's houses as an interloper, beggar or a slave.[22]

The freedom struggle is witness to the fact that India used the challenge posed by the West in creative terms, and consequently various aspects of Indian culture were renewed and regenerated. It was our singular fortune that the first-rank leaders of the freedom struggle—Bal Gangadhar Tilak, Gopal Krishna Gokhale, Mahatma Gandhi, Aurobindo Ghose, Seshadri Srinivasa Iyenger, Sarojini Naidu, C. Rajagopalachari, Abul Kalam Azad, Jawaharlal Nehru, B.R. Ambedkar, Vinoba Bhave, Subhash Chandra Bose, Shyama Prasad Mookerjee, and Jaya Prakash Narayan—were not only political leaders but also cultural leaders.[23]

A civilization that is characterized by a unique moral vision cannot but have a say in the pursuit of various activities of the people. The mechanisms of wealth generation, the character of social and political institutions, and the texture of the moral values represented in India's culture would be required to be viewed in a harmonious manner. As Ravinder Kumar observes:

> The objectives of the liberation struggle—the transformation of an agricultural into an industrial society; the creation of a cohesive pan-Indian State; and the creation also of representative institutions within India—can be achieved with greater facility within the framework of a 'Civilisation-State' than within the framework of a 'Nation State'. However, crucial to such a consummation is the concept of a subcontinental culture resting upon a multiplicity of religious visions; and drawing into its matrix the richness of the regional constituents of Indian society.[24]

In fact, the approach to culture in India must positively encourage regional diversity and not just tolerate it. No region or group should have the feeling of a threat of being swamped. There are no 'majority' and 'minority' cultures. The smallest unit has its contribution to make to the enrichment of the national sum total, and must be respected.

There has been no major debate in India concerning the role of the state *vis-à-vis* the market in the promotion of culture. The way the state has acted during the last five decades in the cultural domain has, by and large, stood the test of time. The state has not greatly interfered in cultural activities, nor has it manipulated culture in a manner which makes it subservient to the government's political philosophy. The contrast, in this respect, between India's cultural policy and those pursued by near-contemporary totalitarian regimes is very clear. At a philosophical level this was perhaps inevitable since both the Indian government and our cultural leaders were deeply influenced by the spirit of freedom, justice, secularism, and democracy, these having been the major features of India's freedom struggle. The change in political complexion of governments or a cabinet crisis within government never made any significant impact on our cultural freedom. It is for this excellent reason that India's Culture Secretaries and Culture Ministers have never got either the attention or the acclaim that goes with holders of similar positions in Home, Defence, Finance and External Affairs. This is bound to change in the coming decades, for culture is going to be a factor in the world's recognition of India. Besides, the increasing role of the market and the foreign media have already sharpened public debates on issues related to culture.

There is a school of thought which strongly believes that although there has been substantive material progresss in India after 1947, this period is marked by a cultural lag.[25] It is felt that as there is no *particular* emphasis on the study of culture and its promotion, the younger generation is choosing 'common' and sometimes debased expressions of our culture, namely those shown in indifferent films and the mass media. The worrying aspect of the matter is that the advent of the middle class and the phenomenal increase in its size, particularly after the liberalization of the economy, have not facilitated any resurgence of Indian values and cultural practices in the way they did during the freedom struggle. We witness the upsurge of an unbridled consumerism and a frenetic pursuit of the pleasure principle. The Gandhian value-system of austerity, plain living, and high thinking has been relegated to the background as a way of life, not to be aspired for in India's march towards modernization and economic progress.

Unfortunately, the tradition of debates on cultural issues during the freedom struggle has not continued beyond. The main concern after partition in 1947 was to evolve a secular democracy, to handle the massive refugee problem, and to dismantle the feudal order of princes and zamindars. The mandarins of our Planning Commission did not devote enough attention to promoting culture or according it its due place in their paradigm of development. The interrelationship between cultural backwardness and economic backwardness was not fully appreciated by the planners in most of our economically backward regions. The need to fight vigorously against illiteracy, communalism, and casteism, and also to work simultaneously towards providing opportunities for employment generation, was not adequately emphasized.

It is not possible, in our development paradigm, to support the concept of art standing apart from social life. Art has to be an active process in the movement of history. An artist, whether writer, poet, painter, sculptor or film-maker, invariably sees his/her work as a dialogue with the wider issues of life. Poets and scholars have repeatedly said that the greatness of art cannot be determined by form alone. It can be judged largely in the light of its alliance with great ends, with the depth of its note of revolt, with the extent of hope in it. Thus, there are certain interventions which we need from the world of culture to allow our democracy and development processes to continue and grow. Such interventions are possible through layers of creative mediations where myth, history, memory and contemporary experience merge to create aesthetic statements on unity, democracy and development. In modern India, where the electronic media are increasingly playing a major role, such cultural mediations would have an important impact on public policy, the social ethos, individual consciousness, and also on the institutions of market and trade.

V
National Culture Fund

The scale, diversity and historical depth of our heritage in terms of monuments, forms of art, music, dance and drama, as well as manuscripts, requires financial support of a massive nature, and an efficient, sensitive administrative infrastructure. Unfortunately, funding at such a level is not available; the administrative arrangements are inadequate, and there is an acute shortage of good culture managers in the country.

State governments allocate very meagre resources to cultural activities in their budgets. Even this small amount faces drastic cuts whenever austerity measures are launched by the state governments to mop up their deficits or to tide over their frequent financial crises. The position in the Government of India is not very attractive either.

The culture sector has not received much financial support under various past Five Year Plans. While the culture sector's allocation in respect of the Ist Plan is not separately available, the expenditure was only Rs 3 crores, Rs 7 crores, Rs 12 crores, Rs 28 crores, Rs 115 crores and Rs 451 crores respectively under the 2nd, 3rd, 4th, 5th, 6th, 7th Five Year Plans; the 8th Five Year Plan expenditure is Rs 800 crores. Although the Standing Committee of Parliament has been recommending an allocation of 1 per cent of GDP on culture, the allocation of funds under the 8th Plan—which is much more liberal than in previous plans—has been only to the tune of 0.19 per cent of the total plan outlay of the Government of India.[26] Notwithstanding the increasing importance of culture, both as a factor of development and in strengthening the country's special status in the world, one does not expect the 9th Five Year Plan allocation to rise very considerably due to financial constraints and a well-established practice in the thinking of the Planning Commission to make only marginal increases except on programmes which come under political or security compulsions.

The schemes to provide grant-in-aid to voluntary organizations of repute for the conservation and preservation of monuments, for the setting up of museums at district level, for the establishment of new regional centres of National Akademies, the National School of Drama, the Zonal Cultural Centres, the Centre for Cultural Resources and Training, the State Akademies, and for new libraries, all deserve a large extent of state support. Cultural education through the Centre for Cultural Resources and Training, as also through schools in general, requires special attention. In view of the magnitude of financial requirements, there is a need to look for support from outside.

In many countries, industrialized and developing alike, new funding mechanisms are being devised, based on the dual recognition that cultural activities can and should be as rationally managed and administered as other development programmes, and that new alliances must be formed between the public and private sector, between the state and society. For example, in the USA the business contribution to the arts has been assessed at $518 million annually, or about 14 per cent of their total contribution to philanthropic activities in that country.[27] The time has come, therefore, to make appropriate adjustments and innovations in the pattern of cultural funding in India as well. It is with this background that it has been decided by the Government of India to set up the National Culture Fund.

The salient features of the National Culture Fund[28] will include income tax exemption to contributions made to the Fund. To attract the corporate sector and business houses, it has been proposed that, while making donations to the Fund, it would be possible for a donor to indicate a project along with any specific location/aspect for funding, and also an agency for the execution of the project, subject to general policy guidelines and rules in this behalf. The authorities of the Fund will respect the choice of the donor to the extent possible. Besides, in the decision-making authorities of the Fund—namely the General Council to be presided over by the

Human Resource Minister, and the Standing Committee to be presided over by the Secretary, Department of Culture—adequate representation will be given to non-official members drawn from different walks of life in the realm of culture, the corporate sector, private foundations, and non-government organizations. This is to give confidence to the donors that the decisions of the Fund shall be exclusively on the basis of the merits of each case.

The Fund will provide a forum for various agencies—whether governmental, public, or private—which are active in the field of culture to come together in dialogue, interaction, and a sharing of common problems, perceptions, and projects. Its resources will be used to provide intellectual, technical and financial collaboration to individuals and institutions active in the field of culture. The Fund will endeavour to keep the criteria of excellence and quality uppermost in its decisions.

In the long run, it should be possible for this Fund to set up small advisory committees in important capitals of the world, in order to attract donations to the Fund. In future, proposals such as entry fees to certain sites and monuments, could be earmarked for the Fund, and the enhancement of funds for the maintenance and upkeep of particular monuments, could also be favourably considered.

If perceived in more objective terms, the National Culture Fund will constitute an important innovation—a basic departure from the prevalent implementational strategies of the government, which presumed that the onus was necessarily and primarily on the government to provide administrative and financial wherewithal for culture-related activities in the country. The Fund will herald an important initiative for enabling institutions and the public at large to contribute to culture-related endeavours, for forging meaningful inter-institution partnerships, for mobilizing extra-budgetary resources for culture, and for heightening awareness that culture indeed constitutes a crucial input to the overall process of development. It will seek in particular to encourage young people to take part in their culture and to translate that pride through a personal commitment to its preservation and renewal. The proposed Fund will cooperate closely therefore with institutions and individuals already active in the cultural sphere and who are committed to practise, revitalize, safeguard, and promote interest in the rich diversity of our culture. It will promote the culture of India, the values that they embody and the forms of expression that ensure their authenticity and identity. Its concrete activities will flow from the priorities set by the Fund's policy-making body and would include dissemination, coordination, and extension.

There is a need to strengthen the managerial capabilities of various organizations under the Department of Culture, such as the Archaeological Survey of India, the National Archives, the National Research Laboratory for the Conservation of Cultural Property, the Anthropological Survey of India, and the various library systems.

The task of service to heritage sites, archival materials, museums and art centres, libraries, and anthropological research have all suffered for want of organized All-India services. It would, therefore, be necessary for the government to move forwards the constitution of an Indian Archaeological Service, an Indian Archival Service, an Indian Museums and Arts Service, an Indian Anthropological Service, and an Indian Library Service. The creation of these service structures[29] could go a long way in boosting the morale of employees in these organizations, improving their promotion prospects, and serving the wider cause of the augmentation of efficiency in these fields of cultural pursuit. To attract talent from outside, provision should be made for lateral entry and eventual absorption into these services, in addition to the regular annual requirements of Grade 'A' culture managers through the Union Public Service Commission from among young and bright graduates of the country.

VI
Culture and the Media Revolution

The last decade of the twentieth century is a landmark decade in more than one way. It not only leads to a new millennium, but it is a decade which has witnessed a new value-system in determining the status of a country in the comity of nations. Hitherto, the traditional military strength of a country, i.e. the size and lethal capacity of its armed forces, its sophisticated nuclear weapons, and its geo-political ambitions, together had a decisive say in determining its place in the world. It was this value-system that saw the emergence of the USA and the Soviet Union as two superpowers after 1945. The end of the cold war in 1991 dramatically replaced the supremacy of military potential of a nation, by its status in the world market. The strength of the market institutions of a country and its size in world trade has become a preponderant factor relegating military strength to a second place in the global power-game. The emergence of culture as a third factor in this power equation is perhaps the most significant development. It is very difficult to ascribe percentages to these three factors but it is perhaps stating the obvious when one says that it is the cultural strength of a counry that gives it cohesiveness, endurance, and a memory to carry the country forward as a civilization in the world. The importance of culture therefore needs to be viewed in this perspective whichever way one looks at it.

The present situation in global affairs where the nation state plays the role of the principal actor is likely to be continued in the 21st century as well. The increasing importance of culture would have two differing influences. First, it would imply association of loyalties to tribal, ethnic, caste, and religious belongingness. In several democratic countries, we are already witnessing politicization of primordial loyalties with the objective of advancing individual or group interests, and also of defining one's identity in these terms. Second, the influence of creative persons in the realm of art and literature would also substantially increase. These influences, on the other hand, would enable people to educate themselves in terms of their history, language, religion, values, customs, and beliefs.

As the world moves towards the next millennium, fears are being expressed about the future of creative diversity and the plural character of culture. The change that we are now witnessing through the media revolution, post-industrial technologies, and global communication networks, has generated apprehensions about the emergence of a uniform, homogenized culture, and more explicitly about the rapid westernization which will eclipse our plurality of thought patterns and ways of living. Simultaneously, a number of scholars are talking about the 'clash of civilizations'[30] in the decades to come. Hegemony of every kind—political, economic, and cultural—always presupposes the destruction of diverse outlooks. Cultural hegemony is bound to give rise in the 21st century to even more resolute conflicts than those generated by the colonial economic order in the nineteenth century. What can be done to preserve and enrich the large numbers of distinct cultures that exist today in the face of this rapid globalization and standardization of ways of life? The authors of the World Commission on Culture and Development have formulated the issue as follows:

> We have a long way to go. We have not yet learned how to respect each other fully, how to share and work together. This truly exceptional time in history calls for exceptional solutions. The world as we know it, all the relationships we took as given, are undergoing profound rethinking and reconstruction. Imagination, innovation, vision and creativity are required. International partnerships and interaction are an essential ingredient for creativity in problem-solving, a quality that requires a willingness to frame bold questions instead of depending on conventional answers. It means an open mind, an open heart, and a readiness to seek fresh definitions, reconcile old opposites, and help draw new mental maps. Ultimately it will be the honesty of introspection that will lead to compassion for the other's experience, and it will be compassion that will lead us to a future in which the pursuit of individual freedom will be balanced with a need for common well-being, and in which our agenda includes empathy and respect for the entire spectrum of human differences.[31]

With this background, people are looking to India to see whether this country, with its 5000 years of uninterrupted civilization, will provide some answers which might lead to a social harmony wherein there is respect for creative diversity.

India's great heritage of arts and crafts, of language and literature, of music and dance, of religion and philosophy, and of the traditional ways of life and actual living, have inspired Indians of course, but also countless others who came to be associated with it. In sheer numerical terms, India is a country of nearly a billion people, 18 languages, 1700 dialects, 4 main castes, thousands of sub-castes, and 5 main religions. This cultural diversity and rich attainment is accompanied by India's immense biological diversity, which encompasses eco-systems, populations, species and their varied genetic make-up. The number of our plant species is estimated to be over 45,000, representing about 7 per cent of the world's flora, and the total number of animal species is estimated at 81,000, representing about 6.4 per cent of the world's fauna. As a result, India is one of the 12 identified mega bio-diversity centres of the world.[32]

Indian cultural unity has successfully tackled problems of political instability and military invasion, social obscurantism and religious bigotry, and has gained renewal at several stages of its history. Among the finest expressions of India's culture, the *Ramayana*, the *Mahabharata*, the Vedas and the *Upanishads*, are rooted in the family, the village, in religious practices and agricultural modes of production. Similarly, Indian arts and crafts are illustrious expressions of Indian religions and spiritual experiences—their concept and speech, doctrines and conventions, symbols and images—in the milieu of India's changing life-patterns. The renewal that has taken place from time to time and which found expression in Sufism, Vaishnavism and in the writings of Kabir and the cultural renaissances of the 19th and 20th centuries, are also deeply rooted within the Indian historical traditions.

The national leaders were conscious of the fact that any rash political intervention in the realm of art and culture could lead to harmful results. While cultural bodies needed sound financial and public support, it was also felt that matters related to culture as well as cultural heritage be brought within the reach of the largest possible number of citizens. In this context, the experience of the state in cultural activities has, in the past five decades, proved that harmony between culture and the state is both possible and desirable for better governance and for the maintenance of an environment conducive to creativity. I would say, in fact, that the contemporary Indian experience is just the opposite of what Nietzsche declared: 'One should not deceive oneself about this. Culture and the State are antagonists. One thrives at the expense of the other.'[33]

At present, it seems apparent from the rapid social and cultural change that India is going through a rather acute crisis in the domain of cultural consciousness. The *sruti* tradition and the *guru-shishya parampara*, which once facilitated the generation of creative persons, teachers, and sages who revitalized Indian cultural responses to pressing problems of the day, have declined. Computers and the electronic media have served us against memory loss, but by themselves cannot provide any substitute for organic renewal processes. On the other hand, they have so accelerated the process of social change that 'culture shock' is the result. As Alvin Toffler puts it.

> The accelerative thrust in society affects the individual. If the rate of change in the society exceeds the limits of adaptability of the individual, 'culture shock' results.[34]

In such a situation, the individual's roots, culture, family, and the advice of elders, are the only pillars that will support him from being blown entirely off gear.

Even the very role of state and market that we envisaged a few years ago is undergoing rapid change. In 1991, while at the global scene the world came to witness the end of the cold war, in India there began the process of economic reforms which sought to translate the high investment rate into a smart and sustainable growth of output and employment and release of the Indian entrepreneurial energy. Major changes focused on the investment regime, financial sector, taxation, and infrastructure; trade policies and public enterprises have provided an impetus to propel India into the international economy. The market is being perceived as a strong factor in the economy and society of India. These, in turn, have strengthened the Indian market and imparted to it a rare capacity of intervention in the world of art and culture not known before.

Liberalization and the dismantling of state control over the economy since 1991 have generated hopes as well as fears. The pace of change has been very rapid and the transformation taking place is making a serious impact on cultural values and ways of living. In the process, one aspect of the matter which strikes the observer relates to the newly acquired freedom of the market from values and mentalities of the Gandhian era in terms of production, possession and consumption. In the 50s and 60s, the market moulded itself to a mind-set that viewed the relationships between individuals and commodities in terms of traditional beliefs and Gandhian values. Not only works of art but even clothes carried the spirit of the maker. The integration of the Indian economy with the global market is already altering this state of relationship.

Three decades ago, John F. Kennedy said of economic growth: 'A rising tide lifts all boats'.[35] Today, this tide of the global market economy is also rising in India but there is a widespread feeling that a number of these boats are not being sufficiently lifted, and that some of them may even sink. Will Indian culture provide the rescue operation? Will business assist the needed cultural efforts? How will the state intervene?

It is curious to notice that the world's best tennis player is a world figure. This is also becoming true of the world's best chess player. However, the world's best tabla player or sarod player, or the world's best Odissi dancer, or Kathak dancer, or Bharatnatyam dancer, are only regional heroes, not even national heroes. For this image to change it is important to realize that such a position prevails. The image-makers have to find new ways of changing such 'absurd features'.

The United States has found a new way of honouring artists. Portraits of artists are the new trend for the cinema, and Hollywood has found in artists a new breed of heroes: wild, free spirits who live recklessly and often die the same way. Film-makers are making an unprecedented number of movies inspired by the most colourful lives of 20th century painters and sculptors. Among those painters who have gained immortality on the screen are Jackson Pollock, Picasso and Modigliani. India has to explore this and several other ways of acclaiming her artists and creative persons.

In this changed business environment, it is imperative that we deepen our understanding of our own cultural forces and capabilities, both in terms of human skills and diverse Indian aspirations, to bring new opportunities before ourselves. Such is the spirit of idealism which made the New Deal and its programmatic offspring so attractive in the USA, and there is no doubt that this sort of potential exists in India today. In the march towards expanding our share of world trade and strengthening our economic institutions, we must not forget that to live without a cultural memory is not to live at all. Our cultural memory is our coherence, our reason, our feeling, even our action. Yet as we have seen, our different ethnic groups have at different periods of their history found solutions to their problems and their culture has helped them resolve their crisis.

It is the national government's programme to move in the direction of establishing museums and cultural centres at the district level. Efforts are being made to strengthen library and information networks at the grassroots level, and to take full advantage of the new leadership, particularly from among women, that is emerging as a result of the new Panchayati Raj democracy. The requirement of funds and also of managerial cadres is massive, and the market's response, to come to the help of the state as a partner in these areas, would be most welcome. Business houses and corporate bodies are not only likely to contribute to the National Culture Fund but are also expected to construct and even manage museums and culture theatres. Similarly, a large number of artists, particularly in the field of dance, drama, music, painting and sculpture, are being supported by the government in running their schools, and the number of these artists needs to be increased with determined support from the market.

India's contribution to world culture, its rich bio-diversity and great plurality have generated awe, fascination, and respect. In 1915 Ananda Kentish Coomaraswamy summed up the position when the wrote:

> Each race contributes something essential to the world's civilization in the course of its own self-expression... the essential contribution of India, is simply her Indianness; her great humiliation would be to substitute or to have substituted for this own character (svahbava) a cosmopolitan veneer, for then indeed she must come before the world empty-handed.[36]

There is acceptance of a firm relationship between secularism and democracy in India. It is also established that democracy is not an obstacle to modernization and economic and social development; on the contrary, it is a basic pre-requisite for progress. Apart from political democracy, the existence of a central administration, common law, nation-wide network of economic, commercial and banking institutions have proved to be strong factors of unity. Cultural plurality found expression under Ashoka and Akbar and in modern times under Mahatma Gandhi and Nehru.

If the liberalized economy in India has to subserve the destiny and aspirations of all of us, we have to think big and plan carefully. Rarely does creative effort spring from the womb of gloom and pessimism: we must not be upset by temporary setbacks. As one perceptive observer has said, India runs like a 16-wheel truck—always blowing one of its tyres. One might add that the basic four wheels of Indian culture: family; religion; arts, music and drama; and literature and philosophy; have all remained functional and have been renewed by successive generations, giving continuity to India as a civilizational force.

The developments in India particularly since 1947 have given us confidence that in the new millennium India will not face the world emptyhanded, and that she will continue to justify Iqbal's dictum that 'there is something that does not allow the Indian continuum to perish'.[37] It is this that makes me believe that the same Indian art, life, and thought which once illuminated human civilization shall find new expressions in India once more.[38]

Notes and References

1. B.P. Singh, 'Culture and Administration: A Study of Interaction as a Means of Social Change in India', *Indian Journal of Public Administration*, vol.xxix, no.1, Jan–March 1983, pp.1–10.
2. Rabindranath Tagore, *Sanchyata* and *Gitanjali*, Poem entitled *Bharat Tirtha*. The original Bengali text reads as follows:

    हेथाय आर्य, हेया अनार्य, हेथाय द्राविड़-चीन,
    शक-हूण-दल, पठान-मोगल एक देहे होलो लीन ।

3. Jawaharlal Nehru, in his Foreward to *Sanskriti Ke Char Adhyaya* by Ramdhari Singh Dinkar, Delhi, Rajpal and Sons, 1956 observes as follows:

    भारत में दोनों बातें एक साथ बढ़ीं । एक ओर तो विचारों और सिद्धांतों में हमने अधिक से अधिक उदार और सहिष्णु होने का दावा किया । दूसरी ओर, हमारे सामाजिक आचार अत्यन्त संकीर्ण होते गये । यह विभक्त व्यक्तित्व, सिद्धांत और आचरण का यह विरोध, आज तक हमारे साथ है और आज भी हम उसके विरुद्ध संघर्ष कर रहे हैं । कितनी विचित्र बात है कि अपनी दृष्टि की संकीर्णता और आदतों और रिवाजों की कमजोरियों को हम यह कहकर नजर-अन्दाज कर देना चाहते हैं कि हमारे पूर्वज बड़े लोग थे और उनके बड़े-बड़े विचार हमें विरासत में मिले हैं । लेकिन, पूर्वजों से मिले हुए ज्ञान एवं हमारे आचरण में भारी विरोध है और जब तक हम इस विरोध की स्थिति को दूर नहीं करते, हमारा व्यक्तित्व विभक्त का विभक्त रह जाएगा ।

    [Thus, in India, we developed at one and the same time the broadest tolerance and catholicity of thought and opinion as well as the narrowest social forms of behaviour. This split personality has pursued us and we struggle against it even today. We overlook and excuse our own failings and narrowness of custom and habit by references to the great thoughts we have inherited from our ancestors. But there is an

essential conflict between the two, and so long as we do not resolve it, we shall continue to have this split personality.] (English Translation).
4. Scientific Policy Resolution, 4 March 1958, Department of Science and Technology, Government of India, New Delhi, 1958.
5. Jawaharlal Nehru (1889–1964) : Jawaharlal Nehru was educated in England. He joined the freedom struggle and held the position of President of the Indian National Congress five times. He was the first Indian Prime Minister after independence and remained in that position until his death. A prolific writer and an impressive public speaker, he was an idealist and a democrat who worked ceaselessly for building a modern India.

Maulana Abul Kalam Azad (1888–1958): Maulana Abul Kalam Azad was a great nationalist, an erudite scholar, one of the most impressive speakers in public life and a charming conversationalist. Although he was brought up in Calcutta, he did not go to any Madrasa nor did he attend any modern institution of western education. In 1912 Azad started an Urdu weekly, the *Al-Hilal* from Calcutta. He was appointed the first Education Minister of India after Independence in 1947 and held this portfolio until his death.

Rajendra Prasad (1884–1963): Dr Rajendra Prasad was born in an obscure village in Bihar. He was a brilliant student, a great scholar and an outstanding nationalist. Rajen Babu, as he was popularly called, was a disciple of Mahatma Gandhi and rose to become the President of the Indian National Congress during the years 1934–1939 and 1947–1948. He was President of the Constituent Assembly—a body which framed the Constitution of India during 1946–50. He was the first President of India (1950–1962).

Sarvepalli Radhakrishnan (1888–1975): Dr Sarvepalli Radhakrishnan was a man of scholarly disposition and was one of the greatest philosophers of modern India. He was Vice President of India from 1952 to 1962 and was President of India from 1962 to 1967.
6. Quoted in *Report of the High Powered Committee*, popularly known as the Haksar Committee, appointed to review the performance of the National Akademies and the National School of Drama, Department of Culture, Ministry of Human Resource Development, Government of India, New Delhi, July 1990, p.19 (unpublished).
7. Kamaladevi Chattopadhyaya (1903–1988): Kamaladevi Chattopadhyaya was an outstanding freedom fighter who after Independence played a major role in the revival of crafts and empowerment of women in India.

She wrote and spoke extensively on this subject and was a source of inspiration for several organizations in this field.

8. Haksar Committee Report, pp. 172–3.
9. Annual Report (part II), Department of Culture, Ministry of Human Resource Development, Government of India, New Delhi, 1994–5, p.1.
10. Anthropological Survey of India : *People of India* Series, Delhi, Oxford University Press. Out of 43 volumes, 22 volumes have been published during 1994–96, and the rest are expected to be available shortly.
11. India has Cultural Agreements with 106 countries, out of which India has live Cultural Exchange Programmes with 78 countries (Information available with Department of Culture, Ministry of Human Resource Development, Government of India).
12. Pupul Jayakar was a distinguished author and was Chairperson of the Festival of India Committee during the eighties. The observation is from papers maintained by the Festival of India Wing of the Department of Culture, Government of India.
13. Report of the High Powered Committee (Ananthamurthy Committee) appointed by the Ministry of Human Resource Development, Government of India to review the Seven Zonal Cultural Centres, New Delhi, 1995, p.16 (unpublished).
14. Haksar Committee Report, pp. 149–50.
15. Krishna Chaitanya: *Art and Social Consciousness*, Coomaraswamy Memorial Lectures, 26 October 1988, Lalit Kala Akademi, Delhi.
16. Deborah E. Klimburg-Salter: *1000 Years of Tabo Monastery*, Institute of Tibetan and Buddhist Studies, University of Vienna, Austria, 1996, pp.1–16.
17. George Michell (ed.) *Temple Towns of Tamil Nadu*, Marg Publications, Bombay, 1993, p.13.
18. Mallika Sarabhai, *Art, Culture and Business in a Liberalized Economy: Towards Synergy Forging New Partnership*, p.2. This paper was presented at a seminar organized by the Federation of Indian Chambers of Commerce and Industry (FICCI), New Delhi, 11 April 1996; the seminar was inaugurated by the author.
19. Ibid, p.4
20. Bana Bhatt (AD 606-48) India's famous poet and literary figure of the 7th century. His monumental work *Harsha Charita* is a narrative of conditions prevalent in his time and is a valuable treatise for understanding the social and political situation of the era.

21. B.P. Singh, North-East India : Demography, Culture and Identity Crisis, *Modern Asian Studies*, Cambridge University Press, London, April 1987. This paper analyses culture and identity crisis prevailing in the region.

22. Quoted by Mahatma Gandhi in *Young India*, 1 June 1921. *The Collected Works of Mahatma Gandhi*, xx (April–August 1921), p.159.

23. B.P. Singh, *The Indian National Congress and Cultural Renaissance*, Allied Publishers, 1987. This book analyses how the Indian National Congress— a political party founded in 1885—combined the freedom struggle with a cultural renaissance lasting up to about 1960. The theory developed in this book attributes success and longevity of the Indian National Congress to the fact that the party addressed cultural issues in its long innings.

24. Ravinder Kumar, *India: A 'Nation State' or a 'Civilization-State'*, Occasional Papers, May 1989, Centre for Contemporary Studies, Nehru Memorial Museum and Library, New Delhi.

25. P.C. Joshi, *Culture, Communication and Social Change*, Vikas Publishing House, New Delhi, 1989. This book makes a detailed analysis of the challenges facing India in the cultural field.

26. Detailed analysis exists in the document *Report of the Working Group of the Planning Commission on Art and Culture for the Ninth Five Year Plan, 1997–2002*, Department of Culture, Ministry of Human Resource Development, Government of India, 1996 (unpublished). The author was Chairman of the Working Group which drafted the Report.

27. Pushpa Sundar, 'Business in the Arts', *The Economic Times*, New Delhi, 1 June 1996.

28. Based on papers available in the Department of Culture in respect of the establishment of the National Culture Fund under the Charitable Endowment Act, 1890. The author was the originator of the idea and chairman of the group of intellectuals and artists who formulated this document. This National Culture Fund was notified on 28 November 1996 and formally launched on 29 March 1997 with the Union Minister for Human Resources Development as Chairman of the Council and the author as the President of the Executive Committee in his official capacity.

29. Based on submissions made by the author before the 5th Pay Commission, on 19 June 1996, and before the Planning Commission in the meeting of the Steering Committee on Arts and Culture on 22 May, 1996. The 5th Pay Commission accepted these recommendations and

suggested the constitution of four organized services on the following lines:

(1) *Central Archaeological Service*: the services will include all Group 'A' technical posts in the Archaeological Survey of India (ASI) and the National Research Laboratory for Conservation of Cultural Property.

(2) *Central Archival Service*: the services will include all Group 'A' posts currently under the control of the National Archives of India.

(3) *Central Museums and Art Organizations*: the services will include all Group 'A' posts in the National Museum and the National Gallery of Modern Art. They will also include the sub-cadreing of museology, chemistry and restoration.

(4) *Central Anthropological Service*: this will include all organized Group 'A' posts of different specialization and the merger should be effected in such a manner that the career and progress of officers is ensured and uniformity is maintained in the promotional prospects of technical posts in different sub-specialities.

30. Samuel P. Huntington, 'The Clash of Civilization?' *Foreign Affairs*, v.72, pt.2, 1993. The author observes: Civilization identity will be increasingly important in the future, and the world will be shaped in large measure by the interactions among seven of eight major civilizations. These include Western, Confucian, Japanese, Islamic, Hindu, Slavic-Orthodox, Latin American and possibly the African civilization. The most important conflicts of the future will occur along the cultural fault lines separating these civilizations from one another. (p.25)

31. *Report of the World Commission on Culture and Development: Our Creative Diversity* (France, 1995), p.12; Javier Perez de Cuellar was the President of this Commission.

32. Based on work done by the author in his capacity as Chairman of the National Committee on Biodiversity Conservation Action Plan, set up by the Ministry of Environment and Forests, Government of India, New Delhi during 1993–5.

33. 'State of Culture' (editorial), *Times of India*, New Delhi, 2 January 1996.

34. Alvin Toffler, *Future Shock*, Bantam Books, New York, 1990, p.3. Toffler further observes as follows : There is... an even more powerfully significant way in which the acceleration of change in society increases the difficulty of coping with life. This stems from the fantastic intrusion of novelty....into our...existence. (p.322).

35. Ralph Buultjens, 'Why I am a democrat', *Book Review*, New Delhi, June 1996.

36. Ananda Kentish Coomaraswamy, 'The Dance of Shiva', *The Athenaeum*, 1915. See *Parkosa*, Coomaraswamy Centenary Seminar Papers, New Delhi, Lalit Kala Akademi, 1984. This makes a valuable contribution to understanding his thought.

37. Muhammad Iqbal, quoted in B.P. Singh, *The Indian National Congress and Cultural Renaissance*.

   The author of the popular song 'Sare Jehan Se Achha' played a leading role in India's freedom struggle and awakening. He concluded this song as follows: 'कुछ बात है कि हस्ती मिटती नहीं हमारी'.

38. A young computer programmer of Indian origin, now a British national, commented at the end of my lecture at the Nehru Centre, London on 10 February 1997, that culture may be important but what is more important is that India is going to become an economic super-power in the 21st century. I answered that like him, I am concerned about poverty, illiteracy, child labour and lack of health care facilities in India and that economic development is an imperative requirement to overcome all these. But the moot point is whether India is going to imitate the west, and become an economic super-power, and in the process lose its Indianness. It would be sad if that happened as once the Indian identity is lost it will be difficult to bring it back. I believe that India is not going to lose its Indianness.

The photograph of Nehru and Azad captures bonhomie and closeness that marked their personal relationship.

(Courtesy Nehru Memorial Museum & Library, New Delhi)

3
Arts, Cultural Pageants and the State: The Nehru-Azad Dialogue

I
The Challenge to Colonial Rule

Cultural creativity, and its widespread dissemination in our society will have a crucial role to play. Culture will help in expanding the horizons of social understanding; in forging new bonds of political association; in reinforcing old and in generating new social values; and in creating a profound sense of civic fraternity and shared concerns crucial to the emergence of modern nationhood. It may be recalled that our forefathers thought of the world as a family and emphatically pronounced: 'the earth is my mother and the world is my father'.[1] This global consciousness was, however, pre-modern and not tethered by modern communication networks of aeroplanes, telephones, satellites, and electronic media. Yet, this ancient consciousness of our people always stressing upon us the fact of our being a part of the cosmos has had a significant influence on creative persons in India throughout the ages and up to modern times.

Prior to 1947 both the British and the leaders of India's freedom struggle addressed themselves to the theme of culture but with different objectives. The British approach in the domain of culture was largely shaped by their policies of *laissez-faire* and paternalism. The British did not interfere either with the market or the social institutions in pursuit of their cultural activities. Similarly, the princes and zamindars, nawabs and nizams were allowed to promote activities of their choice in the realm of promotion of art and culture, as long as these were not considered subversive to colonial interests. The British paternalist attitude was reflected in the protection of India's heritage and the government's support to certain institutions of art, dance, and oriental studies. The aim, however, was that everything that was done in the realm of art must buttress the imperial interests and be viewed by the people as a 'civilizing' act. They went on to establish and fund organizations such as the Asiatic Society of Bengal (1784), the Fine Arts Society of Madras (1860), the Arts Society, Pune (1873), the Bombay Arts Society (1888), the Punjab Fine Arts Society at Lahore (1922), the Delhi Fine Arts Society (1928) and the Imperial Library, Calcutta (1903). Five art schools were set up, namely the Western Art School, Pune (1798), the Calcutta School of Arts (1839), the Madras School of Art (1850), the Bombay School of Art (1851), and the Mayo School of Art, Lahore (1880). For the task of protecting India's ancient and medieval monuments and art objects of archaeological, historical, or artistic interests, and for related conservation work, the Archaeological Survey of India was founded in 1861. The National Archives of India was established in the year 1891 for the preservation of records. Mass-media units like All India Radio were set up, which were primarily for the dissemination of official information, but which also patronized the arts, particularly music. In the universities, there were courses on history and civilization, relating to both Europe and India, but with little thought given to social and cultural developments, and subjects like aesthetics, art history, or folk-arts were mostly non-existent. No state aid—financial or organizational—was made available for the promotion of regional crafts.

All these measures were solely guided by the motive of strengthening the colonial roots. This policy was aptly put by Lord Curzon before the House of Lords on 27 September 1909, when he stated:

Our familiarity, not merely with the languages of the people of the East but with their customs, their feelings, their traditions, their history and religion, our capacity to understand what may be called the genius of the

East, is the sole basis upon which we are likely to be able to maintain in the future the position we have won, and no step that can be taken to strengthen that position can be considered undeserving of the attention of his Majesty's Government or of a debate in the House of Lords.[2]

Five years later, while speaking on the occasion of the establishment of the School of Oriental Studies in London, Curzon went on to observe, almost in a language uncharacteristic of him:

> In my view the creation of a school [of Oriental studies, later to become the London University School of Oriental and African Studies] like this in London is part of the necessary furniture of Empire.[3]

There were, however, several harmful effects within British policy. It completely ignored folk art and rural values. The work done by a tribal girl in decorating her house or the walls of her home never figured as a work of art. However, works of art which could be kept hanging on the walls in museums or in individual homes, or poems and songs which could be sung in praise of the imperialist order, got recognition and promotion.

The leaders of the freedom struggle strived ceaselessly to create an awareness among the people of their cultural heritage, and through this endeavoured to generate and strengthen the spirit of nationalism in the people's consciousness. The national leaders took recourse to 'romantic reconstruction of the past' to imbue a legitimate sense of national pride in India's heritage, as well as to resist the social and cultural challenges posed by the imperialists. All activities, particularly by the Indian National Congress, in the field of the establishment of schools and colleges, or for the removal of untouchability, or the preservation of art objects, went to strengthen the movement for the attainment of independence. During the early era of the nationalist movement, dramatists, novelists and poets presented heroes of popular legends from regional ethnic groups with a pan-Indian consciousness. This helped to introduce the local culture of the various regions to the rest of the country and to develop a feeling of mutual belonging as well as the self-esteem of the regional group. The freedom struggle was accompanied by a renaissance in literature, painting, music, sculpture, science, and philosophy, which in turn became an effective instrument of national cohesion and contributed to further the cause of freedom.

In 1915, Mahatma Gandhi stated that he wanted such creative expressions in the realm of literature and art which reflected the feelings and aspirations of the millions of his countrymen. In holding India up as culturally superior to the West, the leaders of the freedom movement went on to establish their cultural superiority over the British rulers. This contributed substantially in shaking the foundations of the colonial order and in uniting the Indian people.

A few significant all-India institutions of culture were established through purely voluntary efforts; some with a cultural aim in view, others with a national, political or social goal. In this context the valuable work of several individuals and institutions needs to be mentioned.

Rabindranath Tagore's University at Santiniketan and his dramas with dance and song, Vallathol's Kerala Kalamandalam, and Rukmini Devi Arundale's Kalakshetra (originally part of the Theosophical Society), provided institutions which patrons could support through contributions and volunteer service. The Indian People's Theatre Association (IPTA), the Uday Shankar Culture Centre at Almora, the music conferences begun by V.N. Bhatkhande, and the Madras Music Academy with V. Raghavan's keen interest and support, all offered new patronage for performing artists. But it was the mass media of radio, films, and phonograph records which drew artists from their local patrons into a wider regional or national network of cultural performances.

The challenge to colonial rule was thus both political and cultural. By 1900, the spiritual image of India as the counterpoint to European materialism had matured, nourished by western adulation and a new perception of a historic past. In 1925, Lord Ronaldshay, one time Governor of Bengal, observed that the sources from which the revolutionary movement and the Tagore School of Painting drew their inspiration were identical....[but] one called for the severest condemnation, while the other was worthy of all praise.[4]

The British Empire with a strong sense of identity, also consciously pursued the idea that their superiority over India rested on cultural rather than purely on political and military strength. In his famous 'Tryst with Destiny' speech delivered in the Constituent Assembly on 14 August 1947, Jawaharlal Nehru declared that:

> At the dawn of history India started on her unending quest, and trackless centuries are filled with her striving and the grandeur of her success and her failures. Through good and ill fortune alike she has never lost sight of that quest or forgotten the ideals which gave her strength.[5]

To give shape to this quest in independent India was indeed a gigantic task. The establishment of new institutions of culture, like the Sahitya Akademi, Lalit Kala Akademi, Sangeet Natak Akademi, and National School of Drama; the strengthening of cultural institutions already active in the preservation, fostering and dissemination of culture, such as the Archaeological Survey of India, the Indian Museum, and other museums, the publication of textbooks in Hindi, English and other Indian languages to fill the crying need for literature for children, students, scholars and lay persons, the extension of the mass media organizations like All India Radio, television networks, films, etc.; rehabilitation of the traditional artisans, craftsmen and khadi workers; and projecting India's culture abroad through international cultural cooperation networks; all these activities received attention in the post-independence period.

In all these tasks the leaders of the new Republic, particularly Jawaharlal Nehru, Maulana Abul Kalam Azad, Rajendra Prasad and Sarvepalli Radhakrishnan approached the cultural issues with considerable sensitivity and gentleness. This was adequately reflected in the introduction of a cultural pageant in the Republic Day parade every year (in similar functions many other countries exhibit merely their military strength); and the purchase of works of art for the national and regional museums.

II
The Republic Day Parade

During the last three centuries, each nation has drawn considerable strength from its armed forces, and the celebrations of the national day of a country were invariably marked by an impressive military parade, which in turn used to be taken note of not only by the nationals themselves, but also by the friends and adversaries of that country. The need to have a national day was also felt in India and it was decided to celebrate such a national day on 26 January every year—the date of the adoption of the Constitution of India as a Sovereign Democratic Republic. It was decided to celebrate the Republic Day Parade on Delhi's Raj Path with an impressive military parade, and the Ministry of Defence was entrusted with the responsibility of organizing and providing the necessary wherewithal.

However, the leaders in the early years of the Republic were deeply conscious of the age-old cultural unity of India, and were keen to make cultural manifestations a part of the Republic Day celebrations. Accordingly, we have a spectacle of magnificent blending of a military parade with a cultural pageant representing India's plural society and belief-systems. As Ashfaque Husain, the Joint Secretary of the Department of Education in 1952 stated,

> whereas other countries, on similar occasions, hold impressive military parades which are calculated to give to the whole world an idea of the armed might of the country, we have combined the ceremonial military parade with the cultural pageant, which signifies that this young Republic values cultural progress no less than military strength.[6]

Jawaharlal Nehru provided the initial spirit and substance to the cultural pageant that followed the military parade on Republic Day.

He recorded the following critical minute immediately after watching the Republic Day Parade on 26.1.1952.

The cultural pageant which followed the parade this morning, was more ambitious than last year's and in many way it was better. I should like to congratulate those who organised it.

The quality of the different items in the pageant was not uniform. Some were quite good, others might have been better. The first part of it depicting what is called 'Youth and Progress' appeared to be merely an array of people holding up placards. There was nothing artistic or impressive about it.

I rather liked the tableau representing Haryana, Himachal, Gujarat, the Kulu Valley, Malabar, the Punjab, Rajasthan, the Naga warriors and the Majlis of Qawwals. Maharashtra was good, but too long drawn out. Lezim fits in with a procession. Malkhamb does not. Having boxing and the like was rather out of place.

The wedding procession of Rajasthan was very good. The Kashmir Shikara was effective, not so much the Moghul gardens.

The UP Ramlila was feeble. It was just a crowd sitting in a truck.

The school boys and school girls marching at the beginning of the pageant were effective in a way and specially because they had some kind of a uniform dress. But they marched badly and were limp. A little more training is desirable. Also a little more life put into it.

Perhaps in the whole pageant, a little more vigour is necessary. The singing where it took place could not be heard.

This note is not intended to take away from my appreciation of the pageant and my congratulations to those who organised it. I am merely giving my immediate impressions so that they might be of help in subsequent years.[7]

As will be seen, nothing escaped Nehru's discerning eye. Nehru's minute led to the reconstitution of the high-powered Inter-Departmental Committee for the organization of the Republic Day Parade, so as to include a representative of the Ministry of Education. The following correspondence is relevant in this context.

From Humayun Kabir, Secretary, Ministry of Education to B.N. Kaul, (PPS to ARM), 30.1.1952.

We are grateful for the Prime Minister's comments on the cultural pageant held on Republic day. I am writing to Shri Shankar Prasad to convey the Prime Minister's congratulations to the organisers. I am also communicating to Shri Shankar Prasad the substance of the Prime Minister's comments. I am at the same time suggesting that before the programme for next year is finally settled, the Chief Commissioner may consult the Ministry. I would suggest that a Committee, consisting of the Defence Secretary, Home Secretary, Education Secretary and the Chief Commissioner may be generally responsible for the pageant.

From B.N. Kaul to Humayun Kabir, 30.1.1952.

A committee consisting of a representative of the Defence Ministry and of certain other persons already exists for the purpose of making arrangements for the celebration of Republic day. I suggest you should get in touch with the Defence Ministry regarding the composition of this committee if you wish any changes to be made in it.

With regard to your suggestion that the Chief Commissioner should consult the Education Ministry regarding the programme of the pageant, I believe this is a matter which you can take up directly with the Chief Commissioner. You may also, if you like, consult the Committee referred to in the previous paragraph.[8]

Nehru's minute also inspired the Ministry of Education to propose a somewhat more ambitious cultural pageant in the years to come. In fact the following notes constituted a serious effort to actualize Nehru's vision.

Note dated 11.2.1952 submitted by Ashfaque Husain, Joint Secretary, Education, to Maulana Abul Kalam Azad, Minister for Education.

I have now attended two Republic Day Celebrations and have been thinking over the pageant which follows the military parade. This year's pageant was more ambitious than last year's, but it also aroused some criticisms as to the staff work, which might have been stronger, and also in regard to particular tableaux, which might have been presented better. We must nevertheless remember that the pageant is wholly the effort of the Delhi Education Department, with the help of some local institutions. As such, it must be said in fairness that it is a very creditable effort.

The question occurs to me, however, whether a limited local effort, howsoever good, is appropriate for the occasion. It is the biggest occasion of the year and I feel that nothing but the very best we can do is good enough; indeed I would go so far as to say that rather than put up a second rate show we should do without it altogether. It would, however, be a pity to eliminate the pageant altogether, because it is a very happy idea; whereas other countries, on similar occasions, hold impressive military parades which are calculated to give to the whole world an idea of the armed might of the country, we have combined the ceremonial military parade with the cultural pageant, which signifies that this young Republic values cultural progress no less than military strength. From that point of view, however, the quality of this '*beaugeste*' should be such as to impress not only the important representatives of foreign governments who witness the parade but also hundreds of thousands of our own people, to whom the Republic Day celebrations should be both a source of joy and pride and an aspiration. It is for consideration, therefore, whether the Republic Day should not be made an occasion for a cultural festival throughout the country, in districts, in the State headquarters and in the nation's capital. One should like to see for a few days preceding January 26th performances, displays and exhibitions showing something not only of our cultural heritage but also of our cultural progress in the widest sense of the term. There may be art exhibitions, music and dance recitals, literary gatherings, sports meets and so on. In this festival, Delhi, as the nation's capital, should naturally endeavour to occupy the pre-eminent place and, a fortiori, every display that seeks the honour of review by the President, the nation's head and symbol, should be of the highest possible standard.

What has been suggested above may perhaps sound ambitious, but I am inclined to believe that not only is it wholly feasible but that it can also help in no small measure to revitalize our cultural activities, many of which are at present in danger of languishing for want of patronage and encouragement. It will of course cost some money, but the amount will be very small, compared to the benefits which are likely to accrue. Nor is it necessary that the entire cost should fall on Government; it is perhaps not unrealistic to expect that once the Republic Day festival is established as the national festival of the year and participation in it regarded as a privilege and honour, the need for a subsidy from Government will rapidly diminish.

The cultural pageant on Republic Day in Delhi will be a part of the festival proposed above. Even, however, if for any reason it is decided not to proceed with that larger proposal, it is suggested that we should at least try to make a cultural pageant more worthy of the occasion. At present, I understand, the Ministry of Defence gives Rs. 5,000/- to the

Chief Commissioner of Delhi and leaves it to him to arrange the pageant. He obtains some more money from the Delhi and New Delhi Municipal Committees and entrusts the organization of the pageant to the Director of Education and some other officers of Delhi State. If it is accepted that the Republic Day celebrations in Delhi (at least in New Delhi) are not a local affair, it is suggested that the pageant should be organised on an all-India basis. For this purpose, the Ministry of Education should get into touch as early as possible with State Governments and settle the programme in outline, the actual details of the different items of the pageant being left to the State Governments to be worked out by them. By July, the costs should be worked out and the share of the Government of India settled. After that the entire responsibility for their respective units of the pageant will rest with the State Governments, and it will be open to them, if they so decide for reasons of economy, to utilise the services of residents of their States who happen to be in Delhi. The final responsibility for coordination and for the actual 'staging' of the pageant will rest with the Ministry of Education, who will no doubt enlist the cooperation and assistance of other relevant authorities.[9]

Azad's directions, 25.4.1952

...I agree that the Independence Day celebrations on 26th January, as they have been observed for the last two years, could be very much improved and that it is a suitable occasion for organising cultural activities.

The idea of a Cultural Caravan was a very good one and the arrangements made for it by the Delhi Administration were indeed praiseworthy; nevertheless there is still room for improving and bettering them which we should try to do.

I think that whatever programme we plan for the next year should, for the present, be restricted only to Delhi. Later on we may consider how best it can be organised in other places as well.

It is desirable that a committee should be formed to consider this problem in detail. This committee will consider these two aspects:

(i) to improve and make more effective the Cultural Caravan on 26th January.

(ii) to prepare a programme of cultural activities from 26th to 30th January.

The Ministry of Education, the Ministry of Information and Broadcasting, and the Education Ministry of Delhi Government should be represented on this committee.[10]

In a minute recorded on 9.9.1952 (reproduced below) Nehru brought out the importance of the cultural pageant and reflected on its possible character.

I think that steps should be taken from now onwards to consider the programme for January 26th next. There is the military aspect of the programme, which, no doubt, will be drawn up by the Defence Ministry. But, during the last two years, we have had a procession of tableaux usually organised by the schools in Delhi.

I think we should bring out the civilian aspect of that day's programme even more than previously. The tableaux were good. They might be better still if carefully thought out and prepared for some time ahead. They should follow each other and in fairly quick succession. On previous occasions there were too big gaps in between.

The tableaux were historical. This is good. They might be more topical also. Thus we might lay stress on the grow more food problem. I would suggest for consideration that the farmers who have received prizes in competitions held might be invited at Government expense to participate in that day's celebrations.

Then there has been some kind of proposal for some time to have a demonstration of folk dances, more especially by tribal people from various parts of India and particularly the North-East, the Nagas, etc. General Cariappa once mentioned this to me and I liked the idea. If it is possible, I would like these folk dances to be organised round about that time, possibly on the 27th. In fact, two or three shows might be given. If enough people come, the show might be organised in the stadium. On a small scale some of them may dance at the Rashtrapati Bhavan party that afternoon. All the folk dancers who come to Delhi at our invitation should take part in the procession on the 26th. I should like that procession also to contain some more civilian element— boys and girls from schools and colleges, representatives of various professions, more especially representatives of arts and crafts. Indeed, some of our tableaux may represent the famous arts and crafts of India.

These are some odd ideas which should be carefully considered and we should draw up a programme for the 26th as well as a day or two after which would include functions at Rashtrapati Bhavan and of course the main procession down Kingsway.[11]

In a letter written a day after, that is on 10 September 1952, to the Chief Ministers of all States, Nehru very concretely suggested as to what should constitute the cultural pageant. Extracts from that letter given below make interesting reading.

In a little over four months, we shall have the celebrations of our Republic Day, January 26th. During past years we have had a very effective and impressive parade in Delhi followed by tableaux, which represented a kind of historical pageant of India. These tableaux were organised by school children and were fairly good. Nevertheless, there was much room for improvement. I feel that the celebrations on the 26th January should have certainly the military element but should also have an increasingly civil element in them. We might, for instance, in Delhi organize something on a more ambitious scale. There would be the usual procession plus perhaps an exhibition plus also folk dances, more especially by tribal people. The concept of this procession and exhibition and everything else should be to demonstrate both the unity and great variety and diversity of India. This can only be done if States participate in these Delhi celebrations and take some responsibility for them. Each State could represent some distinctive feature of its own in the tableaux or in the exhibition or both. Thus the procession would be a moving pageant of India in its rich diversity. The arts and crafts of each State could be represented in this way.

A part of these demonstrations might be the Grow-More-Food campaign. Peasants and farmers who have won in the competitions could be invited at State expense to participate in these demonstrations and a tableau could represent in various ways this idea of an abundance of food growing to feed this hungry land.

Then there could be folk dances. I would love to see in our procession people from various parts of India, including our tribal people, the Nagas from the North East, the Bhils from Central India, the Santhals and others showing that they are also full partners in this great enterprise of India going ahead. They could display their dances too, which are so attractive.

I have thrown out some ideas about the celebrations on January 26th. All this will require a great deal of organization and full cooperation between the States and the Central Government. There is not much time left and the sooner we begin thinking of this and organizing it, the better. It would be a good thing if we could hold a meeting in Delhi, say in the second week of October, to consider this matter. Each State could send a representative. He need not be a senior officer. It would be better to send a young and enthusiastic person with ideas. At that meeting some general decisions can be taken and we can go ahead preparing accordingly.[12]

So great was Nehru's keenness in this matter that he recorded yet another minute on 17.9.1952 which enunciated that women too should be involved in the organizational effort. It also settled a number of matters relating to the contents and character of the pageant. The minute reads thus:

> The provisional programme for the 26th January is fairly ambitious. Without considering it in detail, there are some suggestions I should like to make.
>
> The committee consists entirely of men. I think in work of this kind, women are very helpful and indeed essential.
>
> We should not try to do too much and thus perhaps lower standards. We should concentrate on some special items. Thus in regard to folk dancing, we can hardly hope to get folk dances from all over India. That would be too expensive a business. We might, therefore, select some areas from which they will be invited. The next year other areas can be invited. It should be clearly understood that we have no amateur dancing. We must have the original stuff.
>
> So also about tableaux. Instead of too many of a mediocre quality, there might be some really good ones.
>
> I am told that there are some other proposals to have a folk dance festival in Delhi. In particular I understand that General Cariappa has thought of organizing some such thing in October. It would be better to concentrate on the January one instead of dividing up our energy.
>
> The procession should not be too long, more especially as children are being included. Perhaps the children need not go the whole way.

As we are trying to put up as expert a show as possible, performances by amateurs should not be included in this programme.[13]

The Republic Day Parade in India is preceded by a 70-minute folk dance festival on 25 January every year in the presence of the President of India. This event is televised to the whole country. The Republic Day parade shows the military strength of India and the state of alertness and readiness of its security forces. It also demonstrates the country's cultural pluralism and integral nature. All those who have witnessed the parade for the first time have been unanimous in their opinion that the Republic Day pageant is not only an impressive spectacle, but it clearly conveys the military and cultural strength of a vibrant nation.

III
The Brunner Paintings

In June 1948, Jawaharlal Nehru, Prime Minister of India, happened to visit Nainital, where he chanced upon a large number of paintings of two Hungarian artists, Mrs Sass Brunner and her daughter Miss Elizabeth Brunner. Those paintings touched the sensitivity of Nehru and he purchased a few of them, including one of Mahatma Gandhi in meditation, for his own collection. On his return to Delhi, he recorded a minute[14] that formally brought on record what transpired between him and the Brunners. At the same time, he wrote a letter to Abul Kalam Azad, Minister of Education,[15] recommending that some of those paintings should be acquired by the Government. The enclosure[16] to that letter, in fact, listed the paintings that Government could acquire together with their value (totalling Rs 15,000/-).

As will be evident from these three documents, Nehru was not sure as to which Ministry would be concerned with this matter, nor was he aware of the procedure involved in such purchases. Yet his letter led to the initiative which eventually created the contour of the art purchase schemes of the Government that later came into being. However, what eventually was realized was not without hiccups. Nor was there any idea, as will be evident from the correspondence that followed, how a small personal initiative of Nehru would grow into an important cultural initiative of the Government in the years that followed.

While acknowledging the letter of Nehru, Azad also conveyed the decision that the matter indeed concerned the Ministry of Education.[17] He also mentioned that the paintings would adorn the walls of the proposed Central Museum. Yet the officials in the Ministry of Education felt that before any such acquisition was made, it was necessary to evaluate the paintings. R.N. Chakravorty, who then happened to be Chief Artist in the Publications Division of the Ministry of Information and Broadcasting, was entrusted with this responsibility. He did not, however, speak very highly about the work of the two Hungarian artists.[18] He also considered that the average price of the eight paintings could be about Rs. 500/- each.[19] This was much lower than what was quoted by the Hungarian artists and informally accepted by the Prime Minister. Thereafter, Barada Ukil of the All India Fine Arts and Crafts Society was approached for a second opinion.[20] He too opined that the paintings were mediocre and did not deserve more than Rs. 500/- a piece as their value.[21] Saddled with these two opinions, the Ministry of Education felt obliged to inform the Prime Minister's Office of the position.[22] The Prime Minister's Office was also requested to ascertain from the Prime Minister whether the Ministry of Education could negotiate with the artists the price of the paintings. While this correspondence apparently looked routine, yet the remarkable openness and transparency that obtained in the Government in those years cannot possibly escape attention. The two artists who evaluated the paintings were not at all influenced by the fact that the paintings had earlier been assessed as being of much higher value by none other than Jawaharlal Nehru, who, besides being the Prime Minister, was also a connoisseur of art.

Nehru, however, had the conviction of his perceptions in this seemingly small matter. He wrote back to Azad, joining the issue and debating the assessment by the artists.[23] What was, however, important was the fact that he did not disregard the opinions of the experts, but offered to purchase the paintings himself in case the Government did not find it possible to buy them.

As the matter proceeded, the Prime Minister's commitment, on behalf of the Government, to buy the paintings of the Brunners without the prior approval of the Ministry of Finance was also incidentally and obliquely commented upon. Nehru clarified the matter in a letter to Azad.[24] The Ministry of Finance also emphasized, in this context, the need to have the prior clearance of that Ministry if any commitment was made on behalf of the Government.[25] The suggestion that even the Prime Minister was not above the need to adhere to routine procedures in the Government was clear. The matter was taken up by Humayun Kabir with Maulana Azad.[26] Finally, Azad passed the order that the Hungarian artists be paid a price of Rs 15,000/- for the eight paintings.[27]

The above mentioned correspondence, which started with Nehru's letter to Azad and concluded with Azad's letter that the bill of the Hungarian artists be settled, touched upon all aspects that formed that basis of various schemes initiated by the Government of India to acquire works of art. These are all reflected in the fourteen documents reproduced below :

[No.1]

Minute, dated 14 June 1948, recorded by J. Nehru, Prime Minister of India and marked to his PPS.

> During my recent visit to Naini Tal I saw a large number of paintings of Mrs Sass Brunner and her daughter Miss Elizabeth Brunner. These paintings have been collected for display at Government House, Naini Tal. Among them were some which, I think, should be acquired by the Government of India. They depict Indian scenes and should be kept in India. I do not think that they should be sent abroad to our Embassies.
>
> I attach a list of some of these. The list mentions seven paintings of scenes on the way to Amarnath cave and the cave itself, one shows Mahatma Gandhi in meditation and another the evening prayer with Gandhiji at sunset. I have personally purchased the picture of Mahatma Gandhi in Meditation. I should like the evening prayer painting as well as the series of seven on Amarnath to be acquired by the Government.
>
> I do not know the exact procedure for this. I have written to the Ministry for Education. I suppose that in any event the Finance Ministry will have to be approached.

[No.2]

Letter, dated New Delhi, 14th June 1948, from J. Nehru, Prime Minister of India, to Abul Kalam Azad, Minister for Education.

My dear Maulana,

During my recent visit to Naini Tal I saw a large number of paintings by Mrs Sass Brunner and Miss Elizabeth Brunner, the Hungarian artists. These paintings have been collected with a view of exhibition in Government House there. The standard of these paintings was very high and I particularly liked some of them. These paintings deal entirely with Indian subjects. I feel strongly that some of these paintings at least should be acquired by the Government of India.

I have personally purchased for my own use some paintings including one of Mahatma Gandhi in Meditation.

Among others there is a painting of Gandhiji at evening prayer and a series of seven paintings depicting scenes on the way to Amarnath cave and the cave itself. I think these should be acquired by us on behalf of the Government. I am not quite sure which Ministry deals with this matter. I imagine it is yours. Anyway I am taking steps towards their requisition. I enclose a list of some of these paintings.

Yours
J. Nehru

[No.3]

Enclosure to Letter dated New Delhi, 14 June 1948, from J. Nehru, Prime Minister of India to Abul Kalam Azad, Minister of Education.

Seven oil paintings, a series of scenes 'on the way to Amarnath Cave' and the Shiva Linga in the Cave

by S. Brunner.

each painting 2 feet by 3 feet. Namely:
1. Shesnag Lake (South view)
2. Shesnag Lake
3. Through the snow bridge
4. Panchtarni
5. Entrance of the Cave

6. Birth of Amarganga
7. Natural Ice Shiva Linga inside Amarnath Cave.
                Total Price : Rs. 10,000/-
Mahatma Gandhi's deep meditation in prison
                    by S. Brunner
size 2'3" × 3'2" oil painting. Price: Rs 3,500/-

Evening Prayer with Gandhiji at sunset
                    by S. Brunner
size: 2'6" × 3'4" oil painting. Price Rs 5,000/-

[No.4]

Letter, dated New Delhi, 21 June 1948, from Abul Kalam Azad, Minister of Education, to J. Nehru, Prime Minister of India.

I thank you for your letter No. 865/PM dated the 14th June 1948, regarding the paintings by Mrs Sass Brunner and Miss Elizabeth Brunner, the Hungarian artists. The matter concerns this Ministry and I shall take the necessary steps to purchase the paintings suggested by you. They will adorn the walls of the proposed Central Museum.

Yours Sincerely,
A.K. Azad

[No.5]

Report, dated Delhi, 26 July 1948, by R.N. Chakravorty, Chief Artist, Ministry of Information and Broadcasting submitted to the Ministry of Education.

At the request of the Ministry of Education, I went by appointment to the Hon'ble Prime Minister's residence on Saturday, the 24th July, 1948 and saw the following eight paintings by Mrs Sass Brunner:

1. Shesnag Lake (South view)
2. Shesnag Lake
3. Through the snow bridge
4. Panchtarni
5. Entrance of the Cave
6. Birth of Amarganga

7. Natural Ice Shiva Linga inside Amarnath Cave

Total Price: Rs 10,000/-

8. Evening prayer with Gandhiji at sunset

Price: Rs 5,000/-

Neither in technique nor in execution does any one of them appear to me to be of high artistic merit, and the prices quoted are, in my opinion exorbitant.

[No.6]

Letter, dated Delhi, 29 July 1948, from R.N. Chakravorty, Chief Architect, Ministry of Information and Broadcasting, to Mrs D. Madhavi, Ministry of Education.

Dear Mrs Madhavi,

In continuation of my letter of the 26th July, 1948, as you desire, I give an assessment of the value of the paintings by Mrs Sass Brunner. In my opinion, the average price of the eight paintings by Mrs Sass Brunner (the list you shall find in my previous letter), may be about Rs 500/- each.

Yours sincerely,
R.N. Chakravorty

[No.7]

Letter, dated 11/12 August 1948, from Janak Kumari Asghar, Ministry of Education, to Barada Ukil, General Secretary of All India Fine Arts and Crafts Society, New Delhi.

Dear Mr Ukil,

The Govt. of India desire to purchase some paintings by Mrs Sass Brunner which are at the moment placed in the Prime Minister's residence, but before any further action is taken in the matter, this Ministry would like to have the paintings valued by an expert artist or art critic. I would be very grateful if you would very kindly examine these pictures and let us know what in your opinion would be the appropriate price to pay for them. I understand that the total cost of these pictures according to the price fixed by the artist is about Rs 15,000.

If you will be able to undertake this task I will be glad to be informed of the time and date convenient to you when you could visit Prime Minister's residence for the purpose, I will then contact the Private Secretary to fix up an appointment for you.

Yours sincerely,
Janak Kumari Asghar

[No.8]

Letter, dated New Delhi, 31 August 1948, from Barada Ukil, All India Fine Art and Crafts Society, New Delhi, to Mrs Janak Kumari Asghar, Education Officer, Ministry of Education and Art, Government of India, New Delhi.

Dear Mrs Asghar,

Thanks for your letter of the 25th August 1948, regarding Mrs Sass Brunner's paintings, which the Government of India desire to purchase.

I was shown 8 paintings of the artist by Captain Yunus Khan, ADC, at the Government House, when I went there for apprising them as asked by you, on Saturday, the 28th August at 10 AM. I have examined those paintings carefully and I am of the opinion that the paintings are not of high quality and the price asked for by the artist is not only exorbitant but absurd and quite out of proportion with the merit of the paintings. If the Government of India are at all keen on purchasing these mediocre work of art, Rs 500/- apiece is the maximum price that I can recommend.

Yours sincerely,
Barada Ukil

[No.9]

Letter, dated New Delhi, 17 September 1948, from Humayun Kabir, Joint Educational Adviser, to M.O. Mathai, Private Secretary to the Prime Minister.

My dear Mr. Mathai

On June 14, 1948, Pandit Nehru wrote to Maulana Saheb about some paintings by Mrs Sass Brunner and Miss Elizabeth Brunner and suggested that they might be purchased by the Government of India. He also sent a minute to the Ministry of Finance who agreed that the pictures should be purchased. We accordingly wrote to the owners and also, in the meantime, requested Mr Ramen Chakravorty to assess the pictures for us. Mr Chakravorty's valuation was about Rs 500/- per picture and Rs 4000/- for the entire lot of 8 pictures. The artists' own valuation was Rs 15,000/-. The divergence was great and we thought we should have the opinion of a second art critic. We accordingly asked Mr Barada Ukil who has also independently suggested the same figure of Rs 4,000/- of the whole lot. I would be grateful if you kindly ascertain from the Prime Minister if we should negotiate with the artists with an offer of Rs 4,000—for the entire lot. We will proceed as soon as we know his views in the matter.

Yours sincerely,

Humayun Kabir

[No. 10]

Letter, dated New Delhi, 21 September, 1948, from J. Nehru, Prime Minister of India, to Abul Kalam Azad, Minister for Education.

My dear Maulana,

Humayun Kabir has written a letter to Mathai about Mrs Sass Brunner's paintings which I brought from Naini Tal and which are now in Government House here. He says that, according to the valuation of some artists or art critics, all the eight pictures should not cost more than Rs. 4,000/-.

I am no expert at this game and it is quite impossible for me to value any pictures. But prima facie the valuation suggested by Mr Chakravorty and Mr Barada Ukil rather surprises me. I have personally bought four pictures from Mrs Sass Brunner. One of them is of Mahatma Gandhi and I have paid Rs 3500/- for it. Three others are mountain scenes, less ambitious than the ones in Government House now. In all I paid Rs 5000/- for these four pictures. The pictures in Government House are on a bigger scale and personally I think they are exceedingly good. Mahatma Gandhi at a prayer meeting appears to me to be a fascinating picture which grows upon one. To value it at Rs 500/- seems to me very wide of the mark.

I might mention that it was with some slight difficulty that I got Mahatma Gandhi's picture from the Brunners. There was another picture (of Tagore) which I wanted to acquire, but they refused to sell it. For my part I did not argue with them about the pictures I have bought and I thought they were worth the money I paid, which was Rs 5000. I adopted more or less the same attitude about the other pictures which are in Government House. I just do not see how we can make an offer of Rs 4000/- to the artist for these pictures now. Perhaps some slight reduction might have been suggested, but even that would have been a suggestion only in the circumstances. If it is not possible for the Government of India to acquire these pictures, I feel I am committed and I should buy them myself at the price stated.

I suggest, however, as a possible step to begin with that a letter might be sent from your Ministry to Mrs Brunner asking her if it is possible for the prices of these pictures to be reduced in view of the fact that the experts and advisers of your Ministry have suggested a considerably lower price than the one asked. I would not mention the figure. You can await Mrs Brunner's answer, but I am almost sure that she will not agree to sell them at any other figure. Even before a letter is sent to Mrs Brunner, Mrs Sarojini Naidu should be contacted because it was through her that this business was done. I am not quite sure if she has already paid for the pictures on our behalf.

Yours sincerely,
J. Nehru

[No.11]

Letter, dated New Delhi, 20 September 1948, from J. Nehru, Prime Minister of India, to Abul Kalam Azad, Minister for Education

My dear Maulana,

Regarding your query about the purchase of pictures, I would suggest that those paintings which have actually been purchased or in regard to which commitments have been made, should certainly be finally purchased and paid for. Apart from these, fresh purchases should be stopped, unless for some very special or exceptional reasons. We should try our utmost to economise in fresh purchases in view of the economic situation. This is what my previous circular meant. If something very special comes up before us and there is a chance of our losing it, we should buy it for the nation. But where possible, the purchases should be postponed.

In regard to the paintings of the Hungarian lady which are now hanging in Government House, obviously these must be paid for. We have definitely purchased them and used them. Regarding the Shah Jehan pictures, if you have entered into any commitment, they should be purchased and paid for. Any fresh proposals for purchases should be very carefully examined.

I am sending a copy of this letter to the Finance Ministry.

Yours sincerely,

Jawaharlal Nehru

[No.12]

Letter, dated New Delhi, 23rd September 1948, from K.R.K. Menon, Ministry of Finance, to Dr Tara Chand, Secretary, Ministry of Education.

My dear Tara Chand,

H.M. Finance has seen the Hon'ble Prime Minister's D.O. letter No. 1290-P.M. dated the 20th September 1948 to H.M. Education regarding the purchase of pictures and paintings etc. In view of the need for the utmost possible economy in this matter H.M. Finance hopes that those exceptional cases where purchase cannot possibly be postponed will be referred to this Ministry well *before* any commitment is made on behalf of Government.

Yours sincerely,

K.R.K. Menon

[No.13]

Note, dated 30th September 1948, of Humayun Kabir, Joint Educational Adviser, submitted to Abul Kalam Azad, Minister for Education.

This Ministry has, for some time, been considering the proposal to buy some paintings of Mrs Sass Brunner and Miss Elizabeth Brunner, two Hungarian artists. The paintings were seen by Hon'ble Prime Minister who liked them very much and suggested that they might be acquired by the Government of India.

There are eight paintings for which the artists want of price a Rs 15,000/-. Two of our art critics, Messrs, R.N. Chakravorty and Barada Ukil think that this price is rather high. It is difficult to have a correct valuation of works of art where personal taste plays an important part. H.M. has also probably seen these pictures.

For H.M.'s orders about the price that should be offered for these paintings.

[No.14]

Minute, dated 23rd September 1948, recorded by Abul Kalam Azad, Minister of Education and marked to Humayun Kabir, Joint Educational Adviser.

I had a talk with the Hon'ble Prime Minister about the price of these paintings. I feel it does not seem appropriate to have any further correspondence in the matter. The bill for the paintings may be sanctioned and the price asked for may be given to the artists.

Azad

I received a letter from the Hon'ble Prime Minister on this subject which I place on the file. At the end of this letter H.P.M. has suggested Her Excellency Mrs Sarojini Naidu can be approached in this connection. But after taking into consideration the various aspects of this matter, I feel that sanction may be given to the bill and the amount paid.

Azad

In another example of purchase of two books from an individual who was in distress, Maulana Azad showed rare sensitivity both for national heritage and individual honour. His note of 5th September 1952 illustrates this point admirably:

These two books have been offered to me for purchase.

(1) This is a volume of Kuliat-e-Sadi written in a very beautiful and elegant hand. It is decorated with several paintings in Persian style of Safvi period. Very likely it was prepared at the command of some king.

(2) This is a manuscript of the Quran in very small size and written in extremely fine hand. Although written in very fine hand, the workmanship is very elegant and uniform from beginning to the end. Manuscripts of Quran of this size are very rare.

The price asked for both these books is Rs 15,000/- but I have fixed the price at Rs 12,500/- (Rupees Twelve Thousand, Five Hundred only). These two books will make very valuable additions to our National Museum.

The cheque for this amount should be made out in my name and I will hand it over to the owner. He does not want that his name should be divulged.[28]

The kind of sensitivity and high level of attention led to the constitution of the Art Purchase Committee for government museums under the Chairmanship of the Vice-President of India, with experts like Moti Chand, Karl Khandalavala, Rai Krishna Das and others as members and the Director General of the National Museum as its member-secretary. The Art Purchase Committee was to meet in the capitals of States so that acquisitions were made from different regional sources. The Art Purchase Committee was not expected to function like the Food Corporation of India which procured the marketable surplus of rice or wheat. This Committee was expected to acquire for the National Museum only objects which were of national standard, and not to buy what remained unsold at exhibitions. The importance of Art Purchase Committees has gradually declined and today the National Museum, National Gallery of Modern Art, Lalit Kala Akademi and other organizations have separate Art Purchase Committees under the chairmanship of persons selected by these organizations.

IV
Social Responsibility in Cultural Leadership

India's culture provides a mirror in which we see India as a land of the past—of myths and legends—and of the future. This has been possible because both the idea and the reality of India have played a central role in her creative manifestations, whether in literature, painting, music, or drama. India's interaction with Europe and the USA in the present century in particular have several positive features. These cultural encounters by themselves are a matter of achievement; they have imparted to creative men and women experiences of modern cultural forms, and have provided forums for experimentation and expression. Many Indian artists have made their homes in Europe and the USA, and periodically visit India to revive tangible relationship with Indian concepts, contemporary arts, and life, and also to absorb inspiration and ideas. The specific cultural experience of such Indian artists is indeed valuable. Their contributions have not only enriched European countries and the USA but India's culture as well.

Looking at it from another angle it may be recalled that several painters, writers, novelists, and poets have received inspiration from their encounters with India. For example, V.S. Naipaul, author and novelist, whose grandfather had migrated from the United Provinces more than a hundred years ago to Trinidad, Amrita Sher-Gil, the painter of Hungarian birth who subsequently made India her home, Salman Rushdie, the novelist who migrated from Bombay and now lives in London. Amrita Sher-Gil (1913–1941), believed that her inspiration in the realm of creativity would come only from India. In 1934, in a letter from Budapest, she explained to her parents her need to return to India in the interest of her artistic development.

> Our long stay in Europe has aided me to discover, as it were, India. Modern art has led me to the comprehension and appreciation of Indian painting and sculpture. It seems paradoxical, but I know for certain, that had we not come away to Europe, I should perhaps never have realized that a fresco from Ajanta, or a small piece of sculpture in the Mussel Gerimet in worth more than the whole Renaissance.[29]

The social concerns of an artiste and a writer are matters of deep significance to any developing society. As E.H. Carr has said,

> The abstract standard of value, divorced from society and divorced from history is as much an illusion as the abstract individual.[30]

Even in a highly developed economy like that of the United States, social concerns are emerging as a powerful factor and have a meaning at the levels of family, community, and the nation. Harry

Belafonte, singer and activist, has effectively put this ethos in the context of his own family as follows:

> My mother was a feisty, fierce battler. And I knew that I would never ever settle for poverty without doing battle, that I'd never settle for second class. When I did discover that I wanted the world of art, it was discovering art as a social power, as a force. And I have gravitated towards people and teachers who held art as having that responsibility.[31]

The persons in the world of art and literature in India have also to gravitate towards their social responsibility as, although the gods of communism might be dead, poverty and inequity are present in the Indian society. In a complex and discriminating relationship between an artiste and his intellectual source, present day realities of life have to play a part. Creative persons in India—poets, musicians, fiction-writers, painters—must show respect for reality, almost in the way Gandhi did in his time. As soon as the supremacy of reality is accepted, the process of improvement can be initiated, strengthened and accelerated. If a creative person lives in a world of his own, in a world which is above this world, he may be able to entertain but cannot be a direct agent of change. Artists and writers are to be viewed as cultural leaders at popular levels as we treat other leaders in the realms of economy and polity.

It needs, however, to be mentioned that in the past, farmers, artisans, and merchants enjoyed a rare degree of autonomy as the state control was limited and the land resources were vast. The seats of civilizational attainments, whether in Bihar, Punjab, Gujarat or Tamil Nadu, all had fairly developed agricultural operations and large fertile tracts of land. Folk songs were developed around agricultural cycles, and artisans played an important role not only in the actual building of a temple or mosque, but also in giving shape to its dome and minarets, paintings and murals, and the nature of its courtyards and gateways. These were in fact collective efforts where poets and painters, architects and merchants played their part as village wards, artisans and farmers, and their separate contributions were indistinguishable.

During the last 50 years the policy pursued by the state in the realm of culture has its several high points as well as a few low points. The policy of the leaders in the early years of the Republic was to allow cultural pluralism in the country, an environment for its uninhibited growth, and more particularly to create conditions in remote areas where tribal people live so that they can develop in terms of their own genius. This has withstood the test of time. Today, India is one of the few countries in the world with more than 100 creative persons of global standard in the realm of literature and the arts who are the word's best in their respective areas.

However, the policy of granting autonomy to the Akademies and other Government-funded organizations has not been without hitches. In more recent years the Lalit Kala Akademi has fallen on evil days. There have been serious charges of financial irregularities, nepotism and gross misuse of government funds on the part of elected members on the Executive Board of the Akademi. These charges have been levelled by artists, social workers, politicians, and the staff of the Lalit Kala Akademi. There have been 'dharnas', and hunger strikes by the affected parties, and vigilance and administrative inquiries have been authorized by the government. The nature of public concern is duly reflected in a letter written by a senior political leader and Member of Parliament to the Culture Secretary to the Government of India about the affairs of the Lalit Kala Akademi. The striking portion of this communication reads as follows:

> I am aghast at the power wielded by the persons who control the Akademi. How petty men who live off government money and indulging in patently criminal activities can survive and prosper is a matter that cannot be brushed aside casually.
>
> I am writing this both in anguish and in anger. Anguish at the sight of the mighty Government of India's reluctance to cleanse the Akademi and anger at my inability to hound out the criminal elements from the Akademi.[32]

One has to be conscious of the fact that in the past these Akademies were chaired by outstanding freedom fighters and creative people. Pandit Jawaharlal Nehru and Dr S. Radhakrishnan were the Chairman and Vice-Chairman of the Sahitya Akademi in the initial years. They were also instrumental in prescribing that the government cannot make changes in the rules of the Akademies. They went on to provide that it would be incumbent on the government to place its proposals before the General Council, and that these would be given effect to only when they received the assent of two-thirds of the members of the General Council present at voting. In the background of mounting criticism and gross abuse of authority on the part of the office-holders of these Akademies, it may be tempting to bring them under tighter bureaucratic control. This would be unwise as full administrative and financial control of the government may not always mean sound practices conducive to creativity. State intervention in times of proven crisis may not be out of place as a medicine, but political and administrative control as daily bread would certainly be against the traditions so assiduously built up in all these years.

It has been said that, 'If our civilization breaks down, it will be because of a breakdown of our administration'.[33] The breakdown of the Lalit Kala Akademi essentially meant the breakdown of its administration and its consequent inability to provide adequate space for talented painters and sculptors within its forum. However, while the inadequacies in the Lalit Kala Akademi have added to its own irrelevance, they have, fortunately, not subverted the creative capacities of talented persons. The breakdown in the administration of the Lalit Kala Akademi is not merely on account of sloth and inefficiency of its office-bearers but it is a by-product of moral breakdown of its leadership. The interventionist role of the state has to equip persons of integrity and vision in positions of leadership that the constitution of the Lalit Kala Akademi provides for. Once that is done, the process of restoration of a not very distant past of glory can recommence and begin to yield positive results.[34] Rembrandt has captured this idea beautifully in a painting which adorns one of the halls of the Hermitage at St. Petersburg. The painting shows the return of the prodigal son to his father's house. In the embrace between father and son, the right hand is one of compassion, characteristics of the mother while the left hand is one of sternness providing the symbol of authority which is associated in the family with the father.

The profession of a painter, a sculptor, a musician and a writer must be regarded not simply as a means of earning a livelihood, though in itself this is very important, but also as an enabling factor in the highest development of the individual personality. Freedom and democracy are therefore essential for art and literature to flourish.

There is an imperative requirement in the realm of culture and the arts to consciously work towards revival of the spirit of the freedom struggle and the transparency with which our leaders and cultural personalities worked in the early years of the Republic. Such a revival would ensure the collective good as well as individual development.[35] Mahatma Gandhi succinctly expressed the individual aspect of the matter when he spoke about himself as follows:

> I cling to India like a child to its mother's breast, because I feel that she gives me the spiritual nourishment I need. She has the environment that responds to my highest aspirations.[36]

The need is to preserve that 'environment' to which Mahatma Gandhi has so feelingly referred, as it is this 'environment' which has provided both continuity and renewal to India's creativity and culture all these years.

Notes and References

1.   'The Earth is my mother and I am a son of the world' (Sanskrit) – (See p.9, 56).
2.   Edward W. Said, *Orientalism*, Routledge and Kegan Paul, London, 1978, p.214.
3.   Ibid., p.214

4. Partha Mitter, *Art and Nationalism in Colonial India 1850–1922, Occidental Orientations,* Cambridge University Press, USA, 1994, p.377.
5. Jawaharlal Nehru, *Selected Speeches,* volume one, 1946–1949.
6. Ministry of Education File No. 6-11/52-G, 2(A), noting by Ashfaque Husain.
7. Ibid.
    Minute dated 26.1.1952 recorded by Jawaharlal Nehru.
8. Ibid.
    Correspondence between Humayun Kabir, Secretary, Ministry of Education and B.N. Kaul, 30.1.1952.
9. Ibid.
    Noting by Ashfaque Husain, 11.2.1952.
10. Ibid.
    Reply by Maulana Abul Kalam Azad, Minister for Education, 25.4.1952.
11. Ibid.
    Minute dated 9.9.1952 recorded by Jawaharlal Nehru.
12. Ibid.
    Letter dated 10.9.1952 from Jawaharlal Nehru to Chief Ministers of States.
13. Ibid.
    Minute dated 17.9.1952 recorded by Jawaharlal Nehru.
14. Minute dated 14 June 1948, recorded by J. Nehru, Prime Minister of India and marked to his PPS. *[Document no. 1]*.
    On 19 March 1997, Elizabeth Brunner was formally conferred the Doctor of Literature (Desikottama) by the Visva-Bharati University, Shantiniketan at a special ceremony where the author was made the Chief Guest and had the rare honour of inaugurating an exhibition entitled 'Homage to Gurudev' presenting paintings by Elizabeth Brunner and her mother Sass Brunner painted in Shantiniketan between 1930 and 1934.
15. Letter dated New Delhi, 14 June 1948, from J. Nehru, Prime Minister of India, to Abul Kalam Azad, Minister for Education. *[Document no.2]*
16. Enclosure to Letter dated New Delhi, 14 June 1948, from J. Nehru, Prime Minister of India, to Abul Kalam Azad, Minister for Education *[Document no.3]*.
17. Letter dated New Delhi, 21 June 1948, from Abul Kalam Azad, Minister for Education, to J. Nehru, Prime Minister of India. *[Document no.4]*.

18. Report dated Delhi, 26 July 1948, by R.N. Chakravorty, Chief Artist, Ministry of Information & Broadcasting, submitted to the Ministry of Education. [*Document no. 5*].

19. Letter dated Delhi, 29 July 1948, from R.N. Chakravorty, Chief Artist, Ministry of Information & Broadcasting, to Mrs D. Madhavi, Ministry of Education. [*Document no. 6*].

20. Letter dated 11/12 August 1948, from Janak Kumari Asghar, Ministry of Education, to Barada Ukil, General Secretary of All India Fine Arts and Crafts Society, New Delhi. [*Document no. 7*].

21. Letter, dated New Delhi, 31 August 1948, from Barada Ukil, All India Fine Arts and Crafts Society, New Delhi, to Mrs Janak Kumari Asghar, Education Officer, Ministry of Education and Art, Government of India, New Delhi [*Document no. 8*].

22. Letter dated New Delhi, 17 September 1948, from Humayun Kabir, Joint Educational Adviser, to M.O. Mathai, Private Secretary to the Prime Minister.[*Document no. 9*].

23. Letter dated New Delhi, 21 September 1948, from J. Nehru, Prime Minister of India, to Abul Kalam Azad, Minister for Education. [*Document no. 10*].

24. Letter dated New Delhi, 20 September 1948, from J. Nehru, Prime Minister of India, to Abul Kalam Azad, Minister for Education.[*Document no. 11*].

25. Letter dated New Delhi, 23 September 1948, from K.R.K. Menon, Ministry of Finance, to Dr Tara Chand, Secretary, Ministry of Education. [*Document no. 12*].

26. Note dated 30 September 1948 of Humayun Kabir, Joint Education Adviser, submitted to Abul Kalam Azad, Minister for Education. [*Document no. 13*].

27. Minute dated 23 September 1948, recorded by Abul Kalam Azad, Minister of Education and marked to Humayun Kabir, Joint Educational Adviser. [*Document no. 14*].

28. Maulana Azad Papers, National Archives, New Delhi.

29. Quoted in Gayatri Sinha, ed., *Expressions and Evocations, Contemporary Women Artists of India*, Marg Publications, 1996.

30. E.H. Carr, *What is History?*, London, 1987, p.84.

31. From an Interview with Harry Belafonte, *Newsweek*, 9 September, 1996, p.56.

32. Letter dated 2 August 1996, from George Fernandes addressed to Secretary Culture, Government of India.

33. Quoted in *Hindustan Times*, New Delhi, 7 September 1996.

34. The Lalit Kala Akademi was set up as an apex cultural body by the Government of India by a Parliamentary Resolution passed on 5 August 1954 to encourage and promote the visual arts such as paintings, graphics, sculpture, etc. Subsequently, the Lalit Kala Akademi was registered as a Society under the Societies Registration Act, 1860 on 11 March 1957. In view of gross mismanagement, favouritism and functional irregularities, the Government of India decided to take over the Akademi by an Ordinance on 24 January 1997 and subsequently went to Parliament for its enactment as law.

Parliament unanimously approved the take-over and desired that all those who indulged in gross irregularities should be brought to book. The law provides for a maximum period of 5 years of management of the Akademi by the government but it is expected that the government shall fulfil its objectives and relinquish the management of the Society from its side and hand it over to the artist community in a year's time or so.

Before suggesting this extreme step of take-over, I had consulted the original records and was surprised to discover that the founders of the Akademi, namely, Jawaharlal Nehru and Maulana Azad had never contemplated that there would be any occasion for the government to intervene in the affairs of such an institution. In fact they were actuated by a strong desire to grant autonomy and had accordingly prescribed that even if the government wanted a change in any rule or regulation of the Akademi, it would be incumbent on the government to make that suggestion, and only in the event of three fourths of the members of the General Council of the Akademi approving it could the necessary changes be effected. This inherent faith in the goodwill of creative persons was in tune with both the idealism of the freedom movement and the personal qualities of these two great leaders of the early Republic.

35. There is a feeling that there has been too much of western influence on Indian art and that there is need to work for the revival of pride in India's culture. In a recent article Rizwan Salim has written as follows :

India's artists who have adopted the sick conventions of 20th century European art must possess zero aesthetic self-confidence that they can create an art of distinction. There are so many Indian images—transient and recurring—that can inspire great art. Are India's 'modern artists' blind to all this overwhelming beauty around them?

He goes on to add:

India's aspiring artists have a historic opportunity to create a great realist art of the beautiful. Experienced artists and young painters alike must generate within themselves a tremendous surge of cultural pride and contemptuously abandon the abstract style, and take up traditional, representational painting with a vengeance. India's young art students as well as mature painters must rouse themselves to look at their own culture and surroundings, objects and situations with new eyes, as it were; they must notice the over-abundance of beauty in nature here.

The Hindustan Times, New Delhi, Sunday, 16 March, 1997.

36. Quoted in *Gandhi Diary,* 1995, Gandhi Smriti and Darshan Samiti, New Delhi.

Both Gautama Buddha (566–486 B.C.) and Mahatma Gandhi (1869–1948) gave everlasting messages of non-violence, compassion and truth which are very relevant to the future of humanity.

This rare painting of Gandhi and Buddha together has been done by Upendra Maharathi (1908–1981)—a gifted painter of this century from Patna, India.

(Courtesy Vishwasanti Stupa Patna)

4

The New Millennium: Harmony Among or Clash of Civilizations

I
Democracy, Ecology and Culture

The twentieth century has been the most disastrous in human history in social and political terms—nearly 200 million men and women have died in military or political conflicts. Three great struggles, spread over more than three-quarters of the century—World Wars I and II, and the Cold War—made cannon fodder out of human beings.[1] Many other battlefields, from anti-colonial movements to civil strife, contributed to this carnage. Apart from the cost of life, vast resources—both material and intellectual—were wasted on weapons. And yet, as this century comes to a close, and a new millennium begins, we clearly see the emergence of three powerful lights, which if properly nurtured, could make the coming century an era of peace and harmony in the world. These three lights are those of democracy, ecology, and culture.

The triumph of democracy over all forms of dictatorship signals that in future, dialogue and debate will decide local, regional and global issues. The triumph of democracy over the totalitarian system in the closing decades of the twentieth century certainly points to the fact that the people of East Germany, Poland, Hungary, Romania, the Czech Republic, Slovakia and the states comprising the erstwhile Soviet Union, could relate to something superior, notwithstanding the fact that the forces of status quo tried to kill that ability in them.

This has surely enhanced our respect for human freedom and its possibility in our time. Nothing would be better for strengthening harmony, non-violence, and goodwill in every society than the exercise of power through public consent.

The ecological crisis is rather serious. For certain animal and vegetable species it is already too late, and restoration of certain areas in India as well as other developing countries even if so intended now, is somewhat beyond our efforts for the next forty to fifty years. A genuine ecological recovery can succeed only through a break with the present trends of a technology-driven consumerist society. Often, restoration of the environment implies working at a loss, as has recently been shown in Arunachal Pradesh in India. The State Government there wishes to continue its programme of felling trees in the name of providing income to the youth, notwithstanding the wise directions to the contrary given by the Supreme Court of India. The direction of the Supreme Court in essence means rejecting the law of profit and reverting to age-old tribal values related to sacred groves and the worship of trees. It is increasingly evident that the concern for the preservation of the environment and protection of ecology could critically help towards ensuring a better life for all species and plant life.

The emergence of culture as an important factor in determining the status of an individual in society, or of a nation in the world is a matter of great significance. Art has a curious way of belonging to its times, and yet of being removed from it. Art has its own agenda, and has habitually risen above the conditions prevailing on the ground in every period of human history. The songs, dance-forms, literary activities and works of art produced in the 20th century have found new expressions and have gone to prove that this century has not only been the greatest in human history but has also been a period of new discoveries and radical renewals. While all the old art forms have exhibited significant achievements, several entirely new ones have been invented and popularized such as cinema, pop music, and television documentary.

Democracy enables people to be themselves. It gives them wide free space and, therefore, encourages diversity and pluralism. The interaction between democracy, ecology and culture in the context of a global economy raises several important questions. One is political. As countries belonging to different cultures blend economically, it is necessary to develop cooperative economic institutions to sustain the independence of each country as well as their inter-dependence. The role of culture in the development of that trust is of importance. In the absence of such trust and institutional frame-work, the rich countries would protect themselves while the developing and economically weak countries would succumb to financial crises. The second danger is in the realm of environment and ecology. The developed countries with their sophisticated technology are in a position to trigger high prices for raw-materials, and since these raw-materials are available in several of the bio-diversity-rich developing countries, this would mean adverse environmental side-effects in the developing countries. It may be recalled that since the profit margins are higher in finished goods, whether in the domain of cosmetics or pharmaceuticals, the benefits would accrue to the developed countries alone. There are, however, some positive features as well. Commerce also has a neutralizing effect on violent behaviour since commerce facilitates prosperity and this, in turn, would give people a stake in peace. The equity factor in global economy therefore becomes very important.

The growing faith in democracy as a form of governance, conservation of ecology and preservation of the environment, and cultural pluralism as a way of living, are integral parts of our common future. As forces of democracy, ecology and culture in different parts of the world interact and support each other, many effects of value and substance would result and would enrich the world community. It is heartening to see that the youth in different societies of the world are concerned not only with their own future, but also with the security of the global value-system. The expansion in television coverage, computer networking, and the press, is going to ensure that the joys of creativity in both the realms of science and culture will be shared by humanity as a whole and will not remain a localized affair. If global transmission of information gives the required focus to the cultural attainments of 'the global village', the present situation will vastly improve in the 21st century.

There is, however, another point of view which advocates that certain civilizations will play a decisive role in the transformation of states and societies in a manner that would lead to conflicts and wars in the 21st century. Professor Samuel P. Huntington of Harvard University in his much talked about paper entitled 'The Clash of Civilizations' published in the 1993 summer issue of *Foreign Affairs,* followed by *The Clash of Civilizations and the Remaking of World Order* published in 1996,[2] has argued that the conflict between civilizations will be the latest phase in the evolution of conflict in the modern world. His thesis is based on the premise that the West would like to continue its domination over the rest of the world, both in the political as well as in the economic domain. With the end of the cold war, the military establishments of the West are in search of an adversary and a philosophy that would justify their sustaining themselves in adequate strength, and persuading their legislatures to fund them. The rationale would be provided by civilizational differences.

Professor Huntington goes on to list eight civilizations in the international system: (1) Western, (2) Confucian, (3) Japanese, (4) Islamic, (5) Hindu, (6) Slavic, (7) Latin American and (8) African. He theorizes that the most important conflicts in future will occur along the cultural fault lines separating these civilizations from one another, and foresees an imminent clash between Western Christianity and Islam. He asserts that the basic differences among civilizations encompass history, language, culture, tradition and, most importantly, religion. These are more fundamental than the divergence in political and ideological beliefs. The enormity of these differences gets heightened as economic regionalism increases and cultural commonality induces economic regionalism. Besides, the process of economic modernization and social change tends to weaken nation-states as the source of identity, while strengthening religion as a bonding force. Above all, the world is shrinking due to communication revolution, and this process on the one hand intensifies civilization consciousness, while on the other it increases the awareness of differences between civilizations. The renewed Asian identity movement, the new Islamic movement, and the movement of Hinduization in India, are all examples of civilizational consciousness. To the extent that these civilizational consciousness movements turn militant or experience oppression, they may lead to war and conflict.

Professor Huntington fails, however, to see that information technology is equally capable of harmonizing cultures. For example, the Hindu view of the cosmos emphasizes that the world is a family (*Vasudhaiva Kutumbakam*), and similar concepts in Confucian, Buddhist, Islamic and Christian philosophies as they become common heritage through shared information would prevent people from thinking of civilizations in terms of separatism and conflict. It is widely recognized that dialogue among cultures contributes towards harmony, that it acts like a lattice-work of thoughts and points of view, that interweave and complement each other. This would help the emergence of truth, not from one point of view but from many. As N.K. Roerich, the great Russian artist and philosopher who made the Himalayas his abode wrote:

It is only the values of culture that will solve the hardest problems of life. And humanity may succeed only in case it acts in the name of cultural values. It is this concept of culture that supposes artistic activity, not just an abstract idea or cold unreality; it is alive due to permanent deeds of life, enlightened labour, creativity. We shall repeat it, not for ourselves, because we already know that, but for the young generations: all the best periods of the human history, renaissance and golden ages were created in those places where the tradition of respecting culture appeared.[3]

One of the major concerns of political scientists and defence analysts of the 20th century has been conflicts, clashes, and war. It is not my contention that they have consciously favoured conflicts, clashes, and wars, but their writings have influenced the mind-set of several politicians, generals, and heads of governments. Samuel P. Huntington with his expertise in political science has emerged as the leading spokesman of such a group of scholars, and his analysis of future conflicts, as also the detailed scenarios painted by him will be read with care as well as with passion by military strategists, and politicians.[4] Huntington writes:

> It is human to hate. For self-definition and motivation people need enemies, competitors in business, rivals in achievement, and opponents in politics. They naturally distrust and see as threats those who are different and have the capability to harm them.[5]

Huntington, in a bid to buttress his theory of 'clash of civilizations', forgets that it is also human to love and to have self-expression. More than enemies, people need a wide range of friendships and sharing for a meaningful existence. As Zakir Husain, an eminent educationist who rose to become the President of India, rightly observes:

> Cultures do not clash, savagery does clash... civilization of two nations would never clash as long as they suppress their savagery, and mix and mingle, and exchange cultural values.[6]

There is no denying that culture and ethnicity could be used by political leaders and military leaders for divisive purposes, as was done in Germany by Adolf Hitler and his ideologues. Huntington draws very interesting conclusions about the role of culture. He writes:

> in the post-Cold War world, culture is both a divisive and unifying force. People separated by ideology but united by culture come together, as the two Germanys did and as the two Koreas and the several Chinas are beginning to. Societies united by ideology or historical circumstances but divided by civilization either come apart, as did the Soviet Union, Yugoslavia, and Bosnia, or are subjected to intense strain, as is the case with Ukraine, Nigeria, Sudan, India, Sri Lanka, and many other countries with cultural affinities cooperating economically and politically. International organizations based on states with cultural commonalities,

such as the European Union, are far more successful than those that attempt to transcend cultures. For forty-five years the Iron Curtain was the central dividing line in Europe. That line has moved several hundred miles east. It is now the line separating the peoples of Western Christianity, on the one hand, from Muslim and Orthodox peoples on the other.[7]

While one may not agree with all his conclusions, the need to stress those aspects of culture which unite people and enable them to develop themselves fully in terms of their potential, cannot be over-emphasized. We firmly believe that governments may come and go, but culture and its set of values survive and persist in binding society. Today the government plays a preponderant role in India, but if it were suddenly withdrawn one would endorse the view that society would, nevertheless, endure. This is not to minimize the importance of the government and political systems in providing the society with certain prerequisites which help the individual genius and creativity to flourish, but to underline the inherent strength of the Indian society which it has gathered over the ages from its civilizational attainments.

The clash of civilizations in history has always been a battle between two visions of this world and/or the other world. This conflict could take place between two religions, or between two philosophies, or two ways of life or even in a single religion. In India, we have had a long tradition of conflict between the followers of Lord Shiva and those of Lord Vishnu, both Hindu Gods. We have also seen conflicts between Hindu belief systems and its rebellious spirit expressed in Buddhist and Jain philosophies, between Hinduism and Islam; and between Indian civilization and Western civilization. These civilizational encounters in India have established one thing very clearly that it is possible for conflicting values to assimilate the strong points of each other and get transformed in the process, and also for religions to co-exist as in case of Hinduism and Islam for over 1000 years. Notwithstanding the partition of India in 1947 in the name of religion, it has not been possible for either Pakistan or Bangladesh to acquire a new civilization or radically alter the character of their inheritance. This is largely because of the fact that civilizations are not created in fifty years or hundred years but take longer and also the fact that religion and civilization are not co-terminus. A Hindu converted to Islam does not change his civilization simultaneously. Similarly, Pakistan or Bangladesh having become separate sovereign states with Islam as their state religion remain a part of the same civilization. The clash of values is also possible within a single religious order like the recent one between Iran and Iraq or between the two wings of Pakistan which led to the creation of Bangladesh in 1971.

India owes to Islam and the Mughal rule admirable works of architecture, painting, music, urban centres and also a pan-Indian empire. The co-existence of Islam and Hinduism, however, had been marked at different times by sporadic violence. Both Hinduism and Islam have undergone a reformation movement—Hinduism through the Bhakti movement and Islam through Sufism.

The *Ramayana*, the *Mahabharata*, the *Upanishads*, the *Bhagvad Gita*, the Buddha's sermon at Sarnath, the holy book of Quran, the Guru Granth Sahib and the Bible are integral parts of Indian civilization. It is this capacity of Indian culture to absorb and also to transform the ideas and creations of other cultures that has helped in the process of renewal of India's age-old culture. The internal criticism provided by Buddhism and Jainism and the outside influence of Islam and Christianity have fortified and revitalized Indian culture which otherwise would have degenerated into mere rites, beliefs and myths.

According to Henry Kissinger

> the international system of the twenty-first century... will contain at least six major powers—the United States, Europe, China, Japan, Russia and probably India—as well as a multiplicity of medium-sized and smaller countries.[8]

The developments in the last decade of the twentieth century have shown that China has emerged as a great economic power, and several China-watchers are of the opinion that the unleashed free market forces may push China past the United States as the world's largest economy in the beginning of the 21st century itself [9]. The process of development in China shows that while, like the erstwhile Soviet Union, it first concentrated on becoming a military power with nuclear capabilities, unlike the Soviet Union it later concentrated on economic development with emphasis on foreign investments. The image of Chinese power, its political stability, and political relationship with the United States attracted the Chinese from overseas and persuaded them to invest in China. Besides China, a number of countries in Asia like Japan, Malaysia, Singapore, Indonesia, and India have given signals that in the new millennium the gravity of global economic, political and cultural systems may shift from the USA and Europe to Asia.

In cultural terms China has the unique experience of achieving coexistence among its three schools of philosophical and religious thought—Confucianism, Buddhism, and Taoism. Scholars are of the opinion that each faith and belief-system was able to propagate its own doctrines, and all three could live side-by-side, as none of them comes in the way of the overriding Chinese tradition of veneration of ancestors and strong family ties. Notwithstanding this cultural attainment, the Chinese have not yet shown that they would move along democratic lines. The faith in democracy that the US, the European countries, and India have shown in the twentith century is particularly missing in China. In fact, India is the only model of simultaneous build-up of economic power and democracy in terms of its cultural genius, but the Indian enterprise has yet to reveal itself as a shining example for the rest of the world because of its slow rate of growth and anomie that characterizes several of its institutions in the arena of the market as well as of democracy.

It is necessary to recall that the famous UNESCO Declaration of 1945 which pronounced that 'since wars begin in the minds of men, it is in the minds of men that the defences of peace must be constructed', also highlighted, in succeeding paragraphs of this Declaration, that the wide diffusion of culture, and the education of humanity for justice and liberty and peace are indispensable to the dignity of man and constitute a sacred duty which all nations must fulfil in a spirit of mutual assistance and concern, ... that peace based exclusively upon political and economic arrangements of governments would not be a peace which could secure the unanimous, lasting and sincere support of the peoples of the world, and that peace must therefore be founded, if it is not to fail, upon the intellectual and moral solidarity of mankind.[10]

But harmonizing cultures, or giving world peace an intellectual and moral content as envisaged in the UNESCO charter is not an easy task. The complexity of the situation has to be understood. At one level a culture or a civilization is distinguishable from another, yet at another level, every culture or civilization reflects highly complex interactions and processes involving different persons, races and societies. Another aspect of the issue is that while harmony among different cultures and respect for pluralism are a must for peace and progress and that we must learn from each other, yet at the same time, harmony as another expression for a compromise could be a myth as intellectual conflict is important. Every age should have the capacity to expose the hollowness of earlier held beliefs, if this is found through its own analysis and power of reasoning.

There is a feeling that the growing influence of western civilization would lead to the emergence of what V.S. Naipaul has called a 'universal civilization'.[11] This 'universal civilization' would be dominated by the West in its values, assumptions, and doctrines. One is aware of the fact that during the nineteenth and twentieth centuries, the colonization system, and subsequently the emergence of the United States of America greatly facilitated the spread of western civilization values in different parts of the world. European civilization, as a distinct enterprise, can be traced to the third century AD. However, it has made enormous contributions, and its predominant role in the twentieth century cannot be denied. One of the chief features of western civilization has been the close interaction between the different nations of Europe and America.

Modernization has generally enhanced the material level of civilization throughout the world. In some respects it has also enhanced the moral and cultural dimensions of civilization. Colonization, slavery, untouchability, torture, and vicious abuse of individuals, are no longer acceptable in the contemporary world. As we step into a new millennium, we find that people are going to use, in varying degrees, the instruments of modern life such as computers, telephones, television, aeroplanes, railways, fast food, pop music, and western attire. However, every society or ethnic group will continue to have its own folklore, poetry, music, dance, artistic expressions, crafts, rituals, forms of worship, language, dialects, and family traditions. It would be very difficult, therefore, for one uniform culture to dominate the world since no such single culture can answer and satisfy the multiple needs and expectations of different world communities.[12]

According to the traditional Indian view, art is a living process. It is not a product that one puts on the wall, or sells in the market. The work of an artist is, therefore, an act of homage to nature, to the creator, and to the community. Coomaraswamy added a significant perspective to this when he said that an artist is not a special kind of person, but every person is a special kind of artist.[13] In this wider perspective one becomes conscious of the fact that, howsoever well-decorated with paintings the walls of a person's living room may be, it is necessary to look for the inner beauty of that person. It is not permissible for one to only put beautiful things on the wall and keep ugly things on his/her body or to indulge in unsavoury thoughts. In this thought process, trees are sacred, earth is sacred, water is sacred, and above all, the environment is sacred. The role of an artist therefore, is to create a sense of reverence and beauty among the people for their environment. A work of art should inspire people, help them to see beauty in nature, and recognize beauty in themselves and in all human endeavours. This itself contributes significantly towards awakening and deepening of spiritual consciousness, compassion and devotion.

A special feature of the Indian cultural ethos is that in drawing lessons from our ancestors as well as from artists, philosophers and teachers, it has always been global in approach. A typical Indian personality is, therefore, drawn not only to the teachings of the Buddha, Gandhi and Tagore, but also to the works of Shakespeare, Beethoven, Bach, Tolstoy, and other great artists which the world has produced. The entire heritage of man has, in a manner of speaking, openly been owned and participated in by Indians, both in the past and more so now.

One is conscious of the fact that modern art in India is very much influenced by the trends prevailing in the West, conditioned as one is by 200 years of western education as well as the information explosion taking place in the world today and influencing young minds. The heritage of the past, the bitter experience of violence, and the global sharing of information about violence and ugliness are helping in the emergence of a new mind-set. The concerns for ecology, human rights, democracy and pluralism will be sharpened by this sharing of information. The artists can help in learning the art of living, and of relating to people, to nature and the environ-ment, which can provide satisfactory inputs towards a more content-ed existence. I have met persons who have been educated in sophisticated schools of urban India in the 1940s, lamenting that their children are not receiving enough of India's cultural ethos from the curriculum in schools and the environment created by satellite television. These parents are educating themselves so as to be able to communicate to their children the art of living based on Indian values and belief-systems.

In the 21st century, the market economy will continue to be a winning formula. The old belief that one can remain materially poor but morally strong will be weakened. Today, and increasingly so tomorrow, many will opt for becoming rich and if necessary, morally poor.

Major challenges facing economic development are not only poverty and illiteracy, but also the breakdown of moral, ecological, and spiritual values. This awareness needs to be disseminated widely in our culture. The training of teachers in cultural values will not only sharpen their consciousness but will also provide the necessary transfusion of cultural knowledge to students at an age when they are receptive and willing to learn about their cultural heritage. There is no denying that there is nothing more shameful than poverty and illiteracy. Poverty may appear soulful in movies, but it is demeaning and, as Indira Gandhi used to say, 'the greatest polluter'.[14] Even if India's long history convinces us intellectually that one can retain one's moral fibre even under indigent circumstances, what is required is to combine economic development with spiritual endurance.

II
India in the Global Cultural Context

What role can India play in the world of tomorrow where cultural attainments and civilizational progress will serve as determining factors? Although India is, in many respects, a peculiar country, isolated and fenced off from the rest of Asia by the Himalayas, yet, by reason of its extraordinary cultural achievements and plurality of religions, faiths and languages, it creates a strong affinity with a large number of countries in the world. It has received Islam from Western Asia and, today, it has the second largest Muslim population in the world; it has given Buddhism to Eastern Asia; and people of Indian origin have preserved their cultural values in different parts of Africa, Latin America, Europe and America.

As the world enters the new millennium, there are many in India who fear that liberalization will play havoc with our values. The unfettered linkage with the global market will lead to showmanship, gross consumerism, and cheap exhibitionism, seeking always to be in the news as stars and superstars, emphasizing the physical rather than the artistic and intellectual aspects, as a result of which concepts of beauty and aesthetics would be increasingly undermined. Another aspect of this fear is linked to the emergence of a 'consumer culture'—the product of the television network. Manufacturers and sellers, in a market-centred capitalist system, resort to indiscriminate television coverage of their products. They prefer to advertise in programmes with the highest viewership. Commercial producers of television programmes are constantly on the lookout for those who can make films, tele-dramas, etc. which would entertain most people, as television-viewing is a leisure activity. Above all, unless we provide an alternative mode to project cultural attainments, the young might well consider commercial programmes on television as part of the cultural value-system of the age.

The relationship between art and society will shift from the existing creative interface, in which the artist is moved by deep values and commitments, to that of increasingly institutionalized sets of contracts and salesmanship. This would mean a loss of real freedom, and social responsibility will increasingly recede from artistic consciousness. Professor Rajni Kothari, one of India's foremost political and social thinkers, would have us believe that the situation is already serious. He writes:

> The commitment to aesthetic values is still very much there but its salience is on the decline, especially given the constantly rising costs of works of art and of musical and dance appearances as a result of which the whole idea of artistic freedom is getting fast distorted and is raising basic questions of freedom for what and towards which whetting of the appetites? Freedom is a highly elusive concept and is vulnerable to a whole range of interpretations from the egotistic and self-serving ones to those that are based on a deep sense of sensibility, commitment and responsibility in its use. The old dichotomy between freedom and licence is taking on ever new forms in this age of growing competition for positions and mounting pressures for consumerist lifestyles, ever growing mobility and movement instead of being satisfied operating from one's own base and *gharana* in which the *guru-chela* tradition played a major role and as a result of all this an expanding arena of art itself becoming an item of elite consumption and middle class consumerism.[15]

Such fears about the future of Indian civilization is not without parallels in the past. In December 1873, Professor Max Mueller, in a lecture delivered in Westminster Abbey on the day of intercession for missions, highlighted that in future the decisive battle for the dominion of the world would have to be fought out among the three missionary religions which are alive, Buddhism, Islam, and Christianity. And the lecturer while admitting that millions still worship Hindu deities, declared that the national religion in India is in a state of living death, and that for the purpose of

> gaining an idea of the issue of the great religious struggle of the future, Brahmanism is dead and gone.[16]

It is neither surprising that Hinduism is alive and is counted as a major world civilization of the future, nor that Indians of all religions continue to have a great deal of respect and regard for Max Mueller despite his forecast of 1873. The uniqueness of Indian culture lies in the fact that people at different periods of history have contributed to its renewal and revival. In this context, one can clearly see two different sources of strength. First, the increasingly important role played by artists and creative persons in Indian society. And second, the social relevance of this role when perceived in the wider framework of society where hitherto backward sections are struggling with the new awareness of their rights and responsibilities; for it is they who will provide a new dimension to the cultural dynamics of tomorrow's India.

Indian artists have acquired a greater accessibility to the Indian people through mass media and have increasingly liberated themselves from elitist confines. There is both a deep-rootedness in tradition and an innovative zeal at work. Many a time they provide a direct and participative feel of living traditions and also help in coping with new challenges and tensions. In an increasingly tense and somewhat aggressive social ethos, they provide spaces of reflection and tranquillity, of patience and creativity, reinvoking the innate desire for a harmonious community. We believe in the assimilative capacity of India's culture. India's history has displayed that the Indian people have an extraordinary ability to absorb and flourish: armies, religions, forms of worship, dynasties, cuisines, languages, customs, and dress.

Much prior to the UNESCO Declaration of 1945, Mahatma Gandhi, through his writings and deeds, made it amply clear that faith in truth and non-violence—the basic tenets of Indian culture—alone can provide peace and harmony in the world. In a letter to his second son Manilal, who was leading the non-violent struggle in South Africa, Mahatma Gandhi wrote that it is necessary

> to understand non-violence and its two distinct aspects—physical and passive. Passive violence in the form of discrimination, oppression, exploitation, hate, anger, and all the subtle ways in which it manifests itself gives rise to physical violence in society. To rid society of this physical violence, we must act now to eliminate passive violence.[17]

Invariably passive violence precedes physical violence. It is within the realm of cultural values to effectively deal with passive violence, whether at the individual, group, or national level. The triumph of democracy over other forms of governance should help in giving a new direction for the propagation of cultural values. Mahatma Gandhi shared this optimism. He said :

> The world of tomorrow will be, must be, a society based on non-violence. It may seem a distant goal, an unpractical utopia. But it is not in the least unobtainable. An individual can adopt the way of life of the future—the non-violent way—without having to wait for others to do so. And if an individual can do it, cannot whole groups of individuals? Human beings often hesitate to make a beginning because they feel the objective cannot be achieved. This attitude of mind is precisely our greatest obstacle to progress.[18]

Art has essentially been an inherent human technology for expressing consciousness in matter. Artists have created objects, rituals, and environments not only for a subjective expression, but also as homage to the creator, to ensure harmony with nature, and to promote the well-being of nature itself.

India is getting increasingly modernized and the influence of western value systems is entering into remote corners of the country. However, western consumerism has not been able to negate renunciatory attributes from the Indian psyche. The religious ideals still guide the Indian people and the Indians of each generation know how to praise and to celebrate their gods and goddesses of creation, learning, joy and beauty.

The common people of India are not only custodians of religious values but also of India's spirit of beauty, dance, music, and crafts. The women of India, who are changing through education and political rights, have in particular lent strength to India's spiritual greatness in every period of India's history; their promise in this realm for the future is noteworthy, for it is they who are bound to carry forward the cultural heritage of India's ancient civilization in the coming millennium.

The de-colonization movement led by Mahatma Gandhi, the collapse of the Communist order in Europe and the dismantling of the 'apartheid policy' under the leadership of Nelson Mandela in South Africa are three major events of the twentieth century. All have contributed greatly to the strengthening of democracy and cultural pluralism in the world. Vaclav Havel has cogently observed,

at the end of the twentieth century, a genuinely new era of modern human history is beginning—an era during which a single culture, or the two great powers that emerged from it, no longer dominates everyone, making room for real multiplicity.[19]

He further adds :

'If the world today is not to become hopelessly enmeshed in increasingly horrifying conflicts, it has, I think, only one possibility. It must deliberately breathe the spirit of multicultural coexistence into the civilization that surrounds it. There is no need at all for different peoples, religions and cultures to adopt to one another. It is enough if they accept one another as legitimate and equal partners. If they respect one another and respect and honour one another's differences, they need not even understand one another. In any case, if mutual understanding is ever to come about anywhere, it can only happen on the terrain of mutual respect.[20]

The assertion that technological society is something higher than what came before, and that it is bound to bring us a better world, has lately fallen open to grave doubts. There is no denying that technology is the most powerful instrument in the removal of poverty and hunger, provisioning of housing and health care, and development of education and the arts. What is required is a meaningful promotion of cultural values that will ensure the curbing of negative effects of technological society such as consumerism, drug abuse, violence, pollution, AIDS and other ailments.   The spectre of ethnic clashes and religious conflicts at local, regional and global levels can be kept away only by reiterating age-old values which emphasize harmony and trust, love and compassion and the linkage between education and culture.

There is no doubt that globalization of commodity markets would result in fiercer competitiveness which may lead to injustice and violence. The global institutions of trade and commerce may strengthen the forces of exploitation of what is called 'structural violence'.   The plight of those who are particularly poor and oppressed and bereft of skills to operate even the local economic structures need to be the concern of sensitive persons.

The movements for human rights and peace must highlight the need to have a spiritual ideal for self-realization. Self-realization is real happiness, whatever terminology we may use to describe it. Once we steadfastly tread this path, we begin to experience the joy of living. There can be no spiritual ideal if it lacks kindness towards all beings, and non-violence in thought, word and deed.

Centuries before Mahatma Gandhi, Gautama Buddha taught mankind the virtues of compassion and peace. After attainment of enlightenment under a Bodhi-tree in Bodhgaya in Bihar, the Buddha continued his untiring efforts of teaching through conversation, lectures, discourses, and silence, for 45 long years until his *Mahaparinirvana*. His disciples subsequently codified these teachings of wisdom and compassion. During the reign of King Ashoka from 268 to 232 BC, Buddhist teachings were carved on stone pillars, or on polished cliff walls at numerous places. Missions were also sent to Syria, Egypt, Macedonia, Ceylon, and to other parts of Asia, as well as to the western world. The Buddha strongly advocated equality of human beings. In the Buddhist conception of *Dhamma*, non-violence and compassion are supreme values. Gautama Buddha stands alone among the religious personalities of history who categorically asserted that nobody is expected to follow his teachings merely because he has said so, but each one should think rationally and act accordingly. The Buddha developed a form of salutation in which one monk greeted the other with an admirable phrase: 'peace to all beings'.[21]

The dialogues and stories associated with conservation of waterbodies and compassion for animals and plants in the Buddhist philosophy are many and are fairly well known. In fact, the conservation of ecology and wise use of natural resources prescribed in Buddhist thought have guided several environmental movements in different parts of the world. However, the Buddha's preference for democratic governance and his faith in democracy are not widely referred to. It may be recalled that in the Buddha's lifetime while the Magadh Kingdom had a pan-Indian suzerainty, there also existed in Vaishali, on the north bank of the Ganga in Bihar, a Republic, the affairs of which were managed completely with the consent of the people. This democratic order is associated with the Lichhivis or the Vijjians, the elected representatives of the people. The following conversation between Lord Buddha and his principal disciple Ananda goes to clearly establish Buddha's abiding faith in democracy:

> And the Blessed One said to him: 'Have you heard, Ananda, that the Vijjians (Confederacy of Republics at Vaishali) hold full and frequent public assemblies?' 'Lord, so I have heard', replied he.

'So long Ananda', rejoined the Blessed One, 'as the Vijjians hold these full and frequent public assemblies; so long may they be expected not to decline, but to prosper'.

(And in like manner questioning Ananda, and receiving a similar reply, the Blessed One declared as follows the other conditions which would ensure the welfare of the Vijjian confederacy.)

'So long, Ananda, as the Vijjians meet together in concord, and rise in concord, and carry out their undertakings in concord—so long as they enact nothing not already established, abrogate nothing that has been already enacted, and act in accordance with the ancient institutions of the Vijjians as established in former days—so long as they honour and esteem and revere and support the Vijjian elders, and deem it a point of duty to hearken to their words—so long as no women or girls belonging to their clans are detained among them by force or abduction—so long as they honour and esteem and revere and support the Vijjian shrines in town or country and allow not the proper offerings and rites, as formerly given and performed, to fall into desuetude—so long as the rightful protection, defence, and support shall be fully provided for the Arahtas among them, so that Arahats from a distance may enter the realm, and the Arahats therein may live at ease—so long may the Vijjians be expected not to decline, but to prosper.[22]

In the long history of Indian culture these two personalities— Gautama Buddha and Mahatma Gandhi—stand out as world figures. If their messages are properly harmonized with the social and economic realities of our life and times, they seem to have the potential to avert any future clash among civilizations and also to strengthen the forces of democracy, ecology, and culture. Mahatma Gandhi's works and philosophy are shining lights amidst the din and chaos of the twentieth century and are of special relevance to the coming years. As the famous novelist Nadine Gordimer in her Richard Hillary Memorial Lecture, 'Our Century' observed: 'the only truly spiritual advance that has been offered is the thinking of Mahatma Gandhi.'[23]   In the current global crisis of strife and violence, ethnic unrest and ceaseless materialism, ecological erosions, and overstretched resources, Mahatma Gandhi offers a human and humanizing alternative in which there would be enough for everybody's needs but not for everybody's greed. A uniform pattern of development—in whatever field—has to make way for alternative and multiple patterns. The Gandhian approach is a self-questioning, self-critical one which, at another level, connects with the Buddhist approach as well, which is exemplified in the axiom: 'Be a lamp unto yourself' (*Appa Deepo Bhav*).

It is believed that the locus of power in the twenty-first century may shift from Europe to Asia. The economic strength of India will no doubt increase, but one is not sure that India, like the USA and China, will emerge as a great world economic power having a decisive say in world trade. Notwithstanding the various shortcomings and failures of India, Indian culture has continued to provide a distinct personality to Indians as well as to the people of Indian origin in different lands. One can be reasonably certain that the growing role of creative persons in India's society, polity and economy will ensure that India will retain this personality. Democratic institutions, ecological concerns and our rich traditions will support each other.

The Polish poet and Nobel Laureate Wislawa Szymborska in her poem 'The Century's Decline' has raised a very pertinent question:

How should we live? someone asked me in a letter.
I had meant to ask him
the same question.
Again, and as ever,
as may be seen above.
the most pressing questions
are native ones.[24]

In the background of the foregoing analysis and the way the Indian experiment of economic development and democracy in terms of its cultural genius is taking place, India may well provide a comprehensive answer to the question, 'How should we live'? In providing that answer, the cultural attainments that flowered in India well before the Christian era would be as relevant as those of the period of the freedom struggle, as well as the achievements and lessons of the second half of the twentieth century. India may reasonably expect to provide a message as well as an example in asserting that happiness lies in leading a simpler life, a life with the family and within the community, and a life of sharing with others. This would be possible in terms of the Indian genius, as expressed by the Buddha, and by Mahatma Gandhi.

Notes and References

1. Ralph Buultjens has developed this theme in several review notes. His book *Windows on India*, Express Books, New York, 1987, sees the Indian experiment since 1947 in the context of India's cultural attainments. He writes:

   Few nations have sought to modernize through accommodation, to preserve the essence of their heritage yet refurbish its forms, to adjust ethics on non-violence and peaceful coexistence to the imperatives of a violent and power-driven world. Sometimes, the critical balance of this endeavour has been harshly jolted by the trauma of events and the machinations of policy. Generally, however, the compass has stabilized and the equilibrium has been restored. The fact that India has not long drifted or been pushed from its chosen path is of major significance to other societies trying to find their way in the contemporary environment. p.34.

2. Samuel P. Huntington: *The Clash of Civilizations and the Remaking of World Order*, Simon & Schuster, New York, 1996.

3. Quoted in *Parkosa*, Coomaraswamy Centenary Seminar Papers, Lalit Kala Akademi, New Delhi, 1984, pp.3–14.

4. There are a large number of scholars in every country who have life-time expertise on defence strategy, and related studies. Samuel P. Huntington has emerged as a point of reference for them as well as several others. Recently, Victor Lee Burke has authored *The Clash of Civilizations: War-Making and State Formation in Europe*, Polity Press, UK, 1997. Numerous articles and papers have been written in several languages.

5. Huntington, *The Clash of Civilizations*, p.130.

6. Quoted in Address by K.R. Narayanan, Vice-President of India at the function to commemorate the birth centenary of Zakir Hussain at New Delhi on 7.5.1997.

7. Ibid., p.28.

8. Henry Kissinger, *Diplomacy*, Simon & Schuster, New York, 1994, pp.23–4.

9. Ibid., p.229.

Huntington very perceptively writes about China as follows :

China's history, culture, traditions, size, economic dynamism and self-image all impel it to assume a hegemonic position in East Asia. This goal is a natural result of its rapid economic development. Every other major power, Britain and France, Germany and Japan, the United States and the Soviet Union, has engaged in outward expansion, assertion, and imperialism coincidental with or immediately following the years in which it went through rapid industrialization and economic growth. No reason exists to think that the acquisition of economic and military power will not have comparable effects in China. For two thousand years China was the preeminent power in East Asia. The Chinese now increasingly assert their intention to resume that historic role and to bring to an end the overlong century of humiliation and subordination to the West and Japan that began with British imposition of the Treaty of Nanking in 1842.

10. UNESCO Declaration was adopted on 16 November 1945 at London.
11. V.S. Naipaul, 'Our Universal Civilization', The 1990 Wriston Lecture, The Manhattan Institute, *New York Review of Books*, 30 October 1990, p.20.
12. This thought is reflected in the Report of the World Commission on Culture and Development entitled : *Our Creative Diversity*, UNESCO, Paris, 1995.
13. Satish Kumar in Suzi Gablik (ed.) *Conversations before the end of time*, Thames and Hudson, New York, 1995, p.137.
14. This is an oft-quoted phrase from the speech delivered by India's Prime Minister, Indira Gandhi, before the Ist World Summit held in Stockholm in 1982.
15. Rajni Kothari, 'Asiatic Freedom and Social Responsibility', Third Sihare Memorial Lecture delivered at India International Centre, New Delhi, 23 December 1996 (unpublished).
16. Alfred C. Lyall, *Asiatic Studies*, vol.1, Cosmo Publication, New Delhi, 1976, (First published in 1882), pp. 98–121.
17. Quoted in a article, 'The Elusive Goal: World Peace' by Arun Gandhi, Director, MK Gandhi Foundation, USA, (Available with the Foundation).
18. Ibid.
19. Vaclav Havel *Towards a Civil Society*, Lidove Noviny, Prague, 1996, pp.269–81.
20. Ibid., pp.269–81.

21. Will Durant, *The Story of Civilization, I. Our Oriental Heritage,* Simon and Schuster, New York, 1954, pp.417–39. Will Durant in his monumental work quotes the Buddha as follows:

And whosoever, Ananda, either now or after I am dead, shall be a lamp unto themselves, and a refuge unto themselves, shall betake themselves to no external refuge, but, holding fast to the Truth as their lamp,... shall not look for refuge to any one besides themselves—it is they...who shall reach the very topmost height! But they must be anxious to learn!

'Now then, O monks,' he said to them as his last words, 'I address you. Subject to decay are compound things. Strive with earnestness.

22. From the *Mahaparinibbana Sutlam* (in Pali), ch. 1 of the *Digha Nikaya* (part II), Professor N.K. Bhagwat (ed.), Bombay, 1936, pp.60–2. English translation from *Sacred Books of the East,* vol. XI, trans. by T.W. Rhys Davids, Oxford, 1900, pp.3–4. Also available in Dialogues of the Buddha, part II, trans. by T.W. Rhys Davids and C.A.F. Rhys Davids, London, 1910, pp.79–80.

23. Nadine Gordimer, 'Our Century', Richard Hillary Memorial Lecture, *Oxford Today,* 1996, vol. 9, no.1, p.3. Similar sentiments have also been expressed by Kathleen Raine and Vaclav Havel. These are reproduced below:

Gandhiji was something else, the tradition in which he stood not the procession of history and its kings and leaders, but of holy men, renunciates and ascetics, representing on earth some divine principle. The veneration given to Gandhiji is not merely accorded to a great historical figure and national leader, nor is it even that he spoke of non-violence to the whole world, a message whose simplicity all ˙understood: he represented a divine principle.

Katheen Raine, *India Seen Afar,* Green Books, Devon, 1990, p.56.

Vaclav Havel has elaborated Mahatma Gandhi's contribution to humanity in the following words:

The spiritual ethos that came to fruition in the work of Gandhi was a thousand years in the making on the great Indian subcontinent. This work is one of the major contributions of your country to modern history. It is an inspiring contribution, the impact of which can be observed again and again in all corners of the globe. I am convinced that the creation of the multicultural civilization I have talked about, the creation of conditions based on mutual respect and tolerance of different cultures, as well as the creation of a new human responsibility that alone can save this threatened and sorely tried planet, will always find one of the most important sources of its vitality in Gandhi's work.

Without the heritage of Gandhi and his Indian precursors and followers, there would be considerably less hope in the world than there is today.

Vaclav Havel, *Towards a Civil Society*, p.281.

24. Debes Roy, The King and the Clown, Some Confabulations on the Relation between the Democracy and the Writer, Sahitya Akademi, New Delhi, 1997 (unpublished document), pp.17–18.

Appendix A:
Culture and Administration: A Study of Interaction as a Means of Social Change in India

Culture is power. It is a pursuit of total perfection to know all that concerns us most. As expressed through language and art, philosophy and religion, education and science, films and newspapers, radio and television, social habits and customs, political institutions and economic organizations, culture heightens the skills of an individual and a society in its totality in all walks of life because it is by culture that a man or a society gets an insight into the whole. Culture includes not only art, music, dance, and drama, but a whole way of life. In part, culture is '*sanskriti*', or a process of refinement. It is in this broader sense that culture has to be viewed.

Administration keeps the fabric of society intact. It is the tool of the state to achieve its goal. It is an instrument of ordering human relations to help individuals in developing their individuality and a consistent, coherent personality. The art of administration comprises direction, coordination, and control of persons constituting a society to achieve some collective purpose or objective. Administrative machinery is entrusted with the responsibility of keeping order in a society without which there would be anarchy and human life would be solitary, poor, nasty, brutish, and short. Administration thus plays a vital role in the preservation of cultural values and the promotion of new value patterns consonant with the goals that the society sets for itself.

The karma dance along with the wheel above symbolizes progress in administration that safeguards cultural values. The dance is a living part of socio–administrative systems prevalent in Chotanagpur area in Bihar and Chhatishgarh in Madhya Pradesh.

Social change is a wider phenomenon and is brought about by a number of factors. It is true that all things change. It is also true that all things do not change drastically. But it is a lesson of history that when a society reflects upon its instruments with foresight, its consciousness for change gets sharpened. Both culture and administration are instruments of social change and their proper articulation can unleash unprecedented energy to bring in desired changes more rapidly. If we ask how some of the greatest social changes of our age—such as the liberation of our country from colonial rule, or the civil rights movement in the United States—were brought about, it is difficult to attribute either of these to the will or education of the colonialists and the whites. India became free because it could no longer be retained as a colony of the imperialist power. The black American was given the vote in the USA because he could not be kept down. The leadership, which is very crucial for social change, has to come from individuals and groups and may include writers, artists, reformers, political leaders, or social workers, who can think independently and objectively with the capacity to look beyond.

Indian Culture

What is our culture? Over the ages, there has gradually developed a composite Indian culture with its own unbroken history. The story of Indian culture is a story of unity and synthesis, of reconciliation and development, of harmony and assimilation, of fusion of old traditions with new values.

Many have viewed Indian culture in compartments of Hindu culture, Islamic culture, Christian culture, etc. There could perhaps be no narrower view of Indian culture than this. For one thing, the roots of our culture go beyond that of the Aryans to the Negritos, who came to India from Africa, the aboriginals who belonged to the proto-Austroloid race, the Mongoloids who came from Tibet and China, and the Dravidians inhabiting southern India. Originating in the Sapta Sindhu region, the land watered by the Indus, the Saraswati and the five rivers of the Punjab, according to the majority view, the Aryans moved eastwards. Their conquests of the various peoples, some with advanced civilizations, as evidenced by the Mohenjodaro and Harappa excavations, culminated finally in a fusion of cultures. But the view that the Aryans alone were conquerors of this land is not correct. Later came the Greeks followed by the Shakas and the Kushanas. Before the Gupta kings as well as during their time, the Hans came followed by the Turks. In Assam, the Ahoms of the Shan race of upper Burma came and settled down for good. In fact, all the communities which came to India before the Muslims, were assimilated in the existing society and lost their identity.

The Muslims, who maintained a separate identity, were, however, also influenced by the prevailing cultural mores affecting their social habits and customs. The advent of the Europeans also brought about far-reaching changes in our cultural heritage. The restless European spirit willy-nilly brought everything under its control. On the one hand, the material conditions underwent a sea change with the induction of western capitalism and technology. On the other, Christianity, with its international character, emerged as another religion on the Indian scene. The introduction of English in the existing educational system, in this context, was momentous. Although it was aimed to provide the Britishers with a large English-speaking ministerial class of Indians to assist in the management of the colony, the consequences were far more significant, as books in the English language exposed the Indian intelligentsia to new ideas like scientific developments, nationalism and democracy.

Thus, the Indian people are neither purely descended from Aryan stock nor from Dravidian stock, but are a community of children of all the great people who came and made India their home. Today, whatever is Indian—whether it be an idea, a word, a form of art, a political institution, or a social custom—is a blend of all these and many other strains and elements. Indian culture includes little pieces of all and is a product of chemical reaction.

One example of assimilation could be that of the ants who carry particles of foodstuff from different places and deposit them all at one place, yet each particle is distinct and identifiable. The process of assimilation is different and is more comparable to 'bee activity' rather than to 'ant activity'. Bees move from one flower to the next, collect nectar, and then assimilate it so that it ultimately becomes honey. The essential feature of honey is that, while the nectar of each flower cannot be separated, the honey from each place will have its own distinctive taste depending on the season, the climate, and the flowers visited by the bees. Similarly, Indian culture is the honey prepared from the nectar of cultural activities from various parts of the country. Although Indian culture may be given the label of 'Aryan', the role of the Aryans is no more important than that of the bees is in preparation of the honey. Rabindranath Tagore summed it up beautifully when he said that all the people who came to India mingled with one another to become one living organism '*Ek deho holo lin*'.

Evolution of the Indian Administration

A look at the administrative history of India reveals that except in certain periods, there was no unity of administration. This does not, however, mean that there was no striving towards unity. From the earliest times, we find kingdoms and principalities seeking to impose one common rule over the whole country. The legendary epics of the Ramayana and the Mahabharata tell a story of unification. One of the first historical figures was Chandragupta who sought to bring the whole country under one rule. Ashoka continued the tradition and in fact brought more of India under a single authority than up to that time. During the reign of the Pathans and the Moghuls, we find the same story repeated time after time.

India's geography has been largely responsible for its cultural unity and fusion. Physical features so sharply mark off India from neighbouring countries that attempts either to divide the country or to expand it beyond its limits have invariably failed in its long history. For example, attempts of the Aryans to keep Afghanistan within India met with failure. The Greek efforts to incorporate Punjab into Afghanistan proved equally futile as also those of the Mauryas to retain Kandahar. The ambition of Mahmud Gazni to rule India from Kabul came to grief. The Mughul empire conveys the same story. Similarly, Sind, though often annexed, could not become a part of Persia for always. The whole course of recorded history tells us of this unbreakable geographical unity.

India's political vicissitudes have been largely conditioned by the inadequacy of her scientific equipment *vis-à-vis* her geography. While her geography demanded unification of the country into one state, the prevalent state of control over the forces of nature rendered this difficult to achieve and almost impossible to maintain. The vastness of the country and absence of modern methods of communication worked against political unification. There has, therefore, been till recently, unity of culture without unity of administration. This was a strange paradox that in spite of a strong consciousness of cultural unity, the people were lacking in the instinct of unified national political action.

The Indian society was highly organized throughout its history. The unit of social life has been the village and this continues to be so even today. The communities described in the Vedas and the Upanishads were popular and democratic. The will of the people found expression in elected assemblies and democratically governed institutions. It conceded the right of free expression and open discussion to all its members and decided not only political questions, but social and religious questions as well. However, the entire gamut of economic activity from production to consumption was restricted to the members of the village and it was this concept of 'self-sufficient village' that led Marx to write about the Asiatic mode of production. Such conditions precluded growth of a social consciousness that transcends the limits of the family or the tribe, *kul* or *jati*. The dependence of the peasant on the forces of nature generated an attitude of facing the blows of providence with fortitude and passivity. The growth of trade and commerce brought expansion in the unit of economic life and consequential growth in economic administration. These also led to the circulation of ideas and a readiness for accepting novelty and change, but unfortunately this was confined to a small group of people and did not permeate through society at large.

The moot point is as to what kind of future we want for our people. This question, to my mind, is settled as the nation has adopted a definite and determined path for egalitarian social order and progress as evolved both through the processes of political events leading to the independence of the country on 15 August 1947, and adoption of the constitution of India on 26 January 1950. The far-reaching changes, both constitutional and social, taking place since then have made the position absolutely clear. We want an egalitarian social order to base our society on equality and to accelerate the process of our economic growth so that a meaningful opportunity for development is available to us. This could be viewed in three perspectives. First, there is the ancient past that we have inherited, both in respect of social forms and structures and the general heritage of arts, sciences, technology and education. The second is our recent past and the emerging pattern of the future wherein we have made enormous progress both in socio-economic and in political fields. And the third is our administration which has provided the necessary infrastructure and is the implementation machinery for bringing about economic growth with social justice.

The Indian Social System

Considering India's long past, we have to remember that we are dealing with a culture which has sustained a highly individualistic ethos and a stratified society. The traditional Indian society gradually became hierarchical both in principle and in practice. It closed its doors and developed institutions of caste and untouchability. In this society, it was considered natural and proper for men to be born unequal and to enjoy unequal rights and privileges. Unfortunately, these inequalities were given some sort of legitimacy by means of a system based on the theories of *dharma* and *karma*. Men were born as Brahmins or Kshatriyas, Vaishayas or as Sudras or Chandals (untouchables) according to the law of *karma,* and in society it was their *dharma* to act in accordance with the station in life into which they were born. The law of Manu, more or less, formalized these inequalities. The forces of rationalism and change did invigorate our society with the rise of Buddhism and Jainism. There was insistence upon the total renunciation of ritual and idol-worship, but this got defeated at the hands of forces which bring division and encourage differences between man and man. Religion was reduced to caste and communal mores. The caste system broke up the unity of Indian life and impeded the growth of democracy. It engendered snobbishness and pride in the higher castes and induced a spirit of inferiority and servility amongst the lower castes. These factors have hindered the development of an open society. During the Islamic era, the dynamism of Islam under the secular, liberal, forward-looking administration of Akbar brought a brief spurt to Indian thought but the bigotry of his successors culminating in the stultifying and narrow-minded rule of Aurangzeb pushed India back to superstition and obscurantism. Macaulay's famous Minute on Education exposed generations of Indians to western scientific thought and rational political and economic principles. But it was the colonial ethos that was the chief force which, in spite of development education, perpetuated the distinction between man and man, according to status, as the dominant feature of social life. All this narrowed our outlook and to a great degree it still persists.

In the recent past, we made frontal attack against the normative order of our society. It was Mahatma Gandhi who was by far the most outstanding exponent of social justice. Through his Harijan movement and denunciation of caste and untouchability, Gandhi paved the way for a non-violent transition to a new social order. It was, however, Jawaharlal Nehru who thought in terms of precise legislation to achieve social equality and to reform social institutions. The basic commitment of Nehru was to egalitarianism. He wanted to abolish inequality, both in terms of opportunities and living standards. This was possible only through economic planning, and he accordingly made economic planning the chief instrument for securing social justice. To both Gandhi and Nehru, synthesis of the goals of social justice and economic development was possible. The Indian National Congress in pre-independent India was the platform on which to channelize and express the national urge in this direction. Gandhi perceived that in a society free from exploitation and violence, social justice and development are fully harmonized. Nehru gave expression to this philosophy in his historic speech proclaiming independence and calling for dedication to fulfil the ambition of the greatest man of our generation, 'to wipe every tear from every eye'. This would entail the ending of poverty, ignorance, and disease, and would remove the inequality of opportunity. Our people, on their part, have always accorded support to this ethos. The general as well as the state elections in 1971, 1977, 1980, 1985, 1989, 1991 and 1996 clearly demonstrated the power of the voters to give directions to their representatives to use the machinery of government for the betterment of the people. The cultural force behind the decision of the electorate was always discernible notwithstanding the propaganda, money power and such other machinations used to counter it.

Administration and Social Change

While participation of the people in the national programmes is a primary prerequisite of a democratic society, the actual operation has to be carried out by the administration. To be purposeful, administration has to reflect and respond to social change. The administration which we have is unfortunately hierarchical and status quo oriented. In this respect, its rationalization is based upon consistency of human activities and it has itself laid down detailed procedures regarding different social functions. However, besides its commitment to established values, the administration must also change in its structure. In this regard, the most discernible impact of social change has been in the growth of administrative functions in our country. Increasingly, a new administrative ethos has been seen in India which tries to reflect the popular will and is developing its organizational competence and inputs to tackle the new challenges. In this context, the administration is continually interacting with the political, economic and socio-cultural value-system of our society. It is both a modifying influence upon these systems and is itself being modified by the activities of these related systems. A new constitutionalism will be required to cope with the forces of challenge in our system both by our political system and administrative system. Unfortunately, declining moral standards in public life have adversely affected the quality of administration at every level. It is in this context that the new public administration has to devise built-in safeguards against forces leading to maladjustment and confusion, corruption and sloth. The support would come from latent cultural forces of the society.

The scientific revolution that the world has witnessed imposes on us the need to conduct our national affairs scientifically. This is, however, different from the substantive employment of science to achieve a political objective. Calling upon atomic scientists to produce atomic bombs does not automatically lead to a scientific society or a scientific government. We would only be justified in speaking of a scientific society if the methodologies of science replace the age-old archaic and arduous procedures. For centuries, the limitations of science and technology restricted the opportunity for any given culture to learn from another, notwithstanding the fact that our culture did influence others and there was also some cultural exchange within our country. But today, science and technology have greatly simplified this process of exchange. Today, the world is shrinking. Each man's world, however, is expanding or could be made to expand. Every culture is influencing every other culture. Moreover, it is not merely that knowledge has divested itself from the parochialism of a state or country, but it is also free from the confines of race, class and sex. Today, the world is witnessing a phenomenon where the entire earth could be viewed on television from outer space. Side by side, science has given us the capacity to liberate humanity from age-old misery of poverty, squalor and disease.

It has to be clearly understood that the eradication of poverty as well as an overall progress can only be achieved through the application of science and technology in our programmes, and by clear and unambiguous understanding of how natural forces work and how they can be harnessed for human betterment. The growth of a scientific climate, in turn, is dependent upon the type of values we cherish and propagate in our society. This growth is hindered if we continue our blind faith in soothsayers, astrologers, palmists, various types of god-men, and other exploiters of ignorance and irrational faith. Analyses of successful scientific and industrial revolutions have clearly demonstrated an interrelationship between cultural values and economic change. Culturally sanctioned values and symbols have served as necessary fertilizers for the seed of economic progress to grow fully.

On examining closely the evolution of key ideas and institutions which have influenced lifestyles and behaviour patterns, history shows that whenever the economic task has become a cultural challenge, economic development has been achieved more easily. The Puritans of England, the Samurais of Japan, and the Bolsheviks of Russia did not appear as economic or industrial leaders, but as the bearers of a new message of all-round development of the nation's destiny. Similar was the message that Mahatma Gandhi gave to his countrymen. All this underlines the fact that without a profound cultural backing, economic advance cannot be sustained or social inequalities eradicated.

Since administration is a vehicle to bring about social change, it must also inculcate scientific values and supplement them by a cultural consciousness. With the responsibility that has devolved upon it to execute socio-economic programmes, there is need for making it politically and culturally sensitive. Failure of the human element in administration cannot be precluded by rules and regulations alone. It is common knowledge that administration is known to have failed not only on account of corruption or sloth, which, of course, are external manifestations, but for lack of consciousness, commitment, ideas, and dedication. An atmosphere of general consciousness of social goals in various aspects of administration would make it more responsive to the needs of the people than by merely introducing a spate of administrative reforms.

Administration and Culture

To some, culture represents the hallowed, the unchanging, and the unchangeable elements of the past divorced from the realm of administration. There could perhaps be no view of culture more myopic and narrow than this. To a social thinker, culture is a dynamic variable and enormously potent and influential, and one which the human community uses to adapt to its changing environment. Administration bears the unmistakable impact of the cultural milieu at the given time and which, if given proper organization and leadership, can act as an instrument of social change. The various developmental policies and programmes of the government have a cultural dimension and a great many state functionaries are continually active in harnessing the values, symbols, and myths of the society for diverse purposes. Administration must play its role as it lies at the centre of a web composed of many different relationships that extend to the citizen, to the state, to the society, and their values, economy and development.

The problem of forging culture and administration into instruments of social change is complex. The first requirement is a determination of the meaning, scope or relevance of these factors in the context of nation-building. At the same time, it is necessary to identify the forces operating in the name of culture against social change and progress. The widest possible propagation of a scientific temper in the society is a must. The question is how to expedite it, what are the impediments, and how they can be surmounted? Science and technology must assist in modernizing our agriculture, ensuring the optimal utilization of our industrial potential, and using our vast manpower to change the face of the country. How can this be achieved? How best can we evolve an appropriate technology relevant to the country's needs and making full use of the existing institutions, knowledge and traditions? The question naturally arises: is science justified merely for the removal of want and the maximization of material affluence? Scientists tell us how to conserve and utilize our natural resources. Should they not also provide an insight for the full development of the inner resources of man? Science involves speed and energy. Does it not also need spirituality to give it direction? How best can one achieve a synthesis between western technological advance and Indian spirituality so that we have a people with an Indian soul and a western exterior? Are we adequately conscious of the need for striking this balance? If not what are the causes and how can they be overcome? Again, if administration is to be the vehicle of social advance, it has to reflect and respond to the people's hopes and aspirations. But there are countervailing forces seeking to perpetuate the status quo, to prevent the administration from coming closer to the people and becoming a partner in their march towards progress. What are these forces and how best can they be neutralized? What is their role in creating and sustaining a false dichotomy between an elitist administration and rural-oriented 'barefoot' administration?

Conclusions

A study of the interaction between culture as manifested in a multifacted value-system of our plural society, and administration with reference to its structure, its programmes, and their implementation, in the context of generating and channelizing forces of social transformation, is an imperative requirement. The study of interaction between culture and administration could be at village, district, and state levels. Such studies need to be encouraged as these could indeed be interesting additions to the existing literature on public administration which up to now, relates mostly to structural changes, the civil services reforms, and the civil servant–politician relationship. The study of the interaction between culture and administration should be of equal relevance to theoreticians on the one hand, and to active participants in social change on the other.

The picture shows the ruins of the Nalanda University Campus (in Bihar) which was one of the greatest centres of learning of all time. This famed university flourished for a millennium and contributed in large measure to the development of Buddhist theology.

Appendix B:
The Monumental Challenge: The Role of the Archaeological Survey of India in India's Culture

I
Establishment of the Archaeological Survey of India

The Archaeological Survey of India—hereafter the ASI or the Survey—established in 1861 is not exactly in the eye of the storm. The following statements, which are a sample of comments and observations made by different persons and institutions in recent years would, however, show that it is no longer a recluse organization standing all by itself in pre-history:

> It shall be the duty of every citizen of India to value and preserve the rich heritage of our composite culture.

Constitution of India, under Fundamental Duties.

> We are of the view that it is the statutory duty of the ASI to protect and secure national monuments in the country.

From an order issued by the Supreme Court of India on 4 September 1996.

> Historical monuments should be liberated from the control of the Archaeological Survey of India (ASI), in order to develop them better

as tourist destinations... Keeping the Taj with the ASI will not solve the problem.

Shri Srikant Jena, Tourism Minister, Government of India, in a Press Conference on 20 September 1996 at New Delhi.

We have just had the Tourism Minister demanding that ASI should be freed from the clutches of archaeologists and handed over to the tourism ministry. That would be like appointing wolves as wardens of deer parks.

H.Y. Sharda Prasad, in *The Asian Age*, 24 September 1996.

In the past this question of entrusting the preservation of monuments with the tourist organizations was mooted surreptitiously but was not agreed to by the Cabinet Ministers like Abul Kalam Azad, Humayun Kabir, M.C. Chagla, S. Nurul Hasan, V.K.R.V. Rao, P.C. Chunder, including Pandit Jawaharlal Nehru, Indira Gandhi, among others. They had realized that the expertise needed for the preservation of monuments is entirely different from that of the Tourist Department which has only a commercial outlook and has little understanding of the ancient architecture, deep symbolism in sculptures and paintings and cultural values of our monuments of different faiths and ethos.

Indian Archaeological Society in a letter dated 23 September 1996 to the Minister for Human Resource Development.

Compliments and best wishes to all those who were associated with the erection and maintenance of one of the most outstanding miracles of the world: the Taj Mahal.

Nelson Mandela, Dy. President, African National Congress, 17 October 1990.

Every time one visits the Taj Mahal, one sees newer and newer glimpses of this masterpiece of architecture. One never feels satisfied with the vision of sheer beauty. The more you see, the more you want and always leave with regret. I am happy to note that this wonder of the world is well maintained. May this monument endure for eternity.

R. Venkataraman, President of India, 16 March 1992.

The Planning Commission should consider having a separate plan allocation for the environmental protection of the Taj Mahal which is a world heritage and one of the wonders of the world. A lot of money is required to protect the environment, save the Taj from pollution and for growth of tourism. For this purpose, it would be advisable that a separate allocation should be made which should be utilized under the supervision of the Central Government. Even a special Cell can be created to look after the Taj Mahal.

From an order issued by the Supreme Court of India on 4 September 1996.

The ASI is not only in charge of the Taj Mahal—India's most well-known monument of beauty and art in the world—but nearly 5000 other monuments, forts, fortresses, palaces and religious buildings like temples, churches, and mosques. Besides, its other responsibilities include the exploration and excavation of ancient sites; the discovery and decipherment of inscriptions; the establishment and maintenance of site museums; the maintenance of archaeological gardens around monuments, archaeological sites and remains; the chemical preservation of monuments and antiquities; the promotion of specialized studies in various branches of archaeology; the architectural survey of secular and religious buildings; studies on different aspects of archaeology both in India and abroad; and publication of authoritative literature by way of guidebooks on monuments, reports on archaeological sites and remains and monographs on architectural studies.

The monumental responsibility facing the ASI and the way it is discharging its responsibility need to the viewed in the perspective of its evolution, its leadership an analysis of its administrative functions and scientific capabilities and its interaction with the people and institutions of governance in the country.

II

The Early Years of the Archaeological Survey of India

In many ways archaeology as a discipline of scientific study began only in the 1840s. The Industrial Revolution, with its consequent excavations for canals and railways, had given a great fillip to the study of field geology and archaeology by providing large ready-cut sections to be studied. India was lucky to be among the first few major civilizations to have a separate organization styled as the Archaeological Survey of India as early as in 1861. Fortunately, the establishment of the ASI was preceded by great interest generated in Indian culture through the Asiatic Society (set up at Calcutta in 1784) with William Jones as its head. In January 1784, Jones called a meeting wherein a resolution for the foundation of a Society was passed with an objective of enquiring 'into the history and antiquities, arts, sciences and literature of Asia', and named it the Asiatic Society.[1] Within the next few years, many papers on ancient ruins, archaeology, epigraphy and numismatics were published in the *Asiatic Researches* and the Society's journal. Further impetus was given in 1837 when James Prinsep, the Secretary of the Society, discovered the key to the Brahmi script of the Mauryan times, and, soon after this event, deciphered the second script prevalent in the North-West, commonly known as Kharosthi.[2] The Asiatic Society provided a forum for dialogue and discussion and eventual publication not only by British officers but also by Indian scholars who looked at the monuments and other manifestations of Indian culture with precision and offered incisive analysis.

Incidentally, no systematic exploration of the antiquarian remains in the country was carried out during all these years. In November 1861, Alexander Cunningham, a Colonel of the Royal Engineers, addressed a long memorandum to Canning, the Governor General, imploring him to institute a careful and systematic investigation of the existing monuments of ancient India by a professional organization.³ The Government acted fast, and on 1 December 1861 Alexander Cunningham was appointed as the Archaeological Surveyor which marked the birth of the Archaeological Survey of India. Initially, he was entrusted with the responsibility of taking up the survey in northern India with a view to giving

> an accurate description illustrated by plans, measurements and drawings or photographs and by copies of inscriptions of such remains as must deserve notice, with the history of them so far as it may be traceable, and a record of the traditions that are retained regarding them.⁴

Barely after five years of its working, Governor-General Lawrence, decided to retrench the post of Archaeological Surveyor of India. This move invited expected criticism, and in 1870 the post of Director General of the Archaeological Survey of India was created and deservedly again offered to Cunningham.

Cunningham and his colleagues were greatly influenced by the details of Buddhist sites enumerated in the accounts of Fa-Hsien and Huien-Tsang. They decided to follow in the footsteps of the Chinese pilgrim Huien-Tsang who had spent several years in the seventh century in Nalanda and at other places. Cunningham's labour and his dedication led to the discovery of twenty-four ruins in Bodh Gaya, including the world famous places where the Buddha had attained Enlightenment in the fifth century BC.

Another area of importance which occupied Cunningham's attention related to the discipline of epigraphy. Cunningham's interest in and contribution to epigraphy can be seen in the series *Inscriptionum Indicarum* of which the first volume, containing texts of Ashokan inscriptions, carefully edited by Cunningham himself, was published in 1877.

Cunningham retired on 1 October 1885. His retirement 'robbed the Indian archaeological scene of its most familiar figure, a colossus which had been striding it for over a quarter of a century.'⁵ His tireless energy and labour and his precision and objectivity, particularly in the recording of remains, have made his *Reports* invaluable, which in Curzon's words, 'constitute... a noble mine of information in which the student has but to delve in order to discover an abundant spoil.'[6]

Cunningham was succeeded by James Burgess as the Director General of the Survey, whose duties he assumed on 25 March 1886. His initiative and efforts led to the passing of Government directives forbidding any person or agency to undertake excavation without prior consent of the ASI; and forbidding officers from disposing of antiquities found or acquired without permission of the Government; prior to this, the officers of the ASI were entitled to their share in antiquities! Burgess started in 1888 the publication of *Epigraphia Indica* which is the most authoritative journal—along with its *Arabic and Persian Supplement*—for the study of inscriptions.

The appointment of Lord Curzon as the Viceroy marked the dawn of a new era in the Survey. On assumption of office, Curzon declared, 'it is, in my judgement, equally our duty to dig and discover, to classify, reproduce and describe, to copy and decipher and to cherish and conserve.'[7] Curzon, time and again, reiterated, 'conservation of ancient monuments... as an elementary obligation of Government....'[8] He also initiated, in the very first year of his administration, steps for preparing legislation for the protection of monuments and antiquities with a threefold objective, namely, to ensure the proper upkeep and repair of ancient buildings which were in private ownership; to prevent unauthorized excavations; and to secure control over traffic in antiquities. The enactment of the Ancient Monuments Preservation Act, 1904, is a landmark in the history of archaeology in India. Yet another important step taken by Curzon was to bring within the purview of the Survey the archaeological work in the Indian States. As has been rightly stated, Curzon 'succeeded in rekindling an archaeological conscience in the country and placing the Archaeological Survey of India for the first time on a sound and secure foundation.'[9]

Curzon's choice of John Marshall as Director General of the Survey proved to be appropriate and resulted in an all-round spurt in the activities of the ASI. Marshall assumed office of the Director General on 22 February 1902 and, as he himself stated, 'our most pressing duty was to attend to the preservation of the national monuments, most of which were in a grievous state of neglect and decay.'[10] With remarkable foresight Marshall envisioned that

> the future of archaeology in India must depend more and more on the degree of interest taken in it by Indians themselves, and that the surest means of strengthening my own Department was to provide it with an increasing number of Indian recruits.[11]

A great volume of work was accomplished by the ASI during Marshall's tenure. In the field of conservation and preservation of national monuments, consistent and large-scale works, gave a new lease of life to the Agra Fort and the structures within it; the Taj Mahal, as well as the Fatehpuri Masjid, including laying out the lawns and gardens of the Taj, and clearing 'the approaches of squalid bazaars'; the Itimad-ud-Daula and the Chini-ka-Rauza, Akbar's tomb at Sikandra; restoration of the embankment with its stately pavilions on the bank of the Anasagar lake; the Arahai-din-ka-Jhompra in Ajmer; the Dilwara temples on Mount Abu; the Chittor Fort; the Quwwatul Islam mosque; Ghiyasuddin Tughlaq's mausoleum as well as that of Humayun with its well-laid-out gardens—the list is, indeed, rather long and covers almost the entire length and breadth of the country. The monuments at Mandu, Khajuraho, Sanchi, etc. in the erstwhile princely states were also conserved. Equally important is the work done by the Survey in Burma, where the monuments at Pagan and Mandalay were dismantled and rebuilt. Moreover, Marshall took up with increased vigour the work of cataloguing the ancient remains of the country, which is indispensable for any systematic programme of conservation and research.

Yet another important contribution that the ASI made during John Marshall's tenure was in the field of excavation. The excavations at Mohenjodaro and Harappa and the discovery of the Indus Civilization (now variously called the Harappa Culture, Harappan Civilization, and, of late the Indus-Saraswati Civilization) have been outstanding. Equally brilliant, though overshadowed, have been the results achieved at Charsada, the ancient Pushkalavati and a principal centre of Indo-Greek civilization, Taxila, Sarnath, Kasia, Rajagriha, Basarh—which represents the ancient Vaisali—, the prehistoric cemetery at Adichanallur, and others. John Marshall codified the principles and methods of conservation in his *Conservation Manual* which was published in the year 1923.[12]

Marshall was responsible for setting up a large number of museums including site-museums at Taxila, Mohenjodaro, Harappa, Sarnath, Nalanda, and Pagan. He was also instrumental in the establishment of the Central Archaeological Library; the commencement of a new series—*Annual Reports of the Archaeological Survey of India,* and of the *Memoirs* of the officers; documentation of photographs; and publication of guidebooks on monuments as well as archaeological museums, written by ASI officers.

Writing in a work published in 1939 about archaeology in India, John Marshall recapitulated:

> Thirty-seven years ago when I took the first step towards Indianizing my Department, I was confident that I was doing the right thing. Today, with half a life-time's experience behind me and my experiment well tried and tested, I can see that that confidence was abundantly justified. The Indians whom we have trained have proved their ability in every direction. They are good conservators, good excavators, good epigraphists; and they are equally sound as curators of museums, chemists and numismatists. [13]

Marshall's successor was H. Hargreaves who held charge of the post of Director General from 8 October 1928 to 29 July 1931, followed by Daya Ram Sahni, the first Indian to occupy this position. Thereafter, J.F. Blakiston became Director General during 1935–37. K.N. Dikshit assumed charge in 1937 and organized the first Indian party to explore the prehistory of the Sabarmati Valley of Gujarat.

In 1944, R.E. Mortimer Wheeler was appointed for a four-year term as successor to K.N. Dikshit. By 1945, Wheeler had reorganized the circles and, more significantly centralized the conservation work which was to be carried out by the Survey itself rather than by the Provincial Public Works Department who were executing the work for the Survey. In 1945, the Government established a Central Advisory Board of Archaeology for the purpose of reviewing and advising the Central Government in Archaeological matters.

In 1948, Wheeler handed over the charge of his office to N.P. Chakravarti. A large exhibition of Indian art-objects was organized at New Delhi; this was earlier taken to London at the request of the Royal Academy. It ultimately formed the nucleus of the National Museum, which was declared open on 15 August 1949. Chakravarti was succeeded by Madhosarup Vats in 1950. In 1951, the Ancient and Historical Monuments and Archaeological Sites and Remains (Declaration of National Importance) Act was passed, extending its application to those monuments and sites which were under the erstwhile Provinces of British India. Vats was succeeded by A. Ghosh in 1953 until 1967. During this period, the Survey observed its centenary celebrations, opened the School of Archaeology, and saw the enactment of the Archaeological Monuments and Ancient Sites Remains Act, 1958 and its Rules in 1959.

The first century of the Survey was definitely a period of great success. Most of the time there was dedicated leadership and hard-working and devoted field staff. Scholarship was the forte of the members of the Survey, and pride in India's civilization a reward of their labour. However, it was also marked by periods of stress and strain, financial stringency, and misunderstanding.

It would be appropriate to give a brief description of the nature of threats which India's historical monuments, magnificent temples, and inestimable works of art faced at human hands in the formative years of the Survey. This is apart from the ravages of a tropical climate and an exuberant flora, and the vicissitudes of fire, earthquake, and decay. One could do no better than to quote a few vignettes from the famous address of Curzon, delivered at the Asiatic Society, Calcutta on 20 December 1900.

In the days of William Bentinck, the Taj was on the point of being destroyed for the value of its marbles. The same Governor General sold by auction the marble bath in Shah Jehan's Palace at Agra, which had been torn up by Lord Hastings for a gift to George IV, but had somehow never been despatched. In the same regime a proposal was made to lease the gardens at Sikandra to the Executive Engineer at Agra for the purpose of speculative cultivation.

At an earlier date when picnic-parties were held in the garden of the Taj, it was not an uncommon thing for the revellers to arm themselves with hammer and chisel, with which they whiled away the afternoon by chipping out fragments of agate and cornelian from the cenotaphs of the Emperor and his lamented Queen.

When the Prince of Wales was at Agra in 1876, and the various pavilions of Shah Jehan's palace were connected together for the purposes of an evening party and ball, local talent was called in to reproduce the faded paintings on marble and plaster of the Moghul artists two and a half centuries before. The result of their labours is still an eyesore and a regret.

In 1857, after the Mutiny, it was solemnly proposed to raze to the ground the Jumma Masjid at Delhi, the noblest ceremonial mosque in the world, and it was only spared at the instance of Sir John Lawrence. As late as 1868 the destruction of the great gateways of the Sanchi Tope was successfully prevented by the same statesman.

When the Prince of Wales came to India in 1876, and held a Durbar in this building [the Red Fort], the opportunity was too good to be lost; and a fresh coat of whitewash was plentifully bespattered over the red sandstone pillars and plinths of the Durbar-hall of Aurungzeb.

Some of the sculptured columns of the exquisite Hindu-Mussulman mosque at Ajmere were pulled down by a zealous officer to construct a triumphal arch under which the Viceroy of the day was to pass.[14]

The type of vandalism, which took place in the nineteenth century at the hands of the rulers that Curzon so candidly mentioned is, of course, no longer there. However, monuments are still being allowed to be misused and encroached upon, or simply left alone to degenerate and decay.

When I visited the Taj Mahal as Director General of the Archaeological Survey of India in April 1996, I was astonished to see a guide coaxing an elderly couple from France to touch the delicate marble work and feel its softness, and the couple trying to convey to the guide the impropriety of their doing so. There has been another experience at policy level as well. For more than a decade, conservationists were demanding that the Taj be closed for one day in a week for rest and chemical preservation work, but for one reason or another, no decision was taken. It was only with effect from 1 April 1996 that the Government of India took the decision to close the Taj every Monday. The hotel/tour operator lobbies wanted this order to be withdrawn. Fortunately, the decision to close the Taj every Monday stands; thereafter similar decisions have been taken with respect to the Ajanta, Ellora, and Elephanta caves.

III
Conservation and Preservation

When the Archaeological Survey of India was founded in 1861, its primary objective was to locate, preserve, conserve, and study the archaeological remains in the country. The ASI has, over the years, developed into a large organization with eighteen Circles, two Mini-Circles, and specialized Branches: Excavations, Prehistory, Building Survey, Temple Survey, Epigraphy, Museums, Conservation, Science, Horticulture and Publication. The eighteen Circles are located at Delhi, Agra, Srinagar, Calcutta, Patna, Chennai, Aurangabad, Jaipur, Hyderabad, Vadodara, Bhopal, Bangalore, Guwahati, Chandigarh, Bhubaneswar, Lucknow, Dharwar, and Trivandrum; the two Mini-Circles at Goa and Shimla. Besides, it has an Institute of Archaeology offering a full-time Postgraduate diploma in Archaeology of 24 months duration and several other specialized courses for in-service personnel and those from the state Departments of Archaeology, Universities and Research Institutions.

The ASI is a multi-cadre organization having not only archaeologists but also civil engineers, chemists, epigraphists, horticulturists, and administrators. While the chemists, epigraphists and horticulturists have their own independent field offices each headed by a Director (the head of the Horticulture Branch is Chief Horticulturist), the conservationists up to the level of the Deputy Superintending Archaeological Engineer work in the Circles under Superintending Archaeologists. Including the watch and ward staff, there are over 8000 personnel in the ASI.

The principal functions of the Survey include preservation and conservation, developing and maintaining archaeological gardens, chemical preservation of monuments and antiquities; archaeological exploration and excavation, documenting and editing of inscriptions; establishment and maintenance of Site Museums; promotion of specialized studies in various branches of archaeology through the Institute of Archaeology; architectural survey, publication of guidebooks on monuments, archaeological sites and remains, excavation reports, monographs on architectural studies, etc. It has also undertaken major conservation works outside India besides carrying out excavations, explorations, iconographical and other studies in different countries such as Afghanistan, Nepal, Cambodia, and Egypt. It has also helped in setting up a museum in Angola. The Survey's functions also include the implementation of the Antiquities and Art Treasures Act, 1972 to regulate export trade in antiquities and art treasures and to prevent smuggling and fraudulent dealings in antiquities; and the Ancient Monuments and Archaeological Sites and Remains Act, 1958 and Rules thereunder.

Of its various activities, the most important are those of conservation and preservation of archaeological heritage which includes monuments and sites as well as loose antiquities in the form of sculptures and architectural members. While only 3500 monuments and sites are included in its protection list, the actual number may exceed 5000 since, in very many cases, groups of monuments are listed singly or monuments located inside large forts covering an extensive area are also included as a single monument.

This archaeological heritage is distributed over almost the entire country, in different climes—from the arid to monsoonal, from high altitude to coastal areas, from mountainous to flat plains, from forests to deserts. A large number of monuments are located in extreme climatic conditions, like those in the freezing cold of Ladakh, deserts of Rajasthan, coastal areas, and areas with heavy rainfall. Coupled with this ecological and geological diversity is the variation from remote villages to densely populated areas including metropolises. Some of the sites have no basic amenities like electricity and water—sometimes even water for conservation works has to be brought from a considerable distance, leave alone the building material.

The archaeological heritage of India comprises both secular as well as religious buildings, and covers almost the whole gamut of human activity. The Survey's protected list includes forts and fortresses covering vast areas; palaces; religious buildings in the form of temples, churches, mosques, monasteries, *agiaris*, synagogues, funerary monuments such as cemeteries, tombs, graves, *chhatris*, mausoleums, menhirs and other megalithic monuments and *dakhmas,* palaces commemorating or connected with some important historical event; residential buildings significant either from a historical, artistic, or architectural point of view; hydraulic structures in the form of man-made reservoirs, tanks, step-wells, etc.; and finally, prehistoric sites containing only a scatter of tools fabricated by early man. This heritage spans a long period of history—from about one hundred thousand years ago to just a few hundred years earlier. Some of these monuments which are under protection of the ASI continue to be used for religious or other purposes.

This variety does not allow any uniform method of conservation to be applied. The conservation of a monument implies preserving a setting which is not out of scale. Wherever a traditional setting exists, it must be conserved. In other words, the original personality of a monument has to be preserved. No new constructions or modifications which would materially alter the relations of mass and colour should be allowed. A monument is inseparable from the history to which it bears witness, and from the setting in which it occurs. The moving of all or a part of a monument, cannot be allowed except where the safeguarding of that monument demands it. Conservation is a process to *prolong* the life of a monument. Each monument or archaeological site has its own unique problems which are to be addressed keeping in view only that particular monument or site. Thus, for example, the problems of conservation of the Leh palace or the brick temples at Bishnupur would be different altogether in comparison with the problems of conservation of the excavated remains at Lothal or the Shore temple at Mamallapuram. These problems are further compounded by several other features such as the materials used in construction, varying stages of disrepair of or damage to the structure, difficulty in regard to availability of materials or even skilled artisans and, finally, the constant threat due to environmental degradation and the drastic change in milieu from when the monuments were built.

While undertaking the conservation of a monument, several factors have to be taken into consideration such as using the same material, preserving its original personality, the degree of intervention required, etc. We may cite an example to illustrate this point. Due to its location on the seashore, considerable damage had been caused to the stones used in the construction of the Dwarakadhish temple in Gujarat. It had, therefore, become necessary to replace the damaged portions of stone members by new ones and the work had to be carried out without interfering with the rites and rituals, or causing inconvenience to the pilgrims. For replacing the badly weathered stones of the temple, a quarry with similar stones was located at Baradia, not far from the site. Eventually, the quarry ran out of stone and another quarry was located at about 200 km from the monument. Transporting the large-sized stones from the quarry to the temple site posed a problem which was eventually solved with great difficulty. It may be mentioned that no heavy machinery such as bulldozers or earth-movers, is used in the execution of conservation works at ancient sites.

The major problems of the ASI, however, relate to excavation, the smuggling of idols, and the increasing threat to land and buildings under the control of the Survey.

IV
Exploration and Excavation

In view of the magnitude of the problem concerning conservation, protection, upkeep, and maintenance, one is inclined to hold the view that excavation of fresh sites should not be a priority item unless careful plans and adequate financial arrangements are available. The old dictum that 'if one cannot properly conserve an object, it is better to re-bury it and wait for a more favourable situation' still holds good. As early as 1945, a Central Advisory Board of Archaeology (CABA) was constituted to advise the Central Government on the needs of scientific archaeology in India. It has been stipulated that all proposals for archaeological field work in the country shall be screened for approval by the Standing committee of CABA, headed by the Director General of the Survey. Licences in respect of approved proposals are issued under the provisions of the Ancient Monuments and Archaeological Sites and Remains Act, 1958 and Rules, 1959. Over the years, the Advisory Board has come to promote closer contacts between the Survey, the Departments of Archaeology of the State Governments, the Universities and other institutions concerned with exploration and excavation of historical sites. With a view to sustaining uniform standards of excavation techniques, the Survey oversees the field work done by different agencies and assists them both in matters of technical guidance as well as in training.

Exploration comprises the discovery and recording of ancient sites still visible on the surface of the ground. It is in this sense often a necessary preliminary both to excavation and to conservation. It may be recalled that in order to cope with the problem oriented explorations of Harappan sites in the Indus Valley,[15] the Survey first created an Exploration Branch which, at places, also took up excavation activities.[16]

The total effort, in quality as well as in quantity, is impressive; as a result, we now have appreciably more information about several aspects of Indian culture. But there is another side to the matter, the considerable and even wasteful dispersal of effort and resources. More serious is the accumulation of *unpublished* excavations. An excavation report gives an accurate statement of facts of the excavation: the plan of a site, its stratigraphy, the relationship of buildings and objects to the culture(s), a brief definition of these cultures in the light of present knowledge, a precise account of the work done.

Apart from the timely publication of excavation reports, the challenge before the Survey as a whole is the preservation of excavated remains. For the purpose of safeguarding movable antiquities and exhibiting them to their best advantage amidst their natural surroundings, the Survey has established Site Museums at a number of excavated sites. At several excavated sites such as Nagarjunkonda, Amaravati, Sanchi, Satdhara, Sravasti, Sarnath, Vaishali, and Nalanda, simultaneous conservation measures have been taken to preserve them for future inspection and appreciation by posterity. Currently, the excavations and simultaneous conservation of immovable residue are going on at two important sites, namely Vaishali, an early historical site, and Dholavira, a Harappan site.

Dholavira is one such excavated site where a site museum is on the anvil but the village lies in the remotest of remote areas, devoid of basic amenities like medical care, education, communication electricity, and social life; the establishment of a site museum is an acid test for the Survey.[17] Nevertheless, the present excavation work going on at Dholavira gives us a clear insight into the magnitude of problems being encountered right from the setting up of camps to surveying of the site, technique of excavation, laying of trenches, the process of digging, retrieval of antiquities, documentation, cleaning and packaging, drawing and photography, conservation, report-writing, and finally display in site museums.

Dholavira, taluk Rapar, District Kachchh is located on one of the islands known as Khadir in the great Rann of Kachchh. The site was explored in 1971–72 by J.P. Joshi.[18] The mound, locally known as Kotara, is being intermittently excavated since January 1990. It has, nevertheless, brought to light a town-plan of the Harappan Civilization, which is unparalleled anywhere on the subcontinent. At its fully developed stage the settlement had three pronounced parts which the excavator has called the Citadel (with its two sub-parts—Castle and Bailey), the Middle Town, and the Lower Town, all interlinked within an elaborate system of fortifications. Vertically, the sequence begins with a short pre-Harappan[19] settlement (stages I and II of the excavator), followed by a long period of the Mature Harappan[20] settlements (stages III, IV and V) and ending in a post-mature Harappan phase (stages VI and VII) constituting Harappan survivals with some extraneous elements.

The first settlement (stage I) was fortified, made primarily of stone-rubble with occasional use of mud bricks, and the fortification wall measured over 11 m in width at the base. The mud bricks used in the fortifications as well as in the houses inside had the typical Harappan proportions, viz. 4:2:1 (35 × 18 × 9 cm). There is also evidence of copper-working during this stage, as indicated by the occurrence not only of finished objects but also of fragments of crucibles, globules of vitrified clay and chiselled stone blocks (proba-bly used in the process of manufacturing)—all associated with a fireplace with a great deal of ash, metal-waste, etc. The pottery included a well-made ware with pinkish slips and incised decora-tions, as also ware with dull-brown, buff, and deep-black slips. Sometimes the surface had white-painted areas bearing simple designs in black pigment. In stage II, there were minor qualitative differences. For example, the pottery tended to be sturdier and the paintings on it included naturalist motifs. There was also an increase in the number of smaller artefacts.

By stage III most of the mature Harappan elements had made their appearance—weights, seals, script, and the characteristic pottery-forms, though not in a big way. However, it needs to be added that in this stage the seals were without inscriptions but did have the animal figures. Stage IV represents the Harappan Civilization in its full bloom. The seals now had their usual inscriptions as well. Even the use of polished pillars, a rarity in Harappan architecture, is assignable to this stage. The thickness of the occupational strata ascribable to stage IV is also the maximum, viz. around five and a half metres. As for the typical mature Harappan pottery, one may note the presence of fragments of perforated jars and of dishes-on-stands. A few examples of the triangular terracotta 'cakes' were also noted.

However, a kind of decline began to set in by stage V. Although the typical Harappan artifacts continued as before, the maintenance of the structures and of the general layout showed a loss of grip by the civic authorities. For whatever reason, the settlement was also deserted at least for some time.

When people reoccupied the site (stage VI), there was a percep-tible change in their material culture. For example, the seals now had only inscriptions but no figures. This was just the opposite of what had been obtained in stage III when figures appeared without inscriptions. However, the typical Harappan weights were there. While some of the Harappan pottery continued, there were other varieties too, such as the black and red and its associated wares. Some of the pottery also resembled that from Jhukar. The size of the settle-ment became smaller and the layout also differed. Once again, after a period of about a century the site was abandoned. The next reoccupation (stage VII) was characterized by a different settlement pattern. The houses were now circular in plan and were largely constructed with stones robbed from the earlier structures. Town planning and drainage were things of the past. Urbanism had yielded place to a rural scenario; the similarity in pottery used during stages VI and VII showed that the people belonged to the same stock.

Trade was very important to Dholavira's economy because this region has never been agriculturally fertile, though it was much greener then. The excavations have led to the discovery of an interesting network of small and large drains which intersect each other. The larger drains are big enough to allow a person to walk through them. 'The drains were probably used to collect and carry monsoon run-off water to a tank for later use. Water conservation was a critical necessity here, and the drying up of water sources—due either to mountain streams changing course radically, or to over-use—might have caused the death of Dholavira.[21]

The first archaeological report on a settlement of the Indus Civilization was written in 1875 by Alexander Cunningham, Director General of the Archaeological Survey of India. It was, however, only in 1931 that the full significance of the excavations at Mohenjodaro in Harappa came to light with the report by one of Cunningham's successors, John Marshall. He wrote:

> Never for a moment was it imagined that five thousand years ago, before even the Aryans were heard of, the Punjab and Sind, were enjoying an advanced and singularly uniform civilisation of their own, closely akin but in some respect even superior to that of contemporary Mesopotamia and Egypt. Yet this is what the discoveries at Harappa and Mohenjodaro have now placed beyond question.[22]

It is fairly obvious that a civilization as advanced as the Indus Valley does not just come into being: it is preceded by long years, decades and even centuries of development. For a long time, Mohenjodaro and Harappa were the only two large townships belonging to this civilization to be excavated. Then, in the 1960s, archaeologists unearthed the ruins of Kalibangan in Rajasthan. Today it stands as one of the most completely excavated Harappan settlements. The fourth major Harappan site to have been discovered and excavated is at Lothal in Gujarat. The discoveries at Dholavira are in that chain and have conclusively proved that geographical territories of Harappan Civilization were well beyond the Indus Valley.

The excavations at various Harappan sites have clearly established that the geographical spread of the Indian civilization comprised present-day India, Pakistan, Bangladesh, Afghanistan, Sri Lanka and Nepal. Besides the well-laid-out towns and cities, the elaborate social structure and the standard of living of the people of the Harappan civilization indicate that the system must have been maintained by a highly developed trade and agricultural productivity in different parts of the region; the seals of the era prove its legitimacy. Unfortunately, the Indus script is still to be deciphered and hence the details are yet to be worked out. The intellectual development in India after the entry of the Aryans and the subsequent development of Vedic culture were not a complete break from the Harappan culture. Archaeologists are of the opinion that the Vedic and the Dravidian speaking peoples were in 'contact situation for a period perhaps of centuries, before the compilation of the *Rigveda*'.[23]

V
The Smuggling of Art Objects

The art objects of culturally rich developing countries were removed forcibly during the colonial era and today well-organized smuggling at international levels is rampant. In India the Antiquities and Art Treasures Act, 1972, which came into force from 5 April 1976, seeks 'to prevent smuggling of, and fraudulent dealings in antiquities, and art treasures'. Under this Act, registration of categories of antiquities as notified from time to time, has become compulsory. Notwithstanding this legal framework, smuggling has assumed alarming proportions as art objects attract very high prices in affluent western countries. The irony is that smugglers are highly sophisticated people with international networks; and auction houses often aid them.

The long odyssey of the Nataraja of Sivapuram of Tamil Nadu in India which came to an end on 15 May 1986 is revealing. An image of no small dimensions, known all over for its exquisite beauty and excellence of craft, and, most importantly, the treasure property of a Nation could still be smuggled out of India. The *ananda tandava* Nataraja image in bronze (height 4'6" and weight 574 seers), was part of the treasure trove cache, found in Sivapuram village, 5 miles from Kumbakonam, in Tamil Nadu on 2 June 1951 by a landlord whose tenant was digging the ground. It was declared in May 1952 as a treasure under the State Treasure Trove Act. The authorities of the local temple (the Sivagurunathaswamy temple) wanted to keep this treasure collection which included one Nataraja, one Somaskanda, one Ganesha (all three of the early Chola period: mid-tenth century AD), two Devi images and one Gnanasambanda figure (all these of a later period), for worship in their temple. The Director, Government Museum, Madras, recommended to the State Government that in view of the danger implicit in keeping such important and priceless figures (particularly the Nataraja) in the custody of the local temple authorities, from whom they could be easily purchased and spirited away from India by any person, these should be acquired by the State Government for the Museum. The Additional District Magistrate, Thanjavur, in the meanwhile, on a submission by the local temple authorities, gave his orders dated 14 December 1952 that the objects be kept in the temple itself. Notwithstanding this, the Director, Government Museum, Madras, continued his efforts to get some of these bronzes including the Nataraja acquired by the State Government; but was ultimately instructed by the State Government in June 1953 not to press for the acquisition of the objects. Accordingly, as an alternative, an agreement was executed between the Government and the temple trustees on 5 May 1957, wherein provision was made for the party to look after the object, keeping it in safe custody.

Subsequent events, however, confirmed the Museum's apprehensions. The temple trustees gave the idols to one Pramanik (the real name withheld) for repairs. One Bajigar and his brother Chalu of Bombay (real names withheld) persuaded Pramanik to make five fake idols in place of the five original ones and, in the early part of 1957, they took the original idols away (except that of Ganesha) after paying him Rs 10,000/-. Thereafter, the idols reached the hands of Wender (real name withheld), a foreigner who was an employee of an advertising company of Bombay. Wender sold some of these pieces including the Nataraja to one Bari (real name withheld) of Bombay for a sum of Rs 25,000/-. Bari in turn sold these to a firm styled as Prithu Telang overseas—a firm located in Delhi (real name withheld) for a sum of Rs 5 lakhs. As the facts of the case go, Prithu Telang or his firm appeared to be an important Indian point in a global context for illegal trafficking in antiquities. He in fact co-masterminded the smuggling of the Nataraja. The other prime figure in this game was one Broomer (real name withheld) of the USA. The Nataraja reached Broomer in the USA some time in 1969. The methods of Telang and Broomer combined misdeclaration, imper-sonation, forgery, tampering with consignments already booked, withholding facts to circumvent rules, and so on.

As to how the Telang-Broomer nexus achieved the smuggling of the Nataraja came to light after the Government of Tamil Nadu conducted an extensive enquiry to find out the facts of this case. The enquiry was a sequel to the cases registered by the Tamil Nadu Police, on the report of scholars that the idols in the temple were fake ones, against Pramanik, Wendar and various others. Krishnaraj conducted his investigation in 1972 and in the course of that he visited the USA and the UK, interviewed, talked to, and took the evidence of many persons and institutions. The bits of information and facts gathered by him, when put together, gave the following sequence:

A passenger of the name F.C. Johnston and his family left New Delhi for Hong Kong on 10 April 1969. The departure certificate was obtained from the British company in New Delhi that P.C. Johnston left for Hong Kong on 10 April 1969 and that a crate containing personal effects was booked by a Japanese airlines by one T.R. Meheta of Kotla Mubarakpur, New Delhi. The package was seen by the Customs authorities on 23 April 1969 and it was found to contain books, old clothes and souvenirs. The crate was handed over, after examination, by about 2.00 p.m. on 23 April 1969 by customs officers at the city office to the consignor to be taken to the airlines office at the airport. The distance between the airport and the city customs office was about 12 miles. The consignment for export needed to be presented two hours before departure of the plane to the airlines. The airlines accepted the package and again presented it to the customs officer on duty at the airport who had merely to satisfy himself as to whether the proper customs seal was affixed to the package. The Japanese airlines plane which was on a scheduled flight on 23 April 1969 night to New York had only one stop at London. The plane was scheduled to leave at 10.30 p.m. and as such the consignor had six hours at his disposal to tamper with the contents—removing the personal belongings and replacing them with the idol. The Japanese airlines also prepared an Air Way Bill for goods styled as personal effects by T.R. Meheta and it reached JFK Airport, New York as personal effects.

However, before the Air Way Bill of the Japanese airlines reached the United States, an invoice was produced for the same consignment dated 21 April 1969 that the consignment, sent by T.R. Meheta of Kotla Mubarakpur, New Delhi to P.C. Johnston, c/o Hotel Statler Milton, New York, contained an art object, namely the dancing Shiva—an early Chola Bronze.

It is significant to note, that, had the US Customs authorities known, when the shipment arrived by air from Delhi, that it contained an idol without a certificate from the Government of India, both the persons who exported and who imported the package would have been prosecuted under the US Customs Laws for false labelling and declaration. To circumvent this an invoice was made out dated 21 April 1969 declaring the consignment to contain the idol. Strangely enough the invoice did not contain the manner in which the consignment was booked and how it was expected to reach the United States. It was left to the customs officers of the United States to presume that this consignment of personal effects contained the goods mentioned in the invoice dated 21 April 1969. This was a ruse adopted by the party to get hold of the package which was imported into the United States under the false label and declaration.

There were two declaration forms which were signed by P.C. Johnston—one dated 2 May 1969 and the other dated 18 July 1969. But the signatures of P.C. Johnston in these two documents varied from each other. There was also no letter from P.C. Johnston to the customs authorities making over the consignment received by him to Broomer. There was, however, a letter dated 30 April 1969 from the secretary to Broomer to R.J. Saundara & Co., referring to the Japanese Air Way Bill which stated that the consignment received by P.C. Johnston was intended for Broomer. The Customs Department had issued a notice to P.C. Johnston c/o Broomer incorporated, Statler Hilton, New York, to produce a certain document in respect of entry No. 221711. It was not known how the consignment was handed over to Broomer without a letter from P.C. Johnston. It was also not clear why, if the letter was available with the customs, the same was not produced at the time of investigation to the Deputy Inspector General of Police, CID, Tamil Nadu when he visited New York.

It was also strange that the identity of T.R. Meheta of Kotla Mubarakpur, New Delhi was not traced as no one of that name was ever living in that area within the previous 10 years.

Obviously, from the time of purchase until the idol was taken delivery of at New York, Broomer had conspired with several persons and adopted dubious means for smuggling the article from India to the United States. A bogus certificate was obtained that P.C. Johnston and family travelled from New Delhi to Hong Kong by Quantas Airways, whereas in reality only P.C. Johnston travelled by that flight. The articles declared as personal effects were booked and shown to the customs and after they were passed by the customs authorities, the idol was put into the crate and the old clothes and books were removed. Even before the idol reached the United States an invoice was prepared as if the shipment contained the idol. The shipment was made in the name of a non-existing person. Delivery was obtained using forged documents. The identity of the persons who sold the idol, who shipped the idol, and in whose name it reached the United States were all fictitious. The letter of authority by which the idol was made over to Broomer was not forthcoming. All these pieces of evidence proved that Broomer entered into a criminal conspiracy with some other persons to smuggle the idol into the United States by infringing the US customs laws.

With Johnston remaining unidentified and Meheta untraced, the whole transaction appeared to be phoney with the prime figures, namely the Telangs of Delhi and Broomer of the USA, deliberately choosing to remain in the background with a view to escape the clutches of the law. Obviously, the whole operation of smuggling the Nataraja idol to the USA was masterminded with consummate skill by these two parties in conspiracy, both of whom were thoroughly and intimately aware of the laws and the systems of the two lands, and who also had the ability to devise ways and means of circumventing them.

The replacement of the idol in the temple premises happened some time in 1957 and its actual smuggling in 1969. There were a good 12 years in between when the Nataraja idol was in India and most probably with the Telangs. It is a poor reflection on the law-enforcing authorities that they could not trace the idol despite it being within the country for such a long period. The Government of India came into the picture only after an alert High Commission of India in London reported, in August, 1970, that the Nataraja idol was being put on sale.

There are still a large number of people in this country who are engaged in this illicit business. The Antiquities and Art Treasures Act 1972 provides for an offence a penalty extending up to three years of imprisonment. This is not enough of a deterrent. The International Convention on the Means of Prohibiting and Preventing the Illicit Import, Export and Transfer of Ownership of Cultural Property, adopted by the General Conference at its sixteenth session, Paris, 14 November 1970, is an important mechanism to prohibit and prevent illicit import, export and transfer of cultural properties. However, the real check to illicit international trade in antiques has necessarily to come at two levels—at the grassroots/institutional level, and through appropriate bilateral treaties between countries. The security of the antiques in the institutions where they may be located should be such as to preempt the possibility of any theft and, if there are appropriate bilateral agreements between countries for the prompt return of stolen property, instances of antique smuggling would surely be substantially reduced.

The story of the Nataraja idol is, however, not as yet complete. Broomer sold the idol to Norton Simon for a price of one million dollars. On receipt of information that Simon had sent the Nataraja to the UK early in 1974 for custody, the CBI contacted the Interpol and Scotland Yard and ultimately the idol was traced from the premises of Ana Plowdel, a professional restorer. The Indian High Commission engaged a solicitor to move for action claiming that the ownership of the idol vested in the Government of India, the Government of Tamil Nadu, and the trustees of the temple who were jointly made plaintiffs. The claim was contested by the lawyers of the Norton Simon Foundation. Ultimately, there was an out-of-court settlement between the Indian side and the Simon Foundation and the Nataraja idol was eventually returned to India on 15 May 1986. It was on this day that this bronze image of extraordinary resplendence of the Hindu deity Nataraja was taken over by the Government of Tamil Nadu at last. Thus the curtain was drawn on a chain of events which ran like a veritable crime thriller.

The whole operation did not, however, expose any defect in the law *per se*. Yet, it proved a point that law in itself is not enough, it needs to be enforced to be effective.

VI
Protection of Heritage Sites

India's rich cultural heritage stands amply demonstrated in its various cultural sites and monuments. They reflect a point of evolution that we had attained in ancient times. Some of these monuments and sites have been acclaimed the world over as of universal importance and they stand included in the World Heritage List of UNESCO. All the monuments are, however, important not only architecturally but also from the point of view of history. It is, therefore, the avowed policy of the Central Government, to protect and conserve these monuments.

The job of the Survey is not, however, an easy one. There are several contemporary pressures of development which often supplant the socio-cultural sensibilities of the people: the increased tourist traffic and the unreasonable demands made in the name of tourism; the rapid urbanization which has made most of our town planning efforts irrelevant and has, in many cases, irreversibly altered the ambience of many of our cultural and historical sites; a population which is bursting at the seams and much of which lives in dire poverty in slums and ghettos; tendency of some persons to exploit religious monuments for commercial ends; and so on. All these pressures taken in totality threaten to damage our tangible heritage irreparably.

Both in the recorded history of civilization and in mythology the finest works of art and sculpture were always meant for places of worship. In fact, the dwellings of the Creator invariably occupied a higher status than those of kings, chieftains, and the ruling elite. Most of our monuments, therefore, are intended as homage to the Creator. In the very nature of things a massive and/or uncontrolled entry of tourists to these places would go against the sacredness of these monuments. Yet, tourism is necessary both for the national economy and for sharing our knowledge, culture and values with the rest of the world. Tourists have also often helped to focus attention on the monuments in several of the developing countries and India is no exception.

A matter of immediate concern is the State's vulnerability in matters of religion. It has been an unfortunate fact of our times that the government has shied away from dealing with the offenders severely for fear that it might be dubbed as partisan—pro-or anti-one or the other religious group. Taking advantage of this fear and this vulnerability of the system, unscrupulous and greedy people act with impunity for commercial gain. Some of these monuments were the places of worship at the time of their creation, but religious prayers were not being held there when they were taken over by the State for conservation and protection and were declared as protected monuments. Such instances are many and are not limited to only one religious group. There are a large number of temples, mosques, churches, and such other places, abandoned at one time, but later openly or stealthily encroached upon in the name of religion, for offering worship, though the real reason was the lure of lucre and/or for gaining political mileage.

The prime issue is how to protect our cultural property. In my view protection of cultural property has two inter-related aspects: the first includes historical sites, buildings, temples and other places of worship, works of art, and other such physical aspects; the second relates to human skills, and attitudes which constitute the driving point in an individual towards the creation of works of glory and excellence. It must also be appreciated that these skills and attitudes are not static, nor can cultural manifestations conform to being replicas of past buildings, temples, dance forms, or lyrics. Cultural manifestations are undergoing transformation in terms of revolution in communication, technology, environment, and the impact that the wider world is increasingly making on us. The ASI is primarily concerned with the physical aspects of conservation of our cultural heritage, but it can perform this task efficiently only when it is sensitive to the second aspect of preservation mentioned above.

In matters relating to the physical aspects of conservation, there is need to appreciate the role that the local people have played in maintaining heritage monuments and also in viewing them as a part of their cultural personality since time immemorial. In fact, cultural heritage plays a critical role in fostering a sense of cultural personality which is an essential condition for development and social stability.

Leadership plays a crucial role in the building up of any organization. The Survey was fortunate in having some highly dedicated persons of intelligence and vision as its Directors General for long tenures. In the first one hundred years of the Survey, Alexander Cunningham, the first Director General and John Marshall, the third Director General occupied this post for 50 years. During the remaining fifty years of the first century of the Survey, there were only 9 other Directors General. The position began to deteriorate thereafter. During 1987–97, in a period of a mere 10 years there were 7 Directors General, two of whom were holding additional charge and two were officiating. The present Director General is an officer belonging to the Indian Administrative Service. The position at the lower levels shows no promise either as a large number of posts are lying vacant for one reason or the other; several of these have been recently filled up at my initiative. In the context of the importance of propagation, preservation and conservation of the cultural heritage of the country, I had proposed to the 5th Pay Commission the constitution of a Central Archaeological Service which, besides including Group 'A' technical posts in the Archaeological Survey of India, would also incorporate the National Research Laboratory for Conservation of Cultural Property (NRLCP) in its ambit. As envisaged, a duly constituted All India Archaeological Service will be able to meet the challenge of the future in a manner that the Indian Forest Service has done during the last 25 years of its functioning.

There is need to complete documentation of each site monument which is under the control of the Archaeological Survey of India and, simultaneously, to move towards the preparation of a National Register of Historic Sites and Monuments. Towards this end, not only does the ongoing survey process need to be given special thrust, but it is also necessary to go in for aerial photography. The documentation must conform to internationally accepted principles.

There is an imperative requirement for creating and/or consolidating conditions for effective conservation of the cultural resources of the country. One has to move towards capacity building in institutions and empowerment of local conservation professionals. An emphasis on collaborative arrangements, particularly with educational institutions, environmental bodies, and NGOs, and on training and awareness programmes is necessary.

The legal framework needs to be strengthened in the light of emerging needs and judicial pronouncements in a number of public interest litigations.

One increasingly feels the need for collaboration between the Survey, the newly constituted National Culture Fund, and the national level voluntary organization INTACH.

The National Culture Fund, launched in March 1997, has opened new and dynamic opportunities for embarking upon programmes involving participation of voluntary organizations, individuals, and government organizations in the national endeavour to protect and preserve India's cultural heritage. The Fund could become an important instrument to expand the areas of concern beyond the monuments protected by the ASI and the State Departments of Archaeology, to several historical sites and buildings facing decay for want of resources and professional care. A unified approach becomes critical as it will ensure that there is no duplication of work or conflicting objectives, and will also assure possible donors as well as the public about the sincerity of action taken. This will also open the area of cooperation and participation of the local community in the decision-making process as well as in implementation of programmes. Such an approach will also help not merely in the utilization of scientific skills and technical knowledge, but will combine this with local knowledge and traditions which form an integral part of India's intellectual legacy. This is essential as the efforts of protection can only be ensured within a social order that is profoundly aware and proud of its individual and collective responsibility.

Qualitative information, coherently compiled, collated and disseminated, can become the single most powerful tool for the protection and preservation of India's rich and diverse cultural heritage. The responsibility for the preservation and protection of the five thousand nationally protected monuments, however, must. rest exclusively with the ASI; this approach suggests that INTACH and other voluntary organizations could cooperate with ASI on specific issues related to the site. This would include planning and development of appurtenant lands and, where applicable the management of such monuments which because of historic reasons, are unprotected but are an integral part of the complex. The voluntary organizations could also assist in infrastructure and community integration works.

Preserving the memory of a civilization as rich and varied as India's is a sacred duty and the vastness of this task is an immense challenge for the Archaeological Survey of India. This challenge can be met only if high standards of excellence, commitment and integrity are maintained and if the work of the Survey is open to public scrutiny. The Survey can discharge its responsibilities well as long as it acts in tandem with concerned individuals, both in the realm of academia and culture. The history of the Survey is its guide and inspiration, and the future role of India in the world its charter.

Notes and References

1. For some time, the West regarded India as the land of mystique, the fabulous and the fantastic. Even as late as 1494, a book printed in Rome depicted India as a land of winged snakes and flying panthers and peopled by one-eyed, dogheaded and headless men. The Asiatic Society became the harbinger of change. For the first time, the Asiatic Society took up in an organized manner, the task of retrieving, restoring, preserving, and studying the ancient remains of the country

which helped in revealing and reconstructing India's past. Valuable works were translated and critical studies made of ancient works like the Vedas and the Puranas, besides works on mathematics, astronomy, and philosophy. As a result, the historical, cultural, and intellectual contours of India, so long neglected, began to take shape.

A detailed analysis of the history of the Asiatic Society is available in O.P. Kejariwal's book entitled: *The Asiatic Society of Bengal and the Discovery of India's Past, 1784–1838*, Oxford University Press, Delhi, 1988.

2. James Prinsep (1799–1840) was Secretary of the Asiatic Society for a period of 6 years (1833–38). He, along with William Jones, was responsible for heralding the golden period of the Asiatic Society. He inspired Alexander Cunningham through his works including the decipherment of Ashokan inscriptions and several other original writings. O.P. Kejariwal's introduction in the recently published book *Benares Illustrated, A Series of Drawings by James Prinsep*, Vishwavidyalaya Prakashan, Varanasi, 1996, is a valuable guide.

3. The story of the birth of the ASI is vividly captured in the following 6 documents:

Document No. 1

Memorandum—By Colonel A. Cunningham, of Engrs., regarding a proposed investigation of the Archaeological Remains of Upper India.

1. During the one hundred years of British dominion in India, the Government has done little or nothing towards the preservation of its ancient monuments, which, in the almost total absence of any written history, form the only reliable sources of information as to the early condition of the country. Some of these monuments have already endured for ages, and are likely to last for ages still to come; but there are many others which are daily suffering from the effects of time, and which must soon disappear altogether, unless preserved by the accurate drawings and faithful descriptions of the Archaeologist.

2. All that has hitherto been done towards the illustration of ancient Indian history has been due to the unaided efforts of private individuals. These researches consequently have always been desultory and unconnected, and frequently incomplete, owing partly to the short stay which individual officers usually make at any particular

place, and partly to the limited leisure which could be devoted to such pursuits.

3. Hitherto the Government has been chiefly occupied with the extension and consolidation of the Empire; but the establishment of the Trigonometrical Survey shows that it was not been unmindful of the claims of science. It would redound equally to the honour of the British Government to institute a careful and systematic investigation of all the existing monuments of ancient India.

4. In describing the ancient geography of India, the elder Pliny, for the sake of clearness, follows the footsteps of Alexander the Great. For a similar reason, in the present proposed investigation, I would follow the footsteps of the Chinese pilgrim Hwen Thsang, who in the 7th century of our era traversed India from west to east, and back again, for the purpose of visiting all the famous sites of Buddhist, history and tradition. In the account of his travels, although the Buddhist remains are described in most detail with all their attendant legends and traditions, yet the numbers and appearance of the Brahminical temples are also noted, and the travels of the Chinese pilgrim thus hold the same place in the history of India, which those of Pausanias hold in the history of Greece.

5. In the North-Western Provinces and Behar the principal places to be visited and examined are the following, which are also shown in the accompanying Sketch Map:

I. *Khalsi*, on the Jumna, where the river leaves the hills. At this place there still exists a large boulder stone, covered with one of Ashoka's inscriptions, in which the names of Antiochus, Ptolemy, Antigonus, Magas, and Alexander are all recorded. This portion of the inscription, which on the rocks of Kassoordigiri (in the Yusufzai Plain) and of Dhauli (in Cuttack) is much mutilated and abraded, is here in perfect preservation. A copy of this inscription and an account of the ruins would therefore be valuable.

II. *Hurdwar*, on the Ganges, with the opposite City of Mayurpoora.

III. *Mundore,* Sunbhul, and Saswan, in Rohilkund.

IV. *Karsana*, near Khasgunj.

V. *Sunkissa*, between Mynpoory and Futtehgurh, where it is known that many remains of Buddhism still exist. This was one of the most sacred places amongst the Buddhists.

VI. *Muttra*. In one of the ancient mounds outside the city, the remains of a large monastery have been lately discovered. Numerous statues, sculptured pillars, and inscribed bases of columns have been brought to light. Amongst these inscriptions, some, which are dated in an unknown era, are of special interest and value. They belong most probably to the first century of the Christian era, and one of them records the name of the great King Huveshka, who is presumed to be the same as the Indo-Scythian King Hushka.

VII. *Delhi.* The Hindoo remains of Delhi are few, but interesting. The stone pillars of Ashoka and the Iron Pillars are well known, but the other remains have not yet been described, although none have been more frequently visited than the magnificent ruined cloisters around the Kutb Minar, which belong to the period of the great Tuar dynasty.

VIII. *Kanouj.* No account of the ruins of this once celebrated capital has yet been published. Several ruins are known to exist; but it may be presumed that many more would be brought to light by a careful survey of the site.

IX. *Kansdmbi*, on the Jumna, 30 miles above Allahabad. The true position of this once famous city has only lately been ascertained. It has not yet been visited, but it may be confidently expected that its remains would well repay examination.

X. *Allahabad.* The only existing relics of antiquity, that I am aware of, are, the well known Pillar of Ashoka and the holy tree in one of the underground apartments of the Fort. Many buildings once existed, but I am afraid that they were all destroyed to furnish materials for the erection of the Fort in the reign of Akber.

XI. To the south of Allahabad there are the ruins of Kajraha and Mahoba, the two capitals of the ancient Chandel Rajas of Bundelkund. The remains at Kajraha are more numerous and in better preservation than those of any other ancient city that I have seen. Several long and important inscriptions still exist, which give a complete genealogy of the Chandel dynasty for about 400 years.

XII. *Benares.* The magnificent Tope of Sarnath is well known; but no description of the Tope, nor of the ruins around it, has yet been published. At a short distance from Benares is the inscribed Pillar of Bhitari, which requires to be re-examined.

XIII. *Jounpoor.* Although the existing remains at this place are Mahomedan, yet it is well known that the principal buildings were originally Hindoo temples, of which the cloisters still remain almost unaltered. These ruins have not yet been described, but from my own success, in the beginning of this year, in discovering a Sanskrit inscription built into one of the arches, I believe that a careful examination would be rewarded with further discoveries of interest, illustrative of the great Rathor dynasty of Kanouj.

XIV. *Fyzabad.* The ruins of Ajoodhya have not been described. Numerous very ancient coins are found on the site, and several ruined mounds are known to exist there; but no account has yet been published. As the birth-place of Rama, and as the scene of one of the early events in Buddha's life, Ajoodhya has always been held equally sacred, both by Brahmins and by Buddhists, and I feel satisfied that a systematic examination of its ruins would be rewarded by the discovery of many objects of interest.

XV. *Sravasti.* Even the site of this once celebrated city is unknown, but it may be looked for between Fyzabad and Goruckpoor.

XVI. *Kapilavastu,* the birthplace of Buddha, was held in special veneration by his followers; but its site is unknown.

XVII. *Kusinagara,* the scene of Buddha's death, was one of the most holy places in India in the estimation of Buddhists; but its site is at present unknown. It may however confidently be looked for along the line of the Gunduk River. At Kapila and Kusinagara, the scenes of Buddha's birth and death, numerous Topes and stately monasteries once existed, to attest the pious munificence of his votaries. The ruins of many of these buildings must still exist, and would no doubt reward a careful search. At Mathiah, Radhyiah, and Bakra, in Tirhoot, stone pillars still remain, and in other places ruined Topes were seen by Major Kittoe; but no description of these remains has yet been made known.

XVIII. *Vaisali.* This city was the scene of the second Buddhist synod, and was one of the chief places of note amongst Buddhists. At Bassar, to the north of Patna, one Tope is known to exist, but no search has yet been made for other remains. The people of Vaisali were known to Ptolemy, who calls them Passalce.

XIX. *Patna,* the ancient Palibothra. I am not aware that there are any existing remains at Patna, but numerous coins, gems, and seals are annually found in the bed of the river.

XX. *Rajagriha,* between Patna and Gaya, was the capital of Magadha, in the time of Buddha. Some of the principal scenes of his life occurred in its neighbourhood, and the place was consequently held in very great veneration by all Buddhists. Every hill and every stream had been made holy by Buddha's presence, and the whole country around Rajagriha was covered with buildings to commemorate the principal events of his life. Numerous ruined topes, sculptured friezes, and inscribed pillars still remain scattered over the country, as lasting proofs of the high veneration in which this religious capital of Buddhism was held by the people.

6. In this rapid sketch of the places that seem worthy of examination, I have confined myself entirely to the N.W. Provinces and Behar, as containing most of the cities celebrated in the ancient history of India. But to make this account of Indian archaeological remains more complete, it would be necessary to examine the ancient cities of the Punjab, such as Taxila, Sakala, and Jalandher on the west, the caves and inscribed rocks of Cuttack and Orissa on the east, and the Topes and other remains of Ujain and Bhilsa, with the caves of Dhumnar and Kholvee in Central India.

7. I believe that it would be possible to make a careful examination of all the places which I have noted during two cold seasons. The first season might be devoted to a survey of Gaya and of Rajagriha, and of all the remains in Tirhoot to the eastward of Benares and Goruckpoor; while the survey of all to the westward of Benares would occupy the second season.

8. I would attach to the description of each place a general Survey of the site, showing clearly the positions of all the existing remains, with a ground Plan of every building or ruin of special note, accompanied by Drawings and Sections of all objects of interest. It would be desirable also to have photographic views of many of the remains, both of archi-tecture and of sculpture; but to obtain these it would be necessary to have the services of a photographer. Careful facsimiles of all inscriptions would of course be made; ancient coins would also be collected on each site, and all the local traditions would be noted down and compared. The description of each place, with all its accompanying drawings and illustrations, would be complete in itself, and the whole, when finished, would furnish a detailed and accurate account of the archaeological remains of Upper India.

Document No. 2

Dated 22nd January 1862: Minute by the Right Hon'ble the Governor General of India in Council, on the Antiquities of Upper India.

In November last, when at Allahabad, I had some communications with Colonel A. Cunningham, then the Chief Engineer of the N.W. Provinces, regarding an investigation of the archaeological remains of Upper India.

It is impossible to pass through that part—or indeed, so far as my experience goes, any part—of the British Territories in India without being struck by the neglect with which the greater portion of the architectural remains, and of the traces of by-gone civilization have been treated, though many of these, and some which have had least notice, are full of beauty and interest.

By 'neglect' I do not mean only the omission to restore them, or even to arrest their decay; for this would be a task, which, in many cases, would require an expenditure of labour and money, far greater than any Government of India could reasonably bestow upon it.

But so far as the Government is concerned, there has been neglect of a much cheaper duty—that of investigating and placing on record, for the instruction of future generations, many particulars that might still be rescued from oblivion, and throw light upon the early history of England's great dependency; a history which, as time moves on, as the country becomes more easily accessible and traversable, and as Englishmen are led to give more thought to India than such as barely suffices to hold it and govern it, will assuredly occupy, more and more, the attention of the intelligent and enquiring classes in European countries.

It will not be to our credit, as an enlightened ruling Power, if we continue to allow such fields of investigation, as the remains of the old Buddhist Capital in Behar, the vast ruins of Kanouj, the plains round Delhi, studded with ruins more thickly than even the Campagna of Rome, and many others, to remain without more examination than they have hitherto received. Every thing that has hitherto been done in this way has been done by private persons, imperfectly and without system. It is impossible not to feel that there are European Governments, which, if they had held our rule in India, would not have allowed this to be said.

It is true that in 1844, on a representation from the Royal Asiatic Society, and in 1847, in accordance with detailed suggestions from Lord Hardinge, the Court of Directors gave a liberal sanction to certain arrangements for examining, delineating, and recording some of the chief antiquities of India. But for one reason or another, mainly perhaps owing to the Officer entrusted with the task having other work to do, and owing to his early death, very little seems to have resulted from this endeavour. A few drawings of antiquities, and some remains, were transmitted to the India House, and some

15 or 20 papers were contributed by Major Kittoe and Major
Cunningham to the Journals of the Asiatic Society; but so far as the
Government is concerned, the scheme appears to have been lost
sight of within two or three years of its adoption.

I enclose a Memorandum drawn up by Colonel Cunningham,
who has, more than any other Officer on this side of India, made the
antiquities of the country his study, and who has here sketched the
course of proceeding which a more complete and systematic
archaeological investigation should, in his opinion, take.

I think it good—and none the worse for being a beginning on a
moderate scale. It will certainly cost very little in itself, and will
commit the Government to no future or unforeseen expense. For
it does not contemplate the spending of any money upon repairs and
preservation. This when done at all, should be done upon a separate
and full consideration of any case which may seem to claim it. What
is aimed at is an accurate description—illustrated by plans, measurements, drawings or photographs, and by copies of inscriptions—of
such remains as most deserve notice, with the history of them so far
as it may be traceable, and a record of the traditions that are retained
regarding them.

I propose that the work be entrusted to Colonel Cunningham,
with the understanding that it continue during the present and the
following cold season, by which time a fair judgement of its utility
and interest may be formed. It may then be preserved in, and
expanded, or otherwise dealt with, as may seem good at the time.

Colonel Cunningham should receive Rs 450 a month, with Rs
250 when in the field to defray the cost of making Surveys and
measurements, and of other mechanical assistance. If something
more should be necessary to obtain the services of a Native
Subordinate of the Medical or Public Works Department, compe-
tent to take photographic views, it should be given.

It would be premature to determine how the results of Colonel
Cunningham's labours should be dealt with; but whilst the Government would of course retain a proprietary right in them for its own
purposes, I recommend that the interests of Colonel Cunningham
should be considered in the terms upon which they may be
furnished to the Public.

Document No. 3

No. 896, dated 31st January 1862: From Lieut. Col. H. Yale, Secy. to Govt. of India, P.W. Dept., to Colonel A. Cunningham, Engineers.

1. With reference to what passed, at your interview with His Excellency the Viceroy at Allahabad in November last, and past demi-official correspondence, His Excellency the Governor General in Council has been pleased to appoint you Archaeological Surveyor to the Government of India, with effect from the 1st December last.

2. Whilst so employed, you will receive a staff salary of Rs 450 a month in addition to the pay and allowances of your rank.

3. You will also be at liberty to expend money not exceeding Rs 250 in any one month, on account of measurements, excavations, drawing, and minor mechanical assistance, for which and for your allowances you can submit monthly contingent bills to the Controller and Examiner, Bengal.

4. The course of your investigations will be that sketched out in the Memorandum which you submitted to H.E. the G.G., passing from South Behar into Tirhoot, Gorukhpoor, and Fyzabad.

5. I am to request that you will be good enough to furnish this Department regularly with a brief monthly Statement of the localities and general character of the objects that have occupied you during the month.

6. The Military Department has been requested to give orders for the loan to you of an elephant from the Commissariat at Dinapoor, should there be one available. You will be at liberty to charge the keep of the elephant in your contingent bill.

Document No. 4

No. 398, dated 31st January 1862: From Lieut. Col. H. Yule, Secy. to Govt. of India, P.W. Dept., to Offg. Contr. and Exmr. of P.W. Accounts, Bengal.

I am directed to forward for your information copy of a letter addressed to Colonel A. Cunningham, of Engineers, appointing him Archaeological Surveyor to the Government of India. Colonel Cunningham's salary and expenses, alluded to in paras 3 and 6, must be charged against the Reserve in the hands of the Government of India in this Department.

Document No. 5

No. 397, dated 31st January 1862: Office Memorandum—From Lieut. Col. H. Yule, Secy. to Govt. of India, P.W. Dept., to Secy. to Govt. of India, Mily. Dept.

His excellency the Governor General in Council having been pleased to appoint Colonel A. Cunningham, of Engineers, to the investigation of the antiquities of Behar, &c., is desirous that Colonel Cunningham should have the use of an elephant whilst so employed. The undersigned is therefore directed to request that if an elephant can be made available by the Commissariat Department at Dinapoor, one may be furnished on Colonel Cunningham's requisition. The Commissariat Department would be relieved of the keep of the elephant whilst so employed.

Document No. 6

No. 24, dated 31st January 1862: Notification—By the Govt. of India, P.W. Dept.

Appointment—Colonel A. Cunningham, of Engineers, is appointed Archaeological Surveyor to the Government of India, for employment in Behar and elsewhere, with effect from 1st December last.

4. Ibid. 3.
5. Sourendra Nath Roy, *The Story of Indian Archaeology (1784–1947)*, New Delhi, 1961, p. 58.
6. Ibid., p. 56.
7. Ibid., p. 83.
8. Quoted from the Address of 20 December 1900 delivered by Lord Curzon at the Asiatic Society, Calcutta from file No. 54 of 1900, National Archives of India, New Delhi.
9. *The Story of Indian Archaeology*, p. 84.
10. Ibid., p. 84
11. John Marshall, 'The Story of the Archaeological Department in India', in John Cunningham, *Revealing India's Past*, The India Society, London, 1939, pp. 1–33.
12. It would be pertinent to quote from the *Conservation Manual* the principles of conservation which have withstood the test of time and are being universally followed. These are:

Archaeological officers charged with the execution of conservation work should never forget that the preservation of any remnant of ancient architecture, however humble, is a work to be entered upon with totally different feelings from a new work or from the repairs of a modern building. Although there are many ancient buildings whose state of repair suggests at first sight a renewal, it should never be forgotten that their *historical value is gone when their authenticity is destroyed*, and that our first duty is not to renew them but to preserve them. When, therefore, repairs are carried out, no effort should be spared to save as many parts of the original as possible, since it is to the authenticity of the old parts that practically all the interest attaching to the new will owe itself. Broken or half decayed original work is of infinitely more value than the smartest and most perfect new work.

13. Marshall, 'The Story of the Archaeological Department', pp. 1–33.
14. Ibid. 8.
15. The earliest urban civilization that flourished in the north and north-west of the Indian subcontinent during a major part of the third millennium BC (circa 2600–1700 BC) was identified first at Harappa and because of its spread in the Indus Valley it is also called the Indus Civilization. However, with the discovery of a large number of sites on the one hand in the Saraswati-Ghaggar-Hakar valley, land in the upper reaches of the Ganga-Yamuna *Doab* and, on the other, in Gujarat and Maharashtra, the epithet Indus Valley no longer encompasses the entire Harappan or Indus Valley Civilization.
16. The Exploration Branch, now termed the Excavations Branch, comprises five locations at Nagpur (Ex.Br.I); New Delhi (Ex.Br.II); Patna (Ex.Br.III); Bhubaneswar (Ex.Br.IV); and Vadodara (Ex.Br.V). Each one is headed by a Superintending Archaeologist.
17. There are at present 31 site museums under the Survey.
18. J.P. Joshi, *Excavation at Surkotada 1971–72 and Exploration in Kutch*, New Delhi, 1990, p. 414.
19. The pre-Harappan cultures which have been found in the Indian subcontinent are determined on the basis of (1) stratigraphy, (2) cultural equipment, (3) pottery, and (4) dates. Stratigraphically the cultural deposit should precede the mature Harappan horizon. The cultural equipment includes small blades of chalcedony and agate, sometimes serrated and backed, beads of steatite, shell and carnelian, terracotta toy-cart wheels and bulls, querns and mullers of stone, bone points, copper celt and axes. The pre-Harappan occupation came to an end by a

seismic catastrophe as evidenced by the fault in the occupation layers in the upper levels. The pre-Harappan pottery basically represented by wheelmade pottery having irregular striation, carelessly potted, paintings in black and white criss-cross moustache-like bifold designs, red ware with sharp incised designs and grey ware. Chronologically pre-Harappan cultures (antecedent to the Harappan) date to *circa* 2600 to 2400 BC. However, the dates would be much earlier if the standard correction of 500 to 550 years is added to this date bracket.

Some amount of town planning and fortification have also been noticed in pre-Harappan levels. The pre-Harappan brick sizes were 30 × 20 × 10 cm (ratio 1:2:3) and were laid in the English bond. A. Ghosh (ed.), *An Encyclopaedia of Indian Archaeology* vol. I, New Delhi, 1989, p. 75, and M. Wheeler, *Civilization of the Indus Valley and Beyond,* London, 1966.

20. To define the mature Harappan culture is not an easy task. The traits that originated earlier and the regional variations complicated the definition. Wheeler tried to define the culture by the alternative or accumulative presence of: (i) Indus Seals; (ii) Indus Script; (iii) motifs like intersecting circles; (iv) ceramic forms like goblets with a pointed base, cylindrical pots with multiple perforations, jars with an s-profile and dishes on stands; (v) triangular terracotta cakes; (vi) kidney-shaped inlays of shell or faience; and (vii) certain beads, notably discoid with tubular holes. To these one may add town-planning (streets in grids, underground drains, fortified townships), brick dimensions in the ratio of 1:2:4 and typical shapes in copper artefacts like bent-blade knives, double-edged razors, barbed triangular arrowheads with holes etc.

The hallmark of the mature Harappan culture in town planning consists of a lower town, a middle town, and an upper town (citadel). The citadel, whether fortified with the lower town or separately, was invariably located in the west (except at Lothal). Houses, with rooms opening from three sides into a central courtyard, provided with water, drains, and latrines, are characteristic of the Harappans. D.P. Agrawal, *The Archaeology of India,* London, 1982, p. 135.

21. Interview with R.S. Bisht, Director of Dholavira Excavation Branch, *Sunday Times of India Review,* New Delhi, 20 April 1997.

22. Quoted in O.P. Kejriwal's paper, 'The Indus Civilization', *Employment News,* New Delhi, 24 January 1997.

23. Bridget and Raymond Allchin, *The Rise of Civilization in India and Pakistan,* Selectbook Service Syndicate, New Delhi, by arrangement with Cambridge University Press, London, 1983, p. 355.

Select Bibliography

1. Allchin, Bridget and Raymond, *The Rise of Civilization in India and Pakistan*, Selectbook Service Syndicate, New Delhi, 1983, by arrangement with Cambridge University Press, London.
    ———— *The Birth of Indian Civilization: India and Pakistan before 500 BC*, Penguin Books, Great Britain, 1968.
2. Anand, Mulk Raj, *The Hindu View of Art*, G. Allen & Unwin, London, 1933.
3. Appadurai, Arjun, (ed.), *The Social Life of Things*, Cambridge University Press, New York, 1986.
4. Archer, W.G., *India and Modern Art*, G. Allen & Unwin, London, 1853.
5. Basham, A.L., *The Wonder that was India*, Sidgwick and Jackson, London, 1954.
    ———— (ed.), *A Cultural History of India*, Clarendon Press, Oxford, 1975.
6. *Bhagvat Gita*, translated into English by Shri Purohit Swami, Faber & Faber, London, 1970 with Introduction by W.B. Yeats.
7. Bose, Nirmal Kumar, *Culture and Society in India*, Asia Publishing House, Bombay, 1977 reprint.
8. Burke, Victor Lee, *The Clash of Civilizations*, Polity Press, Cambridge, UK, 1997.
9. Buultijens, Ralph, *Windows on India*, Express Books, New York, 1987.
10. Carr, E.H., *What is History?*, Macmillan, London, 1987.
11. Comaraswamy, Ananda K., *Essays in National Idealism*, Apothecaries, Colombo, 1909.
    ———— *History of Indian and Indonesian Art*, Edward Goldston, London, 1927.
12. Conze, E., *Buddhism, its Essence and Devlopment*, Philosophical Lib., Oxford, 1951.
13. Cunningham, A., *Archaeological Survey of India: Four Reports* made during the years 1862, 1863, 1864 and 1865, vol. I, Calcutta 1871.

————, ed. S. Majumdar, *The Ancient Geography of India*, Chukervertty, Chatterjee & Co., Calcutta, 1924.

14. De Bary, W.Th. (ed.), *Sources of Indian Tradition*, 2 volumes, Columbia University Press, New York, 1958.
15. Dinkar, Ramdhari Singh, *Sanskriti Ke Char Adhyayay*, Rajpal & Sons, Delhi, 1956.
16. Durant, Will, *The Story of Civilization, Pt.I, Our Oriental Heritage*, Simon and Schuster, New York, 1954.
17. Gablik, Suzi (ed.), *Conversations before the end of time*, Thames and Hudson, New York, 1995.
18. Gandhi, Mohandas K., *An Autobiography, or the Story of My Experiments with Truth*, Navjivan Publishing House, Ahmedabad, 1940; London, 1966.
19. Gerber, William (ed.), *The Mind of India*, Southern Illinois University Press, London, 1908.
20. Ghose, Sisirkumar (ed.), *Tagore for You*, Visva Bharati, Calcutta, 1966.
21. Ghosh, A., Fifty years of the Archaeological Survey of India, *Ancient India, Bulletin of the Archaeological Survey of India*, no. 9, 1953.
22. Goetz, H., *India: Five Thousand Years of Indian Art*, Taraporevala, Bombay, 1959.
23. Halbfass, Wilhelm, *India and Europe: An Essay in Understanding*, State University of New York Press, Albany, 1988.
24. Hall, D.G.E., *A History of South-East Asia*, 3rd ed., St. Martin, London, 1968.
25. Havel, Vaclav, *Towards a Civil Society*, Lidove Noviny, Prague 2.
26. Hawkridge, Emma, *Indian Gods and Kings*, Aryan Books International, New Delhi, 1994.
27. Huntington, Samuel P., *The Clash of Civilizations and the Remaking of World Order*, Simon & Schuster, New York, 1996.
28. Joshi, P.C., *Culture, Communication and Social Change*, Vikas Publishing House, New Delhi, 1989.
29. Karlekar, Hiranmay, National Seminar on Beyond Creativity: Problems Facing the Cultural Life of India at the Turn of the Century, 21–23 February 1997 at IIC, New Delhi, Sahitya Akademi (Unpublished document).
30. Kissinger, Henry, *Diplomacy*, Simon & Schuster, New York, 1994.
31. Klimburg-Salter, Deborah E., *1000 Years of Tabo Monastery*, Institute of Tibetan and Buddhist Studies, University of Vienna, Austria, 1996.
32. Kosambi, D.D., *The Culture and Civilisation of Ancient India*, Routledge and Kegan Paul, London, 1965.

———— *The Culture and Civilization of Ancient India in Historical Outline,* Vikas, New Delhi, reprint 1990.

33. Kroeber, A.L., *Anthropology: Race, Language, Culture, Psychology, Prehistory,* Oxford & IBH Publishing Co., Calcutta, by arrangement with Harcourt, Brace & World, Inc, New York, 1948.

34. Lal, B.B., *Indian Archaeology since Independence,* Motilal Banarsidas, Delhi, 1964.

35. Li, Shaman Hwui, *The Life of Hsuan-Tsang,* Kegan Paul, Trench, Trubner & Co. Ltd., London, 1911.

36. Lukes, Steven (ed.), *Power,* Basil Blackwell Ltd., UK, 1986.

37. Lyall, Alfred C., *Asiatic Studies, vols. I and II,* Cosmo Publications, New Delhi, 1976, first published in 1882.

38. Majumdar, R.C., *Ancient India,* Motilal Banarsidas, Banaras, 1952.
———— (ed.), *History and Culture of the Indian People,* II vols., Bharatiya Vidya Bhawan, London, Bombay, 1952–65.

39. Marshall J., et al., *Mohenjo Daro and the Indus Civilization,* 3 vols., Arthur Probsthain, London, 1931.

40. Michell George (ed.), *Temple Towns of Tamil Nadu,* Marg Publications, Bombay, 1993.
———— The Story of the Archaeological Department in India, in Sir John Cumming's *Revealing India's past,* The India Society, London, 1939.

41. Mills, C. Wright, *The Power Elite,* Oxford University Press, New York, 1956.

42. Mitter, Partha, *Art and Nationalism in Colonial India 1850–1922, Occidental Orientations,* Cambridge University Press, USA, 1944.

43. Nehru, Jawaharlal *The Discovery of India,* Meridian, London, 1951.

44. Octavio Paz, *In Light of India,* Harcourt Brace and Company, New York, 1997.

45. Pande, B.M., *Problems of Conservation of Excavated Remains in India,* paper presented at WAC-3, December, 1994.

46. Radhakrishnan, S., *Eastern Religions and Western Thought,* 2nd ed., Oxford University Press, London, 1940.
———— *The Hindu view of life,* 10th impression, George Allen & Unwin, London, 1957.

47. Raine, Kathleen, *India Seen Afar,* Green Books, Devon, 1990.

48. Rajagopalachari, C., *Mahabharata,* Bharatiya Vidya Bhavan, Bombay, 1972.

49. Rawlinson, H.G., *India, a Short Cultural History,* Cresset Press, London, 1937.

50. Rawson, P.S., *Indian Painting,* Pierre Tisne Editeur, Paris, 1961.
51. Roy, Debes, 'The King and the Clown, Some Confabulations on the Relation between the Democracy and the Writer', Sahitya Akademi, New Delhi, 1997 (unpublished domument).
52. Roy, Sourindranath, *The Story of Indian Archaeology 1784–1947,* Archaeological Survey of India, New Delhi, 1961.
53. Said, Edward B., *Orientalism,* Routledge & Kegan Paul, London, 1978.
———— *Culture and Imperialism,* Chatto & Windus Ltd., Great Britain, 1993.
54. Saraswati, Baidyanath (ed.), *Interface of Cultural Identity and Development,* Indira Gandhi National Centre for the Arts, New Delhi, 1996.
55. Sastri, K.A. Nilakanta, *A History of South India,* 3rd ed., Oxford University Press, London, 1966.
56. Sen, K.M., *Hinduism,* Penguin, Great Britain, 1961.
57. Sharma, R.S., *Indian Feudalism c. 300–1200,* Macmillan, Delhi, 1965.
58. Shastri, Satya Vrat, *Sriramakirtimahakavyam,* Moolamall Sachdev Foundation Amarnath Sachdeva Foundation, Bangkok, 1990.
59. Singh, B.P., *The Problem of Change: A Study of North-East India,* Oxford University Press, New Delhi, 1987.
————, North-East India: Demography, Culture and Identity Crisis, *Modern Asian Studies,* Cambridge University Press, London, April 1987.
———— *The Indian National Congress and Cultural Renaissance,* Allied Publishers, 1987.
———— *Threads Woven: Ideals, Principles and Administration,* First published by Lawyer's Book Stall, Guwahati, 1975, Reprint Virago Publications, New Delhi, 1997.
60. Smith, V.A., *History of Fine Art in India and Ceylon.,* 2nd ed., revised by K. de B. Codrington, Clarendon Press, Oxford, 1930.
61. Tagore, Rabindranath, *Gitanjali,* Macmillan and Co. Ltd., London, 1953.
62. Taylor, Edward B., *Primitive Culture: Researches into the Development of Mythology, Philosophy, Religion, Language, Art and Custom,* Murry, London, 3rd ed., vol. 2, 1871.
63. Toffler, Alvin, *Future Shock,* Bantam Books, New York, 1990.
64. *Towards Universal Man,* Asia Publishing House, Bombay, 1961.
65. Vatsyayan, Kapila, *Some Aspects of Cultural Policies in India,* UNESCO, Paris, 1972.
66. Verhelst, Thierry G., *No Life Without Roots, Culture and Development,* Zed Books Ltd., London, 1990.
67. Verma, Nirmal, *Bharat Aur Europe: Pratishruti ke Shetra,* Rajkamal Prakashan, New Delhi, 1991.

Index
Subject

Name

208   *India's Culture*